SLOW
COOKER
500
RECIPES

SLOW COOKER
500 RECIPES

SARA LEWIS

hamlyn

An Hachette UK Company
www.hachette.co.uk

First published in Great Britain in 2015 by Hamlyn, a division of
Octopus Publishing Group Ltd, Carmelite House
50 Victoria Embankment, London EC4Y 0DZ
www.octopusbooksusa.com

Some of this material previously appeared in *200 Slow Cooker Recipes*,
200 More Slow Cooker Recipes, *200 Light Slow Cooker Recipes*, and
200 Family Slow Cooker Recipes.

Copyright © Octopus Publishing Group Ltd 2015

Distributed in the US by Hachette Book Group
1290 Avenue of the Americas
4th and 5th Floors, New York, NY 10020

Distributed in Canada by Canadian Manda Group
664 Annette Street, Toronto, Ontario, Canada M6S 2C8

ISBN 978-0-600-63245-0

Printed and bound in China

10 9 8 7 6 5 4 3 2 1

 Recipes with this symbol are under 500 calories.

Follow the manufacturer's instructions for your slow cooker
and adjust the cooking time or temperature if necessary.

Standard level cup and spoon measurement are used in all recipes.

Use medium-sized eggs unless otherwise stated. This book contains
dishes made with raw or lightly cooked eggs. For recipes that call for
eggs that are raw or undercooked when the dish is served, the U.S.
Food and Drug Administration recommends that you use shell eggs
that have been treated to destroy Salmonella, by pasteurization or
another approved method, or pasteurized egg products. Treated shell
eggs are available from a growing number of retailers and are clearly
labeled, while pasteurized egg products are widely available.
It is prudent for more vulnerable people such as pregnant and nursing
mothers, invalids, the elderly, babies, and young children to avoid
uncooked or lightly cooked dishes made with eggs. Once prepared
these dishes should be kept refrigerated and used promptly.

Use whole milk unless otherwise stated.

Fresh herbs should be used unless otherwise stated. If unavailable,
use dried herbs as an alternative but halve the quantities stated.

Ovens should be preheated to the specific temperature—if using
a fan-assisted oven, follow manufacturer's instructions for adjusting
the time and the temperature.

All microwave information is based on a 650-watt oven. Follow
manufacturer's instructions for an oven with a different wattage.

Pepper should be freshly ground black pepper unless otherwise stated.

This book includes dishes made with nuts and nut derivatives. It is
advisable for readers with known allergic reactions to nuts and
nut derivatives and those who may be potentially vulnerable to
these allergies, such as pregnant and nursing mothers, invalids,
the elderly, babies, and children, to avoid dishes made with nuts
and nut oils. It is also prudent to check the labels of pre-prepared
ingredients for the possible inclusion of nut derivatives.

CONTENTS

INTRODUCTION

Whether you are new to slow cooking or a seasoned professional, you probably have a handful of favorite recipes you keep going back to. It's true that some classics taste delicious when slow cooked, time after time: lamb stews, beef casseroles, coq au vin.

But a slow cooker isn't just for casseroles and stews, great though they are. You can make a huge variety of other dishes with this gadget, including lighter meals, delicious fish recipes, and child-pleasing suppers. Try warming main-meal soups, children's favorites, such as baked pasta, everyday favorites like chili con carne, easy cheats, such as tortillas and curries, and food to impress for easy dinner parties.

When water is added to the slow-cooker pot it can be used as a bain-marie, or water bath, to cook baked custards, pâtés, or terrines. Or you can pour alcoholic or fruit juice mixtures into the pot and make warming hot party punches or hot toddies.

The slow-cooker pot can also be used to make chocolate or cheese fondues and preserves, such as lemon curd or simple chutneys, and you can even boil up meat bones or a chicken carcass to make them into homemade stock.

In order to explore the wide range of versatile dishes on offer, this bumper cookbook offers 500 recipes to cover any occasion.

NEW TO SLOW COOKING? YOUR QUESTIONS ANSWERED

WILL IT REALLY MAKE MY LIFE EASIER?

If you're unfamiliar with using a slow cooker, the redistribution of time involved may seem odd. Early on in the day, you spend 15 minutes in the kitchen doing a little preparation, add everything to the slow cooker and walk away, and get on with something else. While cooking before you rush out to work in the morning may not be for everyone, getting a lovely supper on to cook before you head out to the golf course or for a day of shopping, or before doing the Saturday taxi run to and from the kids' clubs may seem more manageable.

A slow cooker cooks so gently there is no need to stir or check on the food because there is no danger of it drying out or spoiling. Just enjoy the welcoming aroma of a delicious supper ready and waiting when you walk back in through the door.

ARE ALL SLOW COOKERS THE SAME?

All slow cookers cook food slowly, though they do vary slightly. Oval-shaped slow cookers offer the most flexibility when it comes to cooking a bone-in roast or desserts.

Generally speaking, slow cookers come in three sizes:

- a two-portion size with a capacity of 2½ pints

- a four-portion size with a capacity of 4 pints

- a six- to eight-portion size with a capacity of 7 pints or 8 pints

Newer models might come with cooking pots that can be used on the stove, so you can fry off meat and onions prior to slow cooking in the pot itself, saving on dishwashing later. These types of slow cookers do tend to cost more. Using a good nonstick skillet in conjunction with a slow cooker works just as well.

As with all things, price varies considerably. The larger models are very often on special offer, but unless your family is large or you plan to cook greater quantities in order to freeze half the batch, you may find that, while the machine itself is a good price, you have to cook larger quantities than you had expected in order to even just half-fill it.

When selecting a slow cooker, choose a machine that features a high and low setting and an on/off light at the front of the machine so that you can easily see that it is on.

WHAT TO DO BEFORE I START?

Dull though it sounds, once you have purchased a slow cooker, make sure you read the instructions handbook. The majority of models should not be preheated while empty. If you partly prepare supper

the night before and put the earthenware slow-cooker pot in the refrigerator, all manufacturers agree that you should leave it at room temperature for 20 minutes before adding it to the slow cooker machine and turning it on. We've also provided you with setup notes on page 10.

IS IT SAFE TO LEAVE IT ON ALL DAY?

Yes, the slow cooker runs on such a small amount of power (the equivalent of two lightbulbs) that it is safe to leave it on all day—even if you go out. Because the heat is so low and the lid forms a seal, there is no danger of the food boiling dry. The sides of the slow cooker will feel warm to the touch, so ensure you leave the machine on an uncluttered part of the work surface.

DO I HAVE TO FRY FOODS BEFORE I ADD THEM TO THE SLOW-COOKER POT?

Frying onions and browning meat adds color and flavor to the finished dish, because foods will not brown in a slow cooker. However, frying ingredients before slow cooking them isn't essential, and very much a matter of personal preference. And if the idea of frying ingredients before you rush out to work in the morning does not appeal to you, especially if are dressed for the office, there are plenty of recipes in the book that can be made without precooking. You can also boost color and flavor with spices or herbs, red wine or beer, or tomato paste.

DOES LIQUID HAVE TO BE HOT BEFORE GOING IN THE SLOW COOKER?

The slow cooker works by building up heat to just below boiling point, then safely maintaining the heat so that food cooks gently but without any danger of allowing the bacteria that cause food poisoning to proliferate. If you add all cold ingredients, this will extend the heating-up process, so add 2 to 3 hours to the cooking time, with the first hour on high, especially if the recipe states to use hot stock. But it is much quicker and very simple to dissolve a stock cube in boiling water and add the hot stock to the slow-cooker pot. Always add hot liquid when cooking a large roast.

HOW FULL SHOULD THE POT BE?

Ideally, the slow-cooker pot should be filled halfway and up to three-quarters full for it to work efficiently. When making soup, fill it so that the liquid is 2 inches from the top. If you have a very large slow cooker, make the quantity to serve six to eight people, then freeze the extra in single portions or portion sizes that your family can enjoy on another occasion. As the slow cooker heats up, the steam generated will condense and make a water seal between the lid and top of the slow-cooker pot—this is perfectly normal.

CAN I USE MY ORDINARY RECIPES?

Yes, of course. Stews, casseroles, and pot-roast recipes can all be made in the slow cooker using the same ingredients. However, because the slow cooker creates a seal during cooking, the liquid doesn't evaporate, so you will find that you need to reduce the liquid in your recipes by one-third, and sometimes even by half. For stews or casseroles, just cover the meat or vegetables with stock. Bear in mind, if using fresh tomatoes, that you will need slightly less stock because the tomatoes will pulp down as they cook.

Depending on the size of your slow-cooker pot, you may need to cut down or increase the quantities of ingredients given in the recipes. A medium-sized slow-cooker pot comfortably makes four portions, while a large one makes six to eight portions. Many of the recipes in this book are designed to serve four people—ideal for a medium-sized slow-cooker pot.

The slow cooker can also be used as a bain-marie or steamer. Making steamed puddings works very well and you don't need to top off with boiling water during cooking, since there is no chance the water will boil dry.

As an approximate guide, if a recipe takes 1 to 2 hours on the stove or in the oven, you should cook it in a slow cooker for 3 to 4 hours on the high setting, or 6 to 8 hours on the low setting. If a recipe takes 2 to 4 hours on the stove or in the oven, cook it in the slow cooker for 4 to 6 hours on high, or for 8 to 12 hours on low.

CAN I COOK RICE AND PASTA?

Yes, but because they are both starchy foods they can turn sticky and gluey if overcooked. Choose parboiled (converted) rice instead of ordinary rice where available, since some of the starch has been removed during manufacturing, making it less sticky. If making a risotto, add the stock all at once rather than a ladleful at a time.

Cook pasta in a saucepan of boiling water, then drain and stir it into the slow-cooker pot just before serving. For lasagne, use dried lasagne sheets that do not require precooking, and cook them for no more than 5 to 6¼ hours. Tiny pasta shapes can be added to soups, without cooking first, for the final 15 to 30 minutes of cooking time.

WHAT ABOUT DAIRY FOODS AND SHELLFISH?

Dairy foods, such as milk, heavy cream, and shredded Cheddar-style cheeses, are fine for recipes with short cooking times or in baked dishes that are cooked for up to 3 to 5 hours on a low setting, or they can be stirred into a dish toward the end of cooking so that they have the final 15 to 30 minutes to add richness and flavor. If you cook them too long, they will separate and look somewhat unappetizing.

Shellfish can be added to a dish, but in small quantities only, and again, toward the end of the cooking time when the other ingredients are already piping hot. Make sure that the shellfish is also piping hot before serving, so cook it on high, preferably for 15 minutes, then serve. Do not keep dishes containing shellfish warm. If you are using frozen fish, ensure that it is fully defrosted before adding it to the slow cooker.

REMEMBER THE BASICS

• Always add liquid to a slow-cooker pot, ideally hot or boiling water.

• Test food before serving it to ensure it is thoroughly cooked before serving. Chicken or pork should not release pink juices when they are pierced with a small, sharp knife. Beef and lamb should be tender. Fish should flake into evenly colored flakes when pressed in the center with a knife.

• To serve, remove the slow-cooker pot from the housing when the dish is cooked wearing oven mitts.

• Cover any remaining food, let it cool, then transfer it to the refrigerator as soon as possible.

• If using raw frozen food other than peas or corn, defrost before use.

• Do not reheat food in a slow cooker (Christmas pudding is the exception).

HEAT SETTINGS

All slow cookers have a "high," "low," and "off" setting, and some also have either "medium," "warm," or "auto" settings. In general, the "high" setting will take half the time of the "low" setting when you are cooking a diced meat or vegetable casserole. This can be useful if you plan to eat at lunchtime or are delayed in starting the casserole. Both settings will reach just below 212°F (boiling point), during cooking, but when it is set to "high," the temperature is reached more quickly.

A combination of settings can be useful and is recommended by some manufacturers at the beginning of cooking. See your manufacturer's instruction handbook for more details.

WHICH SETTING IS BEST FOR WHAT?

The following is a general guide to what you should cook at which temperature:

Low
- Diced meat or vegetable casseroles
- Chops or bone-in pieces of chicken
- Soups
- Egg custard desserts
- Rice dishes
- Fish dishes

High
- Sweet or savory steamed puddings or sweet dishes that include a raising agent, such as baking powder
- Pâtés or terrines
- Whole chicken, guinea fowl, or pheasant, bone-in ham, or half a shoulder of lamb

CAN I REHEAT FOODS IN THE SLOW COOKER?

All manufacturers recommend that you only cook foods from raw in the slow-cooker pot. To reheat a casserole or stew, put it in a saucepan, set it on the stove and bring it to a boil, stirring, then cook for at least 10 minutes until thoroughly reheated and piping hot throughout. Only reheat cooked food once.

TIMINGS

All the recipes in the book have variable timings, which means that they will be tender and ready to eat at the lower time but can be left without spoiling for an extra hour or two, which is perfect if you get delayed at work or stuck in traffic.

If you want to speed up or slow down casseroles based on diced meat or vegetables so that the cooking fits around your plans accordingly, adjust the heat settings and timings as suggested below:

Low	Medium	High
6 to 8 hours	4 to 6 hours	3 to 4 hours
8 to 10 hours	6 to 8 hours	5 to 6 hours
10 to 12 hours	8 to 10 hours	7 to 8 hours

The above timings were taken from the Morphy Richards slow-cooker instruction manual.
Note: Do not change timings or settings for fish, whole bone-in roasts, or dairy dishes.

USING YOUR SLOW COOKER FOR THE FIRST TIME

Before you start to use the slow cooker, put it on the work surface, somewhere out of the way, and ensure that the cord is tucked around the back of the machine and not trailing over the front of the work surface.

The outside of the slow cooker does get hot, so warn young members of the family and don't forget to wear oven mitts when you are lifting the pot out of the housing. Set it onto a heatproof mat on the table or work surface to serve the food.

If your slow-cooker lid has a vent in the top, make sure that the slow cooker is not put under an eye-level cupboard or the steam may catch someone's arm when they reach into the cupboard.

Always check that the bone-in roast, pudding bowl, soufflé dish, or individual molds will fit into your slow-cooker pot before you begin work on a recipe to avoid frustration when you get to a critical point.

PREPARING FOOD FOR THE SLOW COOKER

MEAT
Cut meat into equal-sized pieces so they cook evenly, and fry meat before adding it to the slow cooker.

A whole guinea fowl or pheasant, a small ham, or half a shoulder of lamb can be cooked in an oval slow-cooker pot, but make sure that it does not fill more than the lower two-thirds of the pot. Cover it with boiling liquid and cook on high.

Check that it is cooked either by using a meat thermometer or by inserting a skewer through the thickest part and making sure that the juices that are released run clear.

Add boiling stock or sauce to the slow-cooker pot and press the meat beneath the surface of the liquid before cooking begins.

VEGETABLES
Root vegetables can (surprisingly) take longer to cook than meat. If you are adding vegetables to a meat casserole, make sure you cut them into pieces that are a little smaller than the meat and try to keep all the vegetable chunks the same size so they cook evenly. Press the vegetables and the meat below the surface of the liquid before cooking begins.

When you are making soup, purée it while it is still in the slow-cooker pot by using a hand-held stick blender, if you have one.

FISH
Whether you choose to cut the fish into pieces or cook it in one larger piece (weighing about 1 pound), the slow, gentle cooking will not cause the fish to break up or overcook. However, always make sure the fish is covered by the hot liquid so that it cooks evenly right through to the center.

Do not add shellfish until the last 15 minutes of cooking, and ensure that the slow cooker is set to high.

If the fish was frozen, it must be thoroughly defrosted, rinsed with cold water, and drained before use.

PASTA

For best results, cook the pasta separately in a saucepan of lightly salted boiling water, then combine it with the sauce just before serving. Small pasta shapes, such as elbow macaroni or shells, can be added to soups 30 to 45 minutes before the end of cooking. Pasta can be soaked in boiling water for short-cook recipes, such as macaroni and cheese.

RICE

Parboiled (or converted) rice is preferable to use for slow cookers because it has been partially cooked during manufacture and some of the starch has been washed off, making it less sticky.

When you are cooking rice, allow a minimum of 1 cup water for each ½ cup converted rice or up to 2 cups for risotto rice.

DRIED LEGUMES

Make sure you soak dried beans and peas in plenty of cold water overnight. Drain them, put them into a saucepan, cover them with fresh cold water, and bring to a boil. Boil rapidly for 10 minutes, then drain or add with the cooking liquid to the slow cooker. See the recipes for details.

Pearl barley and lentils—red, Puy, or green—do not need soaking overnight. If you are unsure, check the instructions on the package.

CREAM AND MILK

Both cream and milk are generally added at the beginning of cooking only when you are making rice pudding or baked egg custard-style dishes.

Use whole milk where milk is cooked directly in the slow-cooker pot rather than pudding molds, because whole milk is less likely to separate.

If you are making soup, add the milk at the very end, after the soup has been puréed. Stir cream into soups just 15 minutes before the end of cooking.

THICKENING STEWS AND CASSEROLES

Casseroles can be thickened in just the same way as if you were cooking conventionally. You can do it either before slow cooking, by adding the flour after searing meat or frying onions, or you can thicken the casserole with cornstarch mixed with a little cold water 30 to 60 minutes before the end of cooking.

GETTING THE MOST FROM YOUR SLOW COOKER

DON'T BE TEMPTED TO PEEK

A slow cooker cooks so gently there really is no need for you to stir the food; it won't stick or boil dry as it cooks. Don't be tempted to lift open the lid—every time you do so you release some of the heat and can add up to 10 to 15 minutes to the cooking time.

It is much better to peer through the glass lid, and stir just once before serving or when adding extra ingredients toward the end of the cooking time.

TIPS

• Because foods cook so slowly in a slow cooker, you can make use of less expensive beef cuts, such as chuck, brisket, or oxtail—without compromising on flavor. Don't forget neck of lamb shoulder, foreshank, or breast, too. And bear in mind that chicken thighs taste better in the slow cooker than the more expensive chicken breasts.

• Foods will not brown in the slow cooker, so add color to your stews by frying onions and meats first, adding various spices or herbs, tomatoes or tomato paste, wine or beer, gravy browning, or even yeast extract.

• You can reduce the amount of dishes that will need washing later by puréeing soups while they are still in the slow-cooker pot using a hand-held stick blender.

• Getting a steamed pudding out of the slow-cooker pot can be tricky, especially if the pudding bowl fits very snugly in the pot. Tie string around the bowl to make a handle for lifting the pudding dish out of the slow-cooker pot. Alternatively, fold two pieces of foil individually to make two long straps. Form a cross with the straps and place them on the work surface, then place the pudding dish on the cross and use the pieces of foil to lift up and lower the dish into the slow-cooker pot. Tuck the straps over the top of the bowl, then use them to lift out the pudding dish at the end of the cooking time.

• Food at the bottom of the slow-cooker pot will cook more quickly than the rest, so add diced potatoes to the pot first, because these can take longer to cook than meat. Or, if you are adding lots of root vegetables, cut them into chunks the same size or slightly smaller than the meat you are using and mix up the meat and vegetable chunks.

• Short of time? Then cheat! Add a bottle or can of ready-made sauce instead of making your own.

FOR THE FREEZER

The majority of soups and stews in this book can be frozen successfully, and if you don't have a large family or if you live on your own, freezing individual portions for another meal can be a great time-saver. After all, it requires only a little extra effort to make a casserole for four than it does to make one for two.

Defrost portions in the refrigerator overnight or at room temperature for 4 hours, then reheat thoroughly in a saucepan on the stove, or in the microwave on full power.

If you are using raw frozen foods make sure that they are thoroughly defrosted before you add them to the slow cooker. Exceptions to this rule are frozen peas and kernel corn. Raw food that was frozen and is then defrosted and cooked in the slow cooker can be refrozen in its cooked and cooled state.

CARING FOR YOUR SLOW COOKER

If you look after it carefully, you may find that your machine will last for 20 years or more.

Because the heat of a slow cooker is so controllable, it is not like a saucepan with burned-on grime to contend with. Simply lift the slow-cooker pot out of the housing, fill it with hot soapy water, and let it soak for a while. Even though it is tempting to put the slow-cooker pot and lid into the dishwasher, they do take up a lot of space. Also, be sure to check the slow-cooker's manual first, because not all are dishwasher-proof.

Let the machine itself cool down before cleaning it. Turn it off at the controls and unplug it. Wipe the inside with a damp dish towel, removing any stubborn marks with a little cream cleaner. The outside of the machine and the controls can be wiped with a cloth, then buffed up with a duster or, if it has a chrome-effect finish, sprayed with a little multisurface cleaner and polished with a duster. Never immerse the machine in water to clean it. If you are storing the slow cooker in a cupboard, make sure it is completely cold before you put it away.

BREAKFASTS
& BRUNCHES

BREAKFAST BAKED TOMATOES

Serves **4**
Preparation time **10 minutes**
Cooking temperature **low**
Cooking time **8 to 10 hours**
  or **overnight**

1 lb **plum tomatoes**,
  halved lengthwise
leaves from 2 to 3 **thyme sprigs**
1 tablespoon **balsamic vinegar**
salt and **pepper**
chopped **parsley**, to garnish
4 slices of **wholewheat bread**
  (about 1½ oz each), to serve

Preheat the slow cooker if necessary. Arrange the tomatoes, cut-side up, in the slow-cooker pot, packing them in tightly in a single layer. Scatter with the thyme, drizzle with the vinegar, and season to taste. Cover and cook on low for 8 to 10 hours or overnight.

Toast the bread the next morning and place on 4 serving plates. Top with the tomatoes and a little of the juice and serve scattered with parsley.

FOR BALSAMIC TOMATOES WITH SPAGHETTI, follow the recipe above to cook the tomatoes, then chop them and mix with the cooking juices. Cook 7 oz dried spaghetti in a large saucepan of lightly salted boiling water following the package instructions until just tender, then drain and toss with the tomatoes. Scatter each portion with 1 tablespoon freshly shredded Parmesan cheese.

EGGS EN COCOTTE WITH SALMON

Serves **4**
Preparation time **10 minutes**
Cooking temperature **high**
Cooking time **40 to 45 minutes**

2 tablespoons **butter**
4 **eggs**
4 tablespoons **heavy cream**
2 teaspoons chopped **chives**
1 teaspoon chopped **tarragon**
7 oz **sliced smoked salmon**
salt and **pepper**
4 **lemon** wedges, to garnish
4 slices of **toast**, halved diagonally,
   to serve

Preheat the slow cooker if necessary. Liberally butter the inside of 4 4-ounce ramekins, checking first that they will fit in the slow-cooker pot.

Break an egg into each dish. Drizzle 1 tablespoon cream over each egg and sprinkle with the herbs and a little salt and pepper. Transfer the ramekins to the slow-cooker pot and pour boiling water into the pot to come halfway up the sides of the ramekins.

Cover with the lid (there is no need to cover the individual ramekins with foil) and cook on high for 40 to 45 minutes, or until the egg whites are set and the yolks still slightly soft.

Lift the dishes carefully out of the slow-cooker pot with a dish towel and transfer to plates with the smoked salmon. Garnish with the lemon wedges and serve with the triangles of toast.

FOR SPICED EGGS EN COCOTTE, break the eggs into buttered dishes and drizzle 1 tablespoon heavy cream, a few drops of Tabasco sauce, and some salt and pepper over each. Sprinkle them with 3 teaspoons finely chopped cilantro and cook as above. Serve with toast and thin slices of pastrami.

BIG BREAKFAST BONANZA

Serves **4**
Preparation time **20 minutes**
Cooking temperature **low**
Cooking time **9 to 10 hours** or **overnight**

1 tablespoon **sunflower oil**
12 **small sausages with herbs**, about 13 oz in total
1 **onion**, thinly sliced
1 lb **potatoes**, cut into 1-inch chunks
¾ lb **tomatoes**, coarsely chopped
4 oz **blood sausage**, skinned and cut into chunks
1 cup **vegetable stock**
2 tablespoons **Worcestershire sauce**
1 teaspoon **English mustard**
2 to 3 **thyme sprigs**, plus extra to garnish
salt and **pepper**

Preheat the slow cooker if necessary. Heat the oil in a skillet, add the small sausages, and brown on one side, then turn them over and add the onion. Fry, turning the sausages over and stirring the onions, until the sausages are browned but not cooked.

Add the potatoes, tomatoes, and blood sausage to the slow-cooker pot. Lift the sausages and onion from the pan with a slotted spoon and transfer to the slow-cooker pot. Pour off the excess fat, then add the stock, Worcestershire sauce, and mustard. Pick the leaves from the thyme sprigs and add to the pan with some salt and pepper. Bring to a boil and pour over the sausages.

Press the potatoes down so that the liquid covers them. Cover with the lid and cook on low for 9 to 10 hours or overnight. Stir before serving and garnish with extra thyme leaves.

FOR A VEGETARIAN BIG BREAKFAST, fry 13 oz meat-free sausages in the oil with the onion as above. Add the potatoes and tomatoes to the slow-cooker pot with 4 oz halved button mushrooms instead of the blood sausage. Heat the stock with the mustard and thyme and add 1 tablespoon tomato paste instead of the Worcestershire sauce. Season with salt and pepper, then pour the mixture over the sausages in the slow cooker. Cover and cook as above.

EASY SAUSAGE & BEANS

Serves **4**
Preparation time **15 minutes**
Cooking temperature **low**
Cooking time **9 to 10 hours** or **overnight**

1 tablespoon **sunflower oil**
1 **onion**, chopped
½ teaspoon **smoked paprika**
2 × 14 oz cans **baked beans**
2 teaspoons **wholegrain mustard**
2 tablespoons **Worcestershire sauce**
⅓ cup **vegetable stock**
2 **tomatoes**, coarsely chopped
½ **red bell pepper**, cored, seeded, and diced
11½ oz **frankfurters**, chilled and thickly sliced
salt and **pepper**

Preheat the slow cooker if necessary. Heat the oil in a skillet, add the onion, and fry, stirring, for 5 minutes or until softened and just beginning to turn golden.

Stir in the paprika and cook for 1 minute, then mix in the beans, mustard, Worcestershire sauce, and stock. Bring to a boil, then stir in the tomatoes, red bell pepper, and a little salt and pepper.

Add the frankfurters to the slow-cooker pot and pour the baked bean mixture over them. Cover with the lid and cook on low for 9 to 10 hours or overnight.

Stir well, then spoon into shallow bowls and serve with hot buttered toast fingers, if liked.

FOR SAUSAGE WITH CHILES & BEANS, fry the onion in the oil as above, then add ½ teaspoon crushed dried red chiles, ¼ teaspoon cumin seeds, coarsely crushed in a mortar and pestle, and a pinch of ground cinnamon along with the smoked paprika. Omit the mustard and Worcestershire sauce, then continue as above, adding the beans, stock, tomatoes, red bell pepper, and frankfurters. Cook on low for 9 to 10 hours or overnight.

BAKED EGGS WITH TOAST FINGERS

Serves **4**
Preparation time **15 minutes**
Cooking temperature **high**
Cooking time **40 to 50 minutes**

2 tablespoons **butter**
4 wafer-thin slices of **honey-roasted ham**, about 2½ oz in total
4 teaspoons **spicy tomato chutney**
4 **eggs**
2 **cherry tomatoes**, halved
1 **scallion**, finely sliced
salt and **pepper**
4 slices of **buttered toast**, cut into fingers, to serve

Preheat the slow cooker if necessary. Grease 4 heatproof dishes, each 4 ounces in capacity, with a little of the butter, checking first that they will fit in the slow-cooker pot, then press a slice of ham into each to line the bottom and sides, leaving a small overhang of ham above the dish.

Add 1 teaspoon of chutney to the bottom of each dish, then break an egg on top. Add a cherry tomato half to each, sprinkle with the chopped scallion and a little salt and pepper, then dot with the remaining butter.

Cover each dish with a square of foil and set them into the slow-cooker pot. Pour boiling water into the pot to come halfway up the sides of the dishes. Cover with the lid and cook on high for 40 to 50 minutes or until the egg whites are set and the yolks still slightly soft.

Lift the dishes out of the slow-cooker pot using a dish towel and remove the foil. Loosen the ham and the inside edge of the dishes with a knife and turn out. Quickly turn the baked eggs the right way up and arrange each one on a plate with the hot buttered toast fingers.

FOR EGGS BENEDICT, butter 4 dishes as above, then break an egg into each one, sprinkle with salt and pepper and the sliced scallion, and dot with the remaining butter. Cover with foil and cook as above. To serve, broil 8 slices of Canadian bacon until golden. Spread 4 toasted, halved English muffins with butter, divide the bacon between the bottom halves, and arrange on serving plates. Top with the baked eggs and remaining muffin halves and serve drizzled with ½ cup warmed ready-made hollandaise sauce.

BRUNCH POACHED EGGS & HADDOCK

Serves **2**
Preparation time **5 minutes**
Cooking temperature **high**
Cooking time **1 to 1¼ hours**

low-calorie cooking oil spray
2 **eggs**
1 teaspoon snipped **chives**,
    plus extra to garnish
2 **smoked haddock steaks**,
    4 oz each
2 cups boiling **water**
4 oz **baby spinach**
salt and **pepper**

Preheat the slow cooker if necessary. Spray the insides of 2 small ovenproof dishes or ramekins with a little low-calorie cooking oil spray, then break an egg into each. Sprinkle with a few chives and season to taste.

Place the egg dishes in the center of the slow-cooker pot, then arrange a fish steak on each side. Pour the measurement boiling water over the fish so that the water comes halfway up the sides of the dishes. Cover and cook on high for 1 to 1¼ hours until the eggs are done to your liking and the fish flakes easily when pressed in the center with a small knife.

Rinse the spinach with a little water, drain, and place in a microwave-proof dish. Cover and cook in a microwave on full power for 1 minute until just wilted. Divide between 2 serving plates, and top with the fish steaks. Loosen the eggs with a knife and turn out of their dishes on top of the fish. Sprinkle with extra snipped chives, season with salt and pepper, and serve.

FOR BRUNCH POACHED EGGS WITH SALMON, follow the recipe above, using 2 wild salmon steaks, weighing 3½ oz each, instead of the smoked haddock. Arrange 2 sliced tomatoes on the serving plates, top with the cooked salmon and eggs, and serve.

BANANA & CINNAMON PORRIDGE

Serves **4**
Preparation time **5 minutes**
Cooking temperature **low**
Cooking time **1** or **2 hours**

2½ cups boiling **water**
1¼ cups **milk**
2 cups **oatmeal**
2 **bananas**
¼ cup **light** or **dark brown sugar**
¼ teaspoon **ground cinnamon**

Preheat the slow cooker if necessary. Pour the measurement boiling water and milk into the slow-cooker pot, then stir in the oatmeal.

Cover with the lid and cook on low for 1 hour for "runny" porridge or 2 hours for "thick" porridge.

Spoon into bowls, then slice the bananas and divide between the bowls. Mix together the sugar and cinnamon and sprinkle over the top.

FOR HOT SPICED MUESLI, follow the recipe as above, adding 6 oz Swiss-style muesli. When cooked, stir in ¼ teaspoon ground cinnamon and top with ⅓ cup diced ready-to-eat dried apricots. Drizzle with 2 tablespoons liquid honey before serving.

ROLLED OATS & MIXED SEED GRANOLA

Serves **4**
Preparation time **10 minutes**
Cooking temperature **high**
Cooking time **2½ to 3 hours**

1 cup **medium rolled oats**
½ cup **jumbo rolled oats**
3 tablespoons **pumpkin seeds**
3 tablespoons **sunflower seeds**
1½ tablespoons **flaxseeds**
¼ teaspoon **ground cinnamon**
1 tablespoon **olive oil**
3 tablespoons **date syrup**
juice of **½ orange**
3 tablespoons **dried goji berries**

TO SERVE
2½ cups **skim milk**
sliced **banana**
sliced **strawberries**
raspberries

Preheat the slow cooker if necessary. Place the rolled oats and seeds in the slow-cooker pot and stir well. Add the cinnamon, olive oil, date syrup, and orange juice and mix again until thoroughly combined. Cover and cook on high for 1½ to 2 hours, stirring once or twice with a fork to break the mixture into clumps.

Remove the lid and cook for 1 hour more until the granola is crisp. Break up once more with a fork, add the goji berries, then let cool. Store in an airtight jar in the refrigerator until ready to serve.

Serve in bowls, topped with the skim milk and fruit.

FOR HONEYED ROLLED OATS & FRUIT GRANOLA, follow the recipe above, omitting the pumpkin seeds and using 3 tablespoons liquid honey instead of the date syrup. Add 3½ tablespoons dried cranberries and 2½ tablespoons dried cherries instead of the goji berries and serve as above.

VANILLA BREAKFAST PRUNES & FIGS

Serves **4**
Preparation time **5 minutes**
Cooking temperature **low**
Cooking time **8 to 10 hours**
  or **overnight**

1 **English Breakfast teabag**
2½ cups boiling **water**
1 cup **ready-to-eat pitted prunes**
1 cup **dried figs**
⅓ cup **superfine sugar**
1 teaspoon **vanilla extract**
peeled zest of ½ **orange**

TO SERVE
natural yogurt
muesli

Preheat the slow cooker if necessary. Put the teabag into a heatproof bowl or teapot, add the measurement boiling water, and let brew for 2 to 3 minutes. Remove the teabag and pour the tea into the slow-cooker pot.

Add the whole prunes and figs, the sugar, and vanilla extract to the hot tea, scatter with the orange zest, and stir to combine. Cover with the lid and cook on low for 8 to 10 hours or overnight.

Serve hot with spoonfuls of natural yogurt and a sprinkling of muesli.

FOR BREAKFAST APRICOTS IN ORANGE, put 10 oz ready-to-eat dried apricots, ¼ cup superfine sugar, 1¼ cups boiling water, and ¾ cup orange juice in the slow cooker. Cover and cook as above.

BERRY COMPOTE WITH SYLLABUB CREAM

Serves **4**
Preparation time **20 minutes,**
  plus cooling
Cooking temperature **low**
Cooking time **1½ to 2 hours**

1 lb **strawberries**, hulled and halved
  or quartered if large
1¼ cups **blueberries**
grated zest and juice of 1 **lemon**
3 tablespoons **superfine sugar**
3 tablespoons **water**
lemon zest curls or small **herb**
  or **pansy flowers**, to decorate

SYLLABUB CREAM
⅔ cup **heavy cream**
2 tablespoons **superfine sugar**
grated zest of ½ **lemon**
2 tablespoons **dry white wine**

Preheat the slow cooker if necessary. Put the strawberries, blueberries, lemon zest and juice, sugar, and measurement water into the slow-cooker pot. Cover with the lid and cook on low for 1½ to 2 hours or until the fruit is tender but still holds its shape.

Lift the pot out of the housing using oven mitts and let the compote cool. Just before serving, make the syllabub cream. Pour the cream into a bowl, add the sugar and lemon zest, and beat until it forms soft swirls. Add the white wine and beat for another 1 to 2 minutes or until thick again.

Spoon the fruit into tall champagne-style glasses and top with spoonfuls of the syllabub cream. Decorate with lemon zest curls or small herb or pansy flowers and serve immediately.

FOR PEACH COMPOTE WITH VANILLA, halve and stone 6 firm, ripe peaches, then add to the slow-cooker pot with ⅓ cup superfine sugar, ¾ cup Marsala or sweet sherry, ¾ cup water, and a slit vanilla bean. Cover and cook as above. Transfer the peaches to a serving dish. Scrape the seeds from the vanilla bean and add to the syrup, then discard the bean. Mix 2 teaspoons cornstarch with a little cold water to make a smooth paste, stir into the syrup in the slow-cooker pot, cover with the lid, and cook on high for 15 minutes. Stir well, then pour over the peaches. Sprinkle with ¾ cup raspberries and let cool. Serve with spoonfuls of crème fraîche.

TOFFEE APPLE PANCAKES

Serves **4 to 6**
Preparation time **10 minutes**
Cooking temperature **high**
Cooking time **1 to 1½ hours**

3½ tablespoons **butter**
½ cup **light brown sugar**
2 tablespoons **light corn syrup**
4 **apples**, cored and each cut into
    8 slices
juice of 1 **lemon**
12 oz-package or 6
    ready-made pancakes
vanilla ice cream, to serve

Preheat the slow cooker if necessary. Heat the butter, sugar, and syrup in a saucepan or in a microwave-proof bowl in the microwave until the butter has just melted.

Add the apples and lemon juice to the slow-cooker pot and toss together. Stir the butter mixture and pour it over the apples. Cover with the lid and cook on high for 1 to 1½ hours or until the apples are tender but still holding their shape.

Heat the pancakes in a skillet or the microwave following the package instructions. Fold in half and arrange on serving plates. Stir the apple mixture, then spoon it onto the pancakes. Top with scoops of vanilla ice cream.

FOR TOFFEE BANANA PANCAKES, make the recipe as above, replacing the apples with 6 small, thickly sliced bananas and adding ¾ cup boiling water. When ready to serve, reheat 6 pancakes, spread with 3 tablespoons chocolate and hazelnut spread, then top with the bananas and ice cream.

CREPES WITH FRUIT COMPOTE

Serves **4**
Preparation time **15 minutes**
Cooking temperature **high** and **low**
Cooking time **2 to 2½ hours**

10 oz **ripe red plums**, halved, pitted,
    and diced
1 **apple**, quartered, cored, and diced
1 cup **blackberries**
¼ teaspoon **ground cinnamon**, plus
    extra to decorate
1 tablespoon **granulated sweetener**
3 tablespoons **water**
¾ cup **fromage frais or quark**,
    to serve

CREPES
¾ cup **all-purpose flour**
1 **egg** and 1 **egg yolk**
1 cup **skim milk**
sunflower or **vegetable oil**, for oiling

Preheat the slow cooker if necessary. Place all the compote ingredients in the slow-cooker pot, stir well, cover, and cook on high for 2 to 2½ hours until the fruits have softened.

Meanwhile, make the crepe batter. Place the flour in a large bowl, create a well in the middle, and add the whole egg, egg yolk, and milk. Beat, starting from the center, gradually drawing the flour into the eggs and milk. Once all the flour is incorporated, beat until you have a smooth, thick batter. Let stand for 30 minutes.

When ready to serve, heat a 7-inch skillet over medium heat, wipe it with oiled paper towels, and ladle some of the crepe batter into it, tilting the skillet to move the batter around to create a thin and even layer. Let cook for at least 30 seconds before flipping the crepe over to cook on the other side. Transfer to a plate and keep warm. The batter will make 4 crepes. Alternatively, use 4 ready-made crepes, 2 oz each, and heat in a skillet or microwave following the package instructions.

Place each crepe on a serving plate. Top with the fruit compote, then fold the crepes in half and spoon the fromage frais on top. Sprinkle with a little extra cinnamon and serve immediately.

FOR ORCHARD FRUIT SUNDAES, follow the recipe above to make the fruit compote and let cool. Spoon into 4 glasses, top with 1 cup fromage frais or quark (divided between the 4 servings), and drizzle each portion with 2 teaspoons maple syrup.

APPETIZERS

LETTUCE WRAPPERS

Serves **4**
Preparation time **20 minutes**
Cooking temperature **low**
Cooking time **8 to 9 hours**

1 tablespoon **sunflower oil**
1½ lb **beef chuck**, cut into
    small cubes
1 **onion**, chopped
2 **garlic cloves**, minced
2 tablespoons **all-purpose flour**
1½ cups **beef stock**
1 teaspoon **crushed dried red chiles**
½ teaspoon **chili powder**
2 tablespoons **soy sauce**
2 tablespoons **hoisin sauce**
2 tablespoons **rice vinegar**
1 tablespoon **dark brown sugar**
pepper

TO SERVE
1 **iceberg lettuce**
1 small **red onion**, thinly sliced
small handful of **cilantro**,
    coarsely chopped

Preheat the slow cooker if necessary. Heat the oil in a large skillet, add the beef a few pieces at a time, then fry over high heat, stirring, until browned.

Add the onion and garlic and fry for 3 to 4 minutes until softened. Sprinkle with the flour and mix it in, then gradually stir in the stock. Scatter with the chiles and chili powder, then stir in the soy and hoisin sauces, vinegar, and sugar. Season with a little pepper.

Bring to a boil, then transfer to the slow-cooker pot. Press the meat beneath the liquid, cover with the lid, and cook on low for 8 to 9 hours until the beef is tender.

Separate the lettuce leaves, spoon a little of the beef into each lettuce cup, then scatter with the red onion and cilantro. To eat, you fold the leaves over the beef filling to pick up the parcels or eat them with a knife and fork.

FOR BEEF "PEKING DUCK" WRAPPERS, make and cook the beef as above. Warm 16 Chinese pancakes in a steamer following the package instructions. Separate the pancakes, then top with spoonfuls of the hot beef, ½ cucumber, cut into matchstick strips, and a bunch of scallions, cut into matchstick strips. Roll up and serve immediately.

EGGPLANT TIMBALE

Serves **2**
Preparation time **25 minutes**
Cooking temperature **high**
Cooking time **1½ to 2 hours**

4 tablespoons **olive oil**, divided,
   plus extra for oiling
1 large **eggplant**, thinly sliced
1 small **onion**, chopped
1 **garlic clove**, minced
½ teaspoon **ground cinnamon**
¼ teaspoon grated **nutmeg**
3½ tablespoons **pistachio nuts**,
   coarsely chopped
2½ tablespoons **pitted dates**,
   coarsely chopped
3 tablespoons **ready-to-eat dried
   apricots**, coarsely chopped
½ cup **converted long-grain
   white rice**
1¼ cups boiling **vegetable stock**
salt and **pepper**

Preheat the slow cooker if necessary. Lightly oil the bottom of 2 soufflé dishes, each with a capacity of 12 ounces, and line the bottom of each with a disk of nonstick parchment paper, checking first that both dishes will fit in the slow-cooker pot.

Heat 1 tablespoon of the oil in a large skillet, add one-third of the eggplant slices, and fry on both sides until softened and golden. Scoop out of the pan with a slotted spoon and transfer to a plate. Repeat with the rest of the eggplant slices using 2 more tablespoons of oil.

Heat the remaining 1 tablespoon of oil in the pan, add the onion, and fry for 5 minutes or until softened. Stir in the garlic, spices, nuts, fruit, and rice. Add a little salt and pepper and mix well.

Arrange one-third of the eggplant slices in the bottom of the 2 dishes, overlapping the slices. Spoon one-quarter of the rice mixture into each dish, add a second layer of eggplant slices, then divide the remaining rice equally between the dishes. Top with the remaining eggplant slices. Pour the stock into the dishes, cover with lightly oiled foil, and put in the slow-cooker pot.

Pour boiling water into the pot to come halfway up the sides of the dishes. Cover with the lid and cook on high for 1½ to 2 hours or until the rice is tender. Lift the dishes out of the slow-cooker pot using a dish towel and remove the foil. Loosen the edges of the timbales with a knife, invert onto plates, and peel off the lining paper. Serve hot with a green salad and baked tomatoes on the side, if liked.

STICKY RIBS

Serves **4**
Preparation time **20 minutes**
Cooking temperature **high**
Cooking time **5 to 6 hours**

2¾ lb **pork ribs**
1 **onion**, quartered
2 **carrots**, thickly sliced
1 teaspoon **dried mixed herbs**
2 tablespoons **malt vinegar**
2 pints boiling **water**
salt and **pepper**

GLAZE
2 tablespoons **tomato ketchup**
2 tablespoons **honey**
2 tablespoons **Worcestershire sauce**
1 teaspoon **Dijon mustard**

Preheat the slow cooker if necessary. Add the ribs, onion, and carrots to the slow-cooker pot, then scatter with the dried herbs. Mix the vinegar into the measurement boiling water, pour the mixture into the pot, then season with salt and pepper.

Cover and cook on high for 5 to 6 hours or until the meat is almost falling off of the bone.

Line a broiler pan with foil, lift the ribs out of the slow-cooker pot using a slotted spoon, and arrange them in a single layer on the foil. Then add a ladleful of the cooking liquid.

Mix the ingredients for the glaze together, then brush the mixture over the ribs. Cook under a preheated medium broiler for 10 minutes, turning and brushing once or twice, until coated with a sticky glaze.

Arrange the ribs on serving plates and serve with coleslaw and baked beans on the side, if liked.

FOR COLA RIBS, bring 2 pints (34 fl oz) cola to a boil in a saucepan, then pour it over the ribs and vegetables instead of the vinegar and boiling water. Cover, cook, and glaze as above.

BRANDIED DUCK & WALNUT TERRINE

Serves **6**
Preparation time **45 minutes**, plus
    cooling and **overnight chilling**
Cooking temperature **high**
Cooking time **5 to 6 hours**

6 oz **smoked bacon, slices
    rind removed**
1 tablespoon **olive oil**
1 **onion**, chopped
2 **boneless spare rib pork chops**,
    about 9 oz in total
2 **boneless duck breasts**,
    about ¾ lb in total, fat
    removed, divided
2 **garlic cloves**, chopped
3 tablespoons **brandy**
1½ cups **fresh bread crumbs**
½ cup **sun-dried tomatoes in oil**,
    drained and chopped
3 **pickled walnuts**, drained and
    coarsely chopped
1 **egg**, beaten
1 tablespoon **green peppercorns**,
    coarsely crushed
salt

Preheat the slow cooker if necessary. Lay the bacon slices on a cutting board and stretch each one with the flat of a large cook's knife until half as long again. Line the bottom and sides of a 6-inch diameter, deep soufflé dish with the bacon, checking first that the dish will fit in the slow-cooker pot.

Heat the oil in a skillet, add the onion, and fry, stirring, for 5 minutes. Finely chop or grind the pork and 1 of the duck breasts. Cut the second duck breast into long, thin slices and set aside. Stir the garlic and chopped or ground meat into the pan and cook for 3 minutes. Add the brandy, ignite with a match, and stand well back until the flames subside.

Stir in the remaining ingredients. Mix well, then press half the mixture into the bacon-lined dish. Top with the sliced duck, then add the remaining mixture. Fold the bacon ends over the top, adding any leftover slices to cover the gaps. Cover with foil.

Place the dish on an upturned saucer in the bottom of the slow-cooker pot. Pour boiling water around the dish to come halfway up the sides. Cover with the lid and cook on high for 5 to 6 hours or until the meat juices run clear when the center of the terrine is pierced with a knife.

Lift the dish carefully out of the pot using a dish towel, stand it on a plate, remove the foil top, and replace with wax paper. Weigh down the top of the terrine with a heavy can of food, for example, set on a small plate. Transfer to the refrigerator when cool enough and let chill overnight.

To serve, remove the wax paper, then loosen the edge of the terrine with a knife, turn out onto a cutting board, and cut into thick slices.

BAKED BELL PEPPERS WITH CHORIZO

Serves **4**
Preparation time **20 minutes**
Cooking temperature **high**
Cooking time **3 to 4 hours**

2 large **red bell peppers**, halved
    lengthwise, cored, and seeded
2 **scallions**, thinly sliced
2 oz **chorizo**, skinned and finely diced
7 oz **cherry tomatoes**, halved
1 to 2 **garlic cloves**, minced
small handful of **basil**, torn, plus extra
    to garnish
4 pinches of **smoked hot paprika**
1 tablespoon **balsamic vinegar**
salt and **pepper**

Preheat the slow cooker if necessary. Arrange the bell peppers, cut-sides up, in a single layer in the bottom of the slow-cooker pot. Divide the scallions and chorizo between the bell peppers, then pack in the cherry tomatoes.

Sprinkle with the garlic and torn basil, then add a pinch of paprika and a drizzle of balsamic vinegar to each one. Season to taste, cover, and cook on high for 3 to 4 hours until the bell peppers have softened.

Transfer to a platter and scatter with extra basil leaves. Serve hot or cold as a light lunch with salad, if liked.

FOR BAKED BELL PEPPER PIZZAS, follow the recipe above, omitting the chorizo and paprika. When cooked, transfer the bell peppers to a shallow baking dish. Tear 5 oz mozzarella cheese into small pieces, scatter them evenly over the bell peppers, then place under a preheated hot broiler for 4 to 5 minutes until the cheese is bubbling and golden. Garnish with extra torn basil and 4 pitted black olives.

TOMATO, PEPPER & GARLIC BRUSCHETTA ♥

Serves **4**
Preparation time **20 minutes**
Cooking temperature **high**
Cooking time **3 to 5 hours**

1 large **red bell pepper**, quartered, cored, and seeded
1 lb **plum tomatoes**, halved
4 large **garlic cloves**, unpeeled
leaves from 2 to 3 **thyme sprigs**
1 teaspoon **granulated sweetener**
1 tablespoon **virgin olive oil**
8 slices of **French bread**, 6 oz in total
8 **pitted black olives in brine**, drained
salt and **pepper**

Preheat the slow cooker if necessary. Arrange the bell pepper pieces, skin-side down, in the bottom of the slow-cooker pot, arrange the tomatoes on top, then tuck the garlic cloves in among them. Scatter the thyme leaves on top, reserving a little to garnish. Sprinkle with the sweetener and drizzle with the oil.

Season to taste, cover, and cook on high for 3 to 5 hours until the vegetables are tender but the tomatoes still hold their shape.

Lift the vegetables out of the slow-cooker pot with a slotted spoon. Peel the skins off the bell peppers, tomatoes, and garlic, then coarsely chop the vegetables and toss together. Adjust the seasoning if necessary.

Toast the bread on both sides, arrange on a serving plate, then spoon the tomato mixture on top. Arrange the olives and reserved thyme on the bruschetta and serve as a light lunch or starter.

FOR QUICK TOMATO & BELL PEPPER PIZZAS, follow the recipe above to cook the tomato and bell pepper mixture, then spoon onto 2 halved and toasted ciabatta. Sprinkle with ½ cup shredded reduced-fat Cheddar cheese and place under a preheated hot broiler to melt the cheese. Serve with a salad.

CHEESE FONDUE WITH BEER

Serves **4**
Preparation time **15 minutes**
Cooking temperature **high**
Cooking time **40 to 60 minutes**

1 tablespoon **butter**
2 **shallots** or ½ small **onion**, minced
1 **garlic clove**, minced
3 teaspoons **cornstarch**
7 fl oz **blonde beer** or **lager**
7 oz **Gruyère cheese** (rind removed), shredded
6 oz **Emmental cheese** (rind removed), shredded
grated **nutmeg**
salt and **pepper**

TO SERVE
½ **wholewheat French stick**, cubed
2 **celery stalks**, cut into short pieces
8 small **pickled onions**, drained and halved
bunch of **radishes**, tops trimmed
1 **red bell pepper**, cored, seeded, and cubed
2 **endives**, leaves separated

Preheat the slow cooker if necessary. Butter the inside of the slow-cooker pot, then add the shallots or onion and garlic.

Put the cornstarch in a small bowl and mix with a little of the beer to make a smooth paste, then blend with the remaining beer. Add to the slow cooker with both cheeses, nutmeg, and some salt and pepper.

Stir together, then cover with the lid and cook on high for 40 to 60 minutes, whisking once during cooking. Whisk again and serve with the dippers arranged on a serving plate, with long fondue or ordinary forks for dunking the dippers into the fondue.

FOR CLASSIC CHEESE FONDUE, omit the beer from the ingredients above and add ¾ cup dry white wine and 1 tablespoon kirsch. Cook as above and serve with bread for dipping.

DUCK, PORK & APPLE RILLETTES

Serves **4**
Preparation time **30 minutes, plus
    cooling** and **overnight chilling**
Cooking temperature **high**
Cooking time **5 to 6 hours**

2 **duck legs**
1 lb **pork belly slices**, rind
    removed, halved
1 **onion**, cut into wedges
1 **tart apple**, such as Granny Smith,
    peeled, cored, and thickly sliced
2 to 3 **thyme sprigs**
1 cup **chicken stock**
⅔ cup **hard dry cider**
salt and **pepper**

Preheat the slow cooker if necessary. Put the duck and pork belly into the bottom of the slow-cooker pot. Tuck the onion and apple between the pieces of meat and add the thyme.

Pour the stock and hard cider into a saucepan and add plenty of salt and pepper. Bring to a boil, then pour into the slow-cooker pot. Cover with the lid and cook on high for 5 to 6 hours or until the duck and pork are cooked through and tender.

Lift the meat out of the slow-cooker pot with a slotted spoon and transfer to a large plate, then let cool for 30 minutes. Peel away the duck skin and remove the bones. Shred the meat into small pieces and discard the thyme sprigs. Scoop out the apple and onion with a slotted spoon, finely chop, and mix with the meat, then taste and adjust the seasoning, if needed.

Pack the chopped meat mix into 4 individual dishes or small preserving jars and press down firmly. Spoon over the juices from the slow-cooker pot to cover and seal the meat. Let cool, then transfer to the refrigerator and chill overnight.

When the fat has solidified on the top, cover each dish with a lid or plastic wrap and store in the refrigerator for up to 1 week. Serve the rillettes with warm crusty bread, a few radishes, and pickled shallots, if liked.

FOR CHICKEN, PORK & PRUNE RILLETTES, omit the duck and put 2 chicken leg pieces into the slow-cooker pot with the pork belly slices, onion, and thyme, replacing the apple with ½ cup ready-to-eat pitted prunes. Continue as above.

GARLICKY PORK & SAGE PÂTÉ

Serves **6 to 8**
Preparation time **30 minutes, plus
   cooling** and **overnight chilling**
Cooking temperature **high**
Cooking time **5 to 6 hours**

bunch of **sage**
1 tablespoon **olive oil**, plus extra
   for oiling
1 small **onion**, chopped
13 oz or 6 **Toulouse sausages**,
   casings slit and removed
3 oz diced **smoked bacon**
7 oz **boneless pork belly slices**,
   finely diced
5 oz **chicken livers**, rinsed with
   cold water and drained
1 **egg**, beaten
2 tablespoons **sherry vinegar**
salt and **pepper**

Preheat the slow cooker if necessary. Oil a 2-pint rectangular baking dish and line the bottom and 2 long sides with nonstick parchment paper, checking first that it will fit in the slow-cooker pot. Cover the bottom with sage leaves, reserving the remainder.

Heat the oil in a skillet, add the onion, and fry until softened. Transfer to a bowl and add the sausages, bacon, and diced pork. Chop the drained chicken livers, discarding the white cores. Add to the bowl with the egg, vinegar, and plenty of salt and pepper. Mix together, then spoon half the mixture into the dish and press down firmly.

Arrange more sage leaves onto the pâté, then cover with the remaining mixture. Press down firmly and arrange the remaining sage leaves on the top. Cover loosely with foil and place the dish in the slow-cooker pot. Pour boiling water into the pot to come halfway up the sides of the dish. Cover with the lid or foil, and cook on high for 5 to 6 hours, or until the meat juices run clear when the center of the pâté is pierced with a knife.

Lift the dish out of the slow-cooker pot using a dish towel, pour off the excess fat, stand the dish on a plate, then cover the top with a second plate and weigh down with something heavy, such as a can of food. Let cool, then transfer to the refrigerator overnight.

To serve, remove the weights, plate, and foil. Loosen the edges of the pâté with a knife, then invert onto a cutting board and peel off the parchment paper. Cut into slices and serve with toasted bread and salad, if liked.

FISH TERRINE

Serves **6 to 8**
Preparation time **30 minutes,**
   plus cooling
Cooking temperature **high**
Cooking time **3 to 4 hours**

sunflower or **vegetable oil**, for oiling
¾ lb **skinless haddock** or **cod**, cubed
2 **egg whites**
grated zest of ½ **lemon**
juice of 1 **lemon**
1 cup **heavy cream**
4 oz **sliced smoked salmon** or **trout**
5 oz **salmon** or **trout fillet**,
   thinly sliced
salt and **pepper**

Preheat the slow cooker if necessary. Lightly oil a 2-pint soufflé dish and line the bottom with a disk of nonstick baking paper, checking first that the dish will fit in the slow-cooker pot. Blend the haddock or cod, egg whites, lemon zest, half the lemon juice, and salt and pepper in a food processor until coarsely chopped, then gradually add the cream and blend until just beginning to thicken.

Arrange half the smoked fish slices over the bottom of the dish. Spoon in half the fish mousse and spread it level. Mix the fish fillet with a little remaining lemon juice and some pepper, then arrange on top. Top with the remaining fish mousse, then the smoked fish slices.

Cover the top with foil and lower into the slow-cooker pot. Pour boiling water into the pot to come halfway up the sides of the dish. Cover with the lid and cook on high for 3 to 4 hours or until the fish is cooked through and the terrine is set.

Lift the dish out of the slow-cooker pot using a dish towel and let cool for 2 hours. Loosen the edge, invert onto a plate, and peel off the parchment paper. Cut into thick slices and serve with a salad and toast, if liked.

FOR SMOKED HADDOCK & CHIVE TERRINE, make the white fish mousse as above and flavor with ¼ cup chopped chives, 2 tablespoons chopped capers, and the grated zest and juice of ½ lemon. Omit the smoked fish and arrange 1 sliced tomato over the bottom of the dish. Cover with half the fish mousse, 5 oz thinly sliced smoked cod, then the remaining fish mousse. Continue the recipe as above.

TURKEY & CRANBERRY MEATLOAF

Serves **4 to 6**
Preparation time **30 minutes, plus
  cooling** and **overnight chilling**
Cooking temperature **high**
Cooking time **5 to 6 hours**

7 oz **smoked rindless bacon slices**
3¾ oz package **dried orange and
  cranberry stuffing mix**
3½ tablespoons **dried cranberries**
1 tablespoon **sunflower oil**, plus extra
  for oiling
1 **onion**, finely chopped
1 lb **skinless turkey breast steaks**
1 **egg**, beaten
salt and **pepper**

Preheat the slow cooker if necessary. Lightly oil a soufflé dish 5½ inches in diameter and 3½ inches deep, and line the bottom with nonstick parchment paper, checking first that the dish will fit in the slow-cooker pot. Lay the slices of bacon on a cutting board and stretch each one with the flat of a large cook's knife until half as long again. Use about three-quarters of the slices to line the bottom and sides of the dish, trimming to fit.

Put the stuffing mixture into a bowl, add the cranberries, and mix with boiling water following the package instructions. Heat the oil in a skillet, add the onion, and fry for 5 minutes, stirring, until softened. Set aside. Finely chop the turkey steaks in a food processor or pass through the coarse setting on a meat grinder.

Mix the stuffing with the fried onion, chopped turkey, and egg. Season well and spoon into the bacon-lined dish. Press flat and cover with the remaining bacon slices. Cover the top of the dish with foil and lower into the slow-cooker pot. Pour boiling water into the pot to come halfway up the sides of the dish. Cover with the lid and cook on high for 5 to 6 hours or until the juices run clear when the center of the meatloaf is pierced with a knife.

Lift the dish out of the slow-cooker pot using a dish towel and let cool. Transfer to the refrigerator to chill overnight until firm. Loosen the edge of the meatloaf with a knife, invert onto a plate, and peel off the nonstick parchment paper. Cut into thick slices and serve with salad and spoonfuls of cranberry sauce or sweet chutney, if liked.

SMOKED SALMON TIMBALES

Serves **4**
Preparation time **30 minutes, plus
    cooling** and **chilling**
Cooking temperature **low**
Cooking time **3 to 3½ hours**

butter, for greasing
1 cup **crème fraîche**
4 **egg yolks**
grated zest and juice of ½ **lemon**
1 small bunch of **basil**, divided
3½ oz **sliced smoked salmon**, divided
salt and **pepper**
lemon wedges, to garnish

Preheat the slow cooker, if necessary. Lightly butter 4 individual 5-ounce metal molds, and line the bottom with disks of nonstick parchment paper or wax paper, checking first that they will fit in the slow-cooker pot.

Put the crème fraîche in a bowl and slowly beat in the yolks. Add the lemon zest and juice and season with salt and pepper. Chop half the basil and 3 ounces of the smoked salmon. Stir both into the crème fraîche mixture.

Pour the mixture into the prepared molds. Stand the molds in the slow-cooker pot (there is no need to cover them with foil). Pour hot water around the molds to come halfway up the sides, cover with the lid, and cook on low for 3 to 3½ hours or until the mixture is set.

Remove the molds carefully from the slow cooker using a dish towel and let cool at room temperature. Transfer to the refrigerator and chill for at least hours or overnight.

Loosen the edges of the timbales with a knife dipped in hot water, then invert onto serving plates and remove the molds. Smooth any rough areas with the side of the knife and remove the parchment paper disks. Top with the remaining smoked salmon and basil leaves and garnish with lemon wedges.

FOR SMOKED MACKEREL TIMBALES, omit the basil and smoked salmon and stir in 3 tablespoons freshly snipped chives, ½ teaspoon hot horseradish, and 3 oz skinned, flaked smoked mackerel. Continue as above. Serve with a salad, if liked.

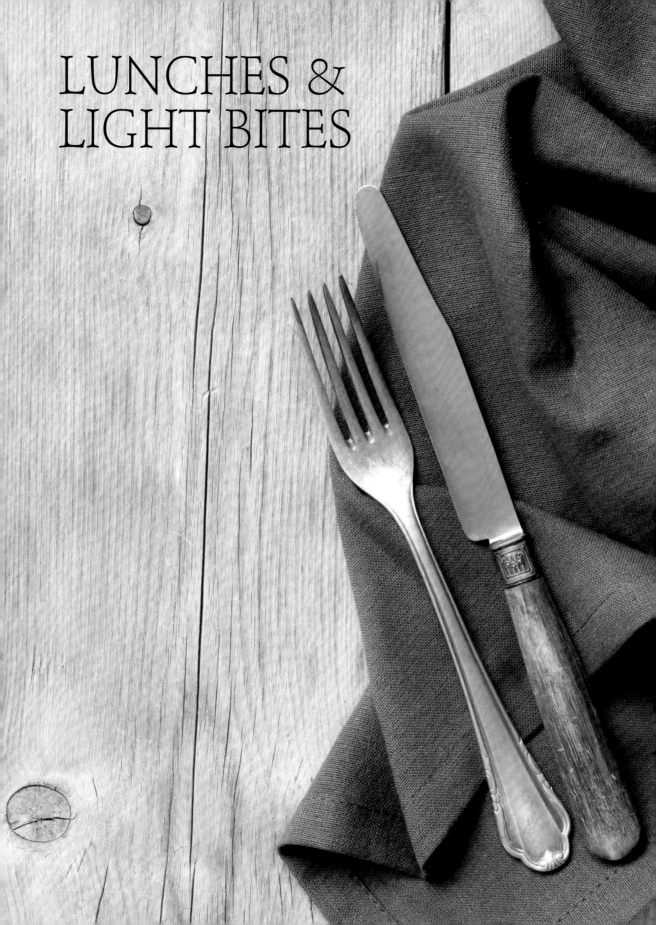

LUNCHES & LIGHT BITES

MUSHROOM & WHEATBERRY PILAU

Serves **4**
Preparation time **20 minutes**
Cooking temperature **high**
Cooking time **3½ to 4 hours**

1 tablespoon **olive oil**
1 **onion**, thinly sliced
2 **garlic cloves**, minced
11 fl oz **brown ale**
2 cups **vegetable stock**
3 **sage sprigs**
¼ teaspoon grated **nutmeg**
2-inch **cinnamon stick**
1 tablespoon **sun-dried tomato paste**
7 oz **wheatberries**
½ lb **cremino mushrooms**, halved
½ lb large **white mushrooms**,
   quartered
salt and **pepper**
¼ cup **parsley**, coarsely chopped,
   to garnish

Preheat the slow cooker if necessary. Heat the oil in a large skillet over medium heat until hot. Add the onion and fry for 4 to 5 minutes, stirring, until just beginning to soften. Add the garlic, brown ale, stock, sage, nutmeg, and cinnamon. Stir in the tomato paste and season well, then bring to a boil.

Place the wheatberries and mushrooms in the slow-cooker pot. Pour in the hot ale mixture, then cover and cook on high for 3½ to 4 hours until the wheatberries are tender and nearly all the liquid has been absorbed. Stir well, then scatter with the parsley. Spoon into shallow bowls to serve.

FOR RED PEPPER WHEATBERRY PILAU, fry 1 sliced red onion in the oil as above, then add 2 minced garlic cloves and 2 cored, seeded, and sliced red bell peppers. Stir in 1 cup red wine, 2½ cups vegetable stock, a small handful of basil leaves, and 1 tablespoon sun-dried tomato paste. Season to taste and bring to a boil, then pour evenly over the wheatberries in the slow-cooker pot and cook as above.

WARM LENTIL & FETA SALAD

Serves **4**
Preparation time **20 minutes**
Cooking temperature **high**
Cooking time **3 to 4 hours**

¾ cup **dried Puy lentils**
1 **onion**, chopped
1 **red bell pepper**, cored, seeded,
    and sliced
½ lb **cherry tomatoes**
2½ cups boiling **vegetable stock**
2 tablespoons **tomato paste**
2 **thyme sprigs**
salt and **pepper**
¼ cup **olive oil**
2 tablespoons **balsamic vinegar**
3½ oz **mixed watercress, spinach,
    and arugula**
1 cup crumbled **feta cheese**
leaves from a small bunch of **mint**

Preheat the slow cooker if necessary. Put the lentils into a sieve, rinse well with cold water, drain, and add to the slow-cooker pot along with the onion, red bell pepper, and tomatoes.

Mix the boiling stock with the tomato paste, thyme, and season generously with salt and pepper. Pour over the lentils, cover with the lid, and cook on high for 3 to 4 hours or until the lentils are tender.

When almost ready to serve, beat the oil and balsamic vinegar together in a salad bowl, add the mixed leaves, and toss gently. Spoon the hot lentils into shallow bowls, draining off any excess cooking liquid. Pile the salad greens on top and scatter with the feta, mint leaves, and a little extra pepper. Serve immediately with warmed pitta bread, if liked. Alternatively, lift the pot out of the housing using oven mitts, let the lentils get cold, then make the dressing and toss together with the salad greens, feta, and mint.

FOR LENTIL SALAD WITH SARDINES & PEAS, cook the lentils as above, adding ¾ cup frozen peas for the last 15 minutes of cooking time. Drain 2 x 3¾ oz cans sardines in tomato sauce, reserving the sauce. Flake the fish into chunky pieces, discarding the bones. Stir the sauce into the lentils. Shred 2 baby gem lettuces and mix with ½ finely chopped red onion, then toss with the juice of 1 lemon, a small bunch of mint, coarsely chopped, and salt and pepper. Spoon the hot lentils into shallow bowls and top with the sardines and the lettuce salad. Serve immediately.

WARM BEET & BEAN SALAD

Serves **4 to 5**
Preparation time **25 minutes**
Cooking temperature **low**
Cooking time **3½ to 4½ hours**

1 tablespoon **olive oil**
1 large **onion**, chopped
1 lb **raw beets**, peeled and finely diced
2 × 14 oz cans **cranberry beans**, rinsed
  and drained
2 cups **vegetable stock**
salt and **pepper**

TO SERVE
¼ **cucumber**, finely diced
1 cup **plain yogurt**
1 **romaine** or **iceberg lettuce**
4 **red-** or **white-stemmed scallions**,
  thinly sliced
¼ cup chopped **cilantro** or **mint leaves**

Preheat the slow cooker if necessary. Heat the oil in a skillet, add the onion, and fry, stirring, for 5 minutes or until pale golden. Add the beets to the pan with the drained beans, stock, and plenty of salt and pepper. Bring to a boil, stirring.

Transfer the beet mixture to the slow-cooker pot. Cover with the lid and cook on low for 3½ to 4½ hours or until the beets are tender. Stir well and lift the pot out of the housing using oven mitts.

Stir the cucumber into the yogurt and season with salt and pepper. Arrange the lettuce leaves on 4 to 5 individual plates. Top with the warm beet salad, then add spoonfuls of the cucumber yogurt. Scatter with the scallions and cilantro or mint and serve at once.

FOR WARM BEET SALAD WITH FETA & TOMATOES, prepare the salad as above. Mix ¾ cup crumbled feta cheese with 2 diced tomatoes. Core, seed, and dice ½ red or orange bell pepper and combine with the cheese and tomatoes. Add ¼ cup chopped mint and 2 tablespoons olive oil. Spoon over the warm salad and top with 2½ cups arugula.

BEEF TORTILLAS WITH CHEESE & CHILES

Serves **4 to 5**
Preparation time **20 minutes**
Cooking temperature **low**
Cooking time **8 to 10 hours**

1 tablespoon **sunflower oil**
1 lb **extra-lean ground beef**
1 **onion**, chopped
2 **garlic cloves**, minced
1 teaspoon **smoked paprika**
½ teaspoon **crushed dried red chiles**
1 teaspoon **ground cumin**
1 tablespoon **all-purpose flour**
14 oz can **chopped tomatoes**
14 oz can **red kidney beans**, drained
¾ cup **beef stock**
1 tablespoon **dark brown sugar**
salt and **pepper**

TOPPING
3½ oz **tortilla chips**
½ **red bell pepper**, cored, seeded
  and diced
chopped **cilantro**
1 cup shredded **sharp Cheddar cheese**

Preheat the slow cooker if necessary. Heat the oil in a skillet, add the ground beef and onion, and fry, stirring and breaking up the beef with a wooden spoon, for 5 minutes until it is browned.

Stir in the garlic, paprika, chiles, and cumin and cook for 2 minutes. Stir in the flour. Mix in the tomatoes, kidney beans, stock, and sugar, season with salt and pepper, and pour the mixture into the slow-cooker pot. Cover with the lid and cook on low for 8 to 10 hours.

Stir the beef mixture then arrange the tortilla chips on top. Scatter with the remaining ingredients, lift the pot out of the housing using oven mitts, and place under a preheated hot broiler until the cheese just melts. Spoon into bowls to serve.

FOR TURKEY FAJITAS WITH GUACAMOLE, make the recipe as above, using 1 lb ground turkey instead of the beef. For the guacamole, halve, seed, and peel 1 avocado, then mash the flesh with the juice of 1 lime, a small bunch of torn cilantro, and some salt and pepper. Spoon the turkey mixture onto 8 warmed, medium-sized soft flour tortillas, top with spoonfuls of the guacamole, and 1 tablespoon each sour cream, if liked, and roll up to serve.

ZUCCHINI & FAVA BEAN FRITTATA

HOT QUINOA & BELL PEPPER SALAD

Serves **4**
Preparation time **15 minutes**
Cooking temperature **high**
Cooking time **1½ to 2 hours**

3 tablespoons **butter**
4 **scallions**, sliced
1 **zucchini**, about 7 oz, thinly sliced
¾ cup **fresh fava beans**
6 **eggs**
1 cup **crème fraîche**
2 teaspoons chopped **tarragon**
2 tablespoons chopped **parsley**
salt and **pepper**

Preheat the slow cooker if necessary. Heat the butter, scallions, and zucchini in a saucepan or in a microwave-proof bowl in the microwave until the butter has melted.

Line the slow-cooker pot with nonstick parchment paper, add the zucchini and butter mixture, then add the fava beans. Lightly beat together the eggs, crème fraîche, herbs, and a little salt and pepper in a bowl, then pour into the pot. Cover with the lid and cook on high for 1½ to 2 hours or until set in the middle.

Lift the pot out of the housing using oven mitts. Loosen the edge of the frittata with a knife, carefully invert onto a large plate and peel off the parchment paper. Cut into wedges and serve with salad, if liked.

FOR ZUCCHINI, SALMON & ASPARAGUS FRITTATA, add ¾ cup sliced asparagus tips to the butter, scallions, and zucchini when heating and replace the fava beans with 3½ oz chopped smoked salmon. Continue as above.

Serves **4**
Preparation time **15 minutes**
Cooking temperature **high**
Cooking time **3 to 4 hours**

3 **bell peppers**, cored, seeded, and cut into chunks
2 **celery stalks**, sliced
2 **zucchini**, halved lengthwise and thickly sliced
½ lb **plum tomatoes**, coarsely chopped
2 **garlic cloves**, finely chopped
4 oz **quinoa and bulgur wheat grain mix**
¼ cup **red wine**
1¼ cups hot **vegetable stock**
1 tablespoon **tomato paste**
1 teaspoon **granulated sweetener**
½ cup coarsely torn **basil leaves**
salt and **pepper**

Preheat the slow cooker if necessary. Place the bell peppers, celery, zucchini, and tomatoes in the slow-cooker pot and scatter with the garlic and the grain mix.

Mix the red wine with the stock, tomato paste, and sweetener, season to taste and pour into the slow-cooker pot. Stir the ingredients together, then cover and cook on high for 3 to 4 hours until the vegetables have softened and the grains have absorbed the liquid.

Stir the salad, then divide between 4 shallow bowls and serve topped with the torn basil leaves.

FOR HOT QUINOA & SHRIMP SALAD, follow the recipe above to make the quinoa salad and divide between 4 bowls. Omit the basil and divide 3½ oz mixed spinach, watercress, and arugula and 6 oz cooked shelled shrimp between the bowls.

BEET & CARAWAY RISOTTO

Serves **4**
Preparation time **15 minutes**
Cooking temperature **low**
Cooking time **5 to 6 hours**

1 cup **converted brown rice**
10 oz **raw beets**, peeled and diced
1 **red onion**, finely chopped
2 **garlic cloves**, minced
1 teaspoon **caraway seeds**
2 teaspoons **tomato paste**
2½ pints hot **vegetable stock**
salt and **pepper**

TO SERVE
¼ cup **Greek yogurt**
4 oz **smoked salmon slices**
handful of **arugula**

Preheat the slow cooker if necessary. Place the rice in a sieve, rinse well under cold running water, and drain well.

Place the beets, onion, and garlic in the slow-cooker pot, add the drained rice, caraway seeds, and tomato paste, then stir in the hot stock and season generously. Cover and cook on low for 5 to 6 hours until the rice and beets are tender.

Stir the risotto, spoon into shallow bowls, and top each portion with a tablespoonful of the yogurt, some of the smoked salmon, and a few arugula leaves. Serve immediately.

FOR PUMPKIN & SAGE RISOTTO, peel, seed, and cube a 10-ounce pumpkin and add it to the slow-cooker pot with 1 finely chopped white onion and 2 minced garlic cloves. Mix in 1½ cups rinsed converted brown rice and flavor with 2 sage sprigs, 1 teaspoon paprika, and 2 teaspoons tomato paste. Add 2½ pints hot vegetable stock, season, and cook as above. Serve scattered with ¾ cup finely grated Parmesan cheese.

SPINACH & ZUCCHINI TIAN

Serves **4**
Preparation time **20 minutes**
Cooking temperature **high**
Cooking time **1½ to 2 hours**

¼ cup **converted white rice**
butter, for greasing
1 **tomato**, sliced
1 tablespoon **olive oil**
½ **onion**, chopped
1 **garlic clove**, minced
1 **zucchini**, about 6 oz,
    coarsely grated
¼ lb **spinach**, rinsed, well drained,
    and thickly shredded
3 **eggs**
½ cup **milk**
pinch of grated **nutmeg**
¼ cup **fresh mint**
salt and **pepper**

Preheat the slow cooker if necessary. Bring a small saucepan of water to a boil, add the rice, bring back to a boil, then simmer for 8 to 10 minutes or until tender. Meanwhile, butter the inside of a soufflé dish 5½ inches in diameter and 3½ inches deep and line the bottom with a disk of nonstick parchment paper. Arrange the tomato slices, overlapping, on top.

Heat the oil in a skillet, add the onion, and fry, stirring, for 5 minutes or until softened and just beginning to turn golden. Stir in the garlic, then add the zucchini and spinach and cook for 2 minutes or until the spinach is just wilted.

Beat together the eggs, milk, nutmeg, and a little salt and pepper. Drain the rice and stir into the spinach mixture with the egg mixture and mint. Mix well, then spoon into the dish. Cover loosely with buttered foil and lower into the slow-cooker pot.

Pour boiling water into the slow-cooker pot to come halfway up the sides of the dish. Cover and cook on high for 1½ to 2 hours or until the tian is set in the middle. Lift the dish out of the slow cooker using a dish towel, let stand for 5 minutes, then remove the foil, loosen the edge, and invert onto a plate. Cut into wedges and serve warm with salad, if liked.

FOR CHEESY SPINACH & PINE NUT TIAN, omit the zucchini and instead stir in ½ cup freshly grated Parmesan cheese, a small bunch of chopped basil, and ¼ cup toasted pine nuts.

ROASTED VEGETABLE TERRINE

Serves **4**

Preparation time **30 minutes,**
   plus cooling

Cooking temperature **high**

Cooking time **2 to 3 hours**

¾ lb **zucchini**, thinly sliced

1 **red bell pepper**, quartered, cored,
   and seeded

1 **orange bell pepper**, quartered, cored,
   and seeded

2 tablespoons **olive oil**, plus extra
   for oiling

1 **garlic clove**, minced

2 **eggs**

¾ cup **milk**

¼ cup freshly grated **Parmesan cheese**

3 tablespoons chopped **basil**

salt and **pepper**

Preheat the slow cooker if necessary. Line a broiler rack with foil. Arrange all the vegetables on the foil in a single layer, with the bell peppers skin-side up. Drizzle with the oil and scatter with the garlic and season with salt and pepper. Cook under a preheated medium broiler for 10 minutes or until softened and browned. Transfer the zucchini slices to a plate and wrap the bell peppers in the foil. Let stand for 5 minutes to loosen the skins.

Oil a 1 lb loaf pan and line the bottom and 2 long sides with nonstick parchment paper, checking first that it will fit in the slow-cooker pot. Beat together the eggs, milk, Parmesan, basil, and salt and pepper in a bowl. Unwrap the bell peppers and peel off the skins with a knife.

Arrange one-third of the zucchini slices onto the bottom of the pan. Spoon in a little of the milk mixture, then add the bell peppers and a little more milk mixture. Repeat, ending with a layer of zucchini and the milk mixture. Cover the top with foil and place in the slow-cooker pot. Pour boiling water into the pot to come halfway up the sides of the pan. Cover with the lid and cook on high for 2 to 3 hours or until the milk mixture is set.

Lift the pan out of the slow cooker using a dish towel and let cool. Loosen the edges with a knife, invert onto a cutting board, and peel off the parchment paper. Cut into slices and serve with Romesco Sauce (*see* below), if liked.

FOR ROMESCO SAUCE TO ACCOMPANY THE TERRINE, fry 1 chopped onion in 1 tablespoon olive oil over medium heat until softened. Stir in 2 minced garlic cloves, 4 skinned and chopped tomatoes, ½ teaspoon paprika, and ½ cup ground almonds. Simmer for 10 minutes until thick.

BABA GANOUSH

Serves **4**
Preparation time **20 minutes**
Cooking temperature **high**
Cooking time **3 to 4 hours**

1 large **eggplant**, about 10 oz,
   halved lengthwise
1 tablespoon **olive oil**
2 tablespoons **0% fat**
   Greek-style yogurt
3 tablespoons chopped
   cilantro leaves
1 large **garlic clove**, minced
juice of ½ **lemon**
seeds from ¼ **pomegranate**
salt and **pepper**

TO SERVE
4 **pitta bread**
1 **red bell pepper**, cored, seeded,
   and cut into batons
½ **cucumber**, seeded, and cut
   into batons

Preheat the slow cooker if necessary. Cut criss-cross lines over the cut side of each eggplant half, rub with salt and pepper, then drizzle with the oil. Arrange, cut-sides down, in the bottom of the slow-cooker pot, cover, and cook on high for 3 to 4 hours or until the eggplant is soft. Let cool.

Use a spoon to scoop the flesh out of the eggplant skins and chop it coarsely. Place in a mixing bowl with the yogurt, cilantro, garlic, and lemon juice. Season to taste, spoon into a serving dish, and scatter with the pomegranate seeds.

Warm the pitta bread under a preheated hot broiler, then cut into thick strips. Arrange on a serving plate with the bell pepper and cucumber batons, and serve with the baba ganoush.

FOR GRILLED STEAKS WITH EGGPLANT SAUCE, make the baba ganoush following the recipe above. Trim the fat from 4 sirloin steaks, 4 oz each, and season to taste. Spray with a little low-calorie cooking oil spray and cook on a preheated hot ridged grill pan for 2 to 3 minutes, turning once, or until cooked to your liking. Serve the steaks with the baba ganoush and an arugula salad tossed with lemon juice.

RED BELL PEPPER & CHORIZO TORTILLA

Serves **4**
Preparation time **20 minutes**
Cooking temperature **high**
Cooking time **2 to 2½ hours**

1 tablespoon **olive oil**, plus extra
    for oiling
1 small **onion**, chopped
3 oz **chorizo sausage**, casing
    removed, diced
6 **eggs**
¾ cup **milk**
3½ oz **roasted red pepper** (from a
    jar or can), drained and sliced
½ lb cooked **potatoes**, sliced
salt and **pepper**

Preheat the slow cooker if necessary. Lightly oil a 2½-pint soufflé dish and line the bottom with a disk of nonstick parchment paper, checking first that the dish will fit in the slow-cooker pot.

Heat the oil in a skillet, add the onion and chorizo, and fry for 4 to 5 minutes until the onion is softened. Beat the eggs, milk, and a little salt and pepper in a bowl, then add the onion and chorizo, the red bell pepper, and sliced potatoes and mix together.

Tip the mixture into the oiled dish, cover the top with foil, and place the dish in the slow-cooker pot. Pour boiling water into the pot to come halfway up the sides of the dish. Cover with the lid and cook on high for 2 to 2½ hours or until the egg mixture has set in the center.

Lift the dish out of the slow-cooker pot using a dish towel and remove the foil. Loosen the edge of the tortilla with a knife, invert it onto a plate, and peel off the lining paper. Cut the tortilla into slices and serve hot or cold with a salad, if liked.

FOR BACON, CHEESE & ROSEMARY TORTILLA, replace the chorizo sausage with 3 oz diced smoked bacon and fry with the onion as above. Beat the eggs and milk in a bowl with the chopped leaves from 2 small rosemary sprigs and ¼ cup freshly shredded Parmesan or Cheddar cheese and salt and pepper. Replace the red bell pepper with 1 cup sliced button mushrooms and continue as above.

CORN WITH CHILES

Serves **4**
Preparation time **15 minutes**
Cooking temperature **high**
Cooking time **2 to 3 hours**

1 tablespoon **sunflower oil**
1 **onion**, finely chopped
1 **orange bell pepper**, cored, seeded,
   and diced
¾ cup **frozen corn kernels**, defrosted
1 **garlic clove**, minced
large pinch of **crushed dried
   red chiles**
½ teaspoon **ground cumin**
1 teaspoon **ground coriander**
14 oz can **mixed beans**, drained
14 oz can **diced tomatoes**
¾ cup **vegetable stock**
2 teaspoons **brown sugar**
salt and **pepper**

TO SERVE
½ cup **crème fraîche**
shredded **Cheddar cheese**

Preheat the slow cooker if necessary. Heat the oil in a large skillet, add the onion, and fry for 5 minutes, stirring, until softened.

Stir in the orange bell pepper, kernel corn, garlic, and spices and cook for 1 minute. Add the beans, tomatoes, stock, sugar, and a little salt and pepper and bring to a boil.

Pour the mixture into the slow-cooker pot, cover with the lid, and cook on high for 2 to 3 hours or until cooked through. Spoon into bowls and serve with the crème fraîche and cheese.

FOR MUSHROOMS & CHILES, fry the onion as above, then add 3½ cups quartered white mushrooms instead of the bell pepper and corn. Fry for 2 to 3 minutes, then add the garlic and spices, and continue as above.

SOUPS

CARAMELIZED ONION SOUP

Serves **4**
Preparation time **25 minutes**
Cooking temperature **low**
Cooking time **4 to 5 hours**

2 tablespoons **butter**
2 tablespoons **olive oil**
1 lb **onions**, thinly sliced
1 tablespoon **superfine sugar**
2 tablespoons **all-purpose flour**
8 fl oz **brown ale**
3¼ cups **beef stock**
2 **bay leaves**
1 tablespoon **Worcestershire sauce**
salt and **pepper**

CHEESE CROUTES
8 slices of **French bread**
¾ cup shredded **sharp**
   Cheddar cheese
2 teaspoons **Worcestershire sauce**

Preheat the slow cooker if necessary. Heat the butter and oil in a large skillet, add the onions, and fry over medium heat, stirring occasionally, for 15 minutes or until softened and just beginning to turn golden. Stir in the sugar and fry for 10 minutes, stirring frequently as the onions begin to caramelize and turn a deep golden brown.

Stir in the flour, then add the ale, stock, bay leaves, and Worcestershire sauce. Add a little salt and pepper and bring to a boil, stirring. Pour into the slow-cooker pot, cover with the lid, and cook on low for 4 to 5 hours or until the onions are very soft.

When almost ready to serve, toast the French bread slices on both sides under a preheated medium broiler. Scatter with the cheese and drizzle with the Worcestershire sauce, then broil until the cheese is bubbling. Ladle the soup into shallow bowls and float the croutes on top.

FOR FRENCH ONION SOUP, fry the onions as above and stir in the flour. Replace the ale with 1 cup red wine and add with the stock, bay leaves, and salt and pepper, omitting the Worcestershire sauce. Continue as above. For the croutes, toast the French bread, then rub one side of each piece with a cut garlic clove, sprinkle with ¾ cup shredded Gruyère cheese, and broil. Serve as above.

MULLIGATAWNY SOUP

Serves **4 to 6**
Preparation time **15 minutes**
Cooking temperature **low**
Cooking time **6 to 8 hours**

1 **onion**, chopped
1 **carrot**, diced
1 **apple**, cored and coarsely grated
2 **garlic cloves**, minced
14 oz can **diced tomatoes**
½ cup **dried red lentils**, rinsed
    and drained
¼ cup **golden raisins**
3 teaspoons **mild curry paste**
2½ pints boiling **vegetable** or
    chicken stock
salt and **pepper**

CROUTES
½ stick **butter**
2 **garlic cloves**, minced
3 tablespoons chopped **cilantro**
8 to 12 slices of **French bread**,
    depending on size

Preheat the slow cooker if necessary. Put the vegetables, apple, garlic, tomatoes, lentils, and golden raisins into the slow-cooker pot.

Add the curry paste, then stir in the boiling stock and add a little salt and pepper. Cover and cook on low for 6 to 8 hours or until the lentils are soft and the carrots are tender.

When almost ready to serve, make the croutes. Beat together the butter, garlic, and chopped cilantro in a bowl. Toast the bread on both sides, then spread with the butter. Ladle the hot soup into soup bowls and serve with the croutes.

FOR GINGER AND CARROT SOUP, put 1 lb diced carrots and a 1½-inch piece of peeled and finely chopped fresh ginger root into the slow-cooker pot with the onion, lentils, and curry paste as above, omitting the other ingredients. Pour in 2½ pints boiling vegetable stock and continue as above. Purée with a hand-held stick blender, mix in 1¼ cups milk, and cook on high for 15 minutes until piping hot. Ladle into bowls and serve with swirls of plain yogurt.

CHICKEN NOODLE BROTH ♥

Serves **4**
Preparation time **10 minutes**
Cooking temperature **high**
Cooking time **5 hours 20 minutes to 7½ hours**

1 **chicken carcass**
1 **onion**, cut into wedges
2 **carrots**, sliced
2 **celery stalks**, sliced
1 **bouquet garni**
2½ pints boiling **water**
3 oz **dried vermicelli**
¼ cup chopped **parsley**
salt and **pepper**

Preheat the slow cooker if necessary. Place the chicken carcass in the slow-cooker pot, breaking it in half if necessary to make it fit. Add the onion, carrots, celery, and bouquet garni. Pour in the measurement boiling water and season to taste. Cover and cook on high for 5 to 7 hours.

Strain the soup through a large sieve, then return the liquid to the slow-cooker pot. Remove any meat from the carcass and add to the pot. Adjust the seasoning if necessary, add the vermicelli pasta, and cook for another 20 to 30 minutes until the pasta is just cooked. Scatter with the parsley, ladle into bowls, and serve.

FOR CHICKEN & MINTED PEA SOUP, follow the recipe above to make the soup, then strain and pour it back into the slow-cooker pot. Add 2 cups finely sliced leeks, 2½ cups frozen peas, and a small bunch of mint leaves. Cover and cook for a further 30 minutes. Purée the soup while still in the slow cooker using a hand-held stick blender. Alternatively, transfer to a blender and purée, in batches if necessary, until smooth, then return to the pot and reheat on high for 15 minutes. Stir in 5 oz mascarpone cheese until melted. Ladle into bowls and scatter with extra finely chopped mint, if liked.

CHUNKY BEEF & BARLEY BROTH ♥

Serves **4**
Preparation time **15 minutes**
Cooking temperature **high**
Cooking time **5¼ to 6¼ hours**

10 oz **lean beef chuck**, diced
2 cups finely diced **turnips**
2 cups finely diced **carrots**
1 **onion**, finely chopped
¼ cup **pearl barley**
¼ cup **dried red lentils**, rinsed and drained
2 pints hot **beef stock**
1 teaspoon **dried mixed herbs**
1 teaspoon **mustard powder**
1 tablespoon **Worcestershire sauce**
2 cups finely shredded **green cabbage**
salt and **pepper**

Preheat the slow cooker if necessary. Place the beef, turnip, carrots, and onion in the slow-cooker pot, then add the pearl barley and lentils.

Mix the hot stock with the herbs, mustard powder, and Worcestershire sauce, then pour over the meat and vegetables. Stir well, season to taste, cover, and cook on high for 5 to 6 hours until the beef and barley are tender.

Stir, then add the cabbage. Cover again and cook for 15 minutes until the cabbage is just tender. Ladle into bowls and serve.

FOR CHICKEN & BARLEY BROTH, follow the recipe above, using 10 oz diced boneless, skinless chicken thighs, and 1 sliced leek instead of the beef and onion. Use 2 pints chicken stock instead of the beef stock, and ½ cup diced ready-to-eat pitted prunes instead of the Worcestershire sauce. Cook as above, adding the cabbage for the last 15 minutes.

CALDO VERDE

Serves **6**
Preparation time **20 minutes**
Cooking temperature **low** and **high**
Cooking time **6¼ hours to 8 hours 20 minutes**

2 tablespoons **olive oil**
2 **onions**, chopped
2 **garlic cloves**, minced
5 oz **chorizo sausage** in one piece, casing
   removed, diced
1¼ lb or 3 small **baking potatoes**, cut into ½-inch dice
1 teaspoon **smoked paprika**
2½ pints hot **chicken stock**
2 cups finely shredded **green cabbage**
salt and **pepper**

Preheat the slow cooker if necessary. Heat the oil in a
large skillet, add the onions, and fry, stirring, for
5 minutes or until lightly browned. Add the garlic,
chorizo, potatoes, and paprika and cook for 2 minutes.

Transfer the mixture to the slow-cooker pot, add the
hot stock, and season to taste with salt and pepper.
Cover with the lid and cook on low for 6 to 8 hours.

Add the cabbage, replace the lid, and cook on high for
15 to 20 minutes or until the cabbage is tender. Ladle
into bowls and serve with warm crusty bread, if liked.

FOR CALDO VERDE WITH PUMPKIN, prepare the
soup as above, reducing the baking potatoes to ¾ lb
and adding ½ pound diced, peeled, seeded pumpkin.
Reduce the chicken stock to 2 pints and add a 14 oz can
diced tomatoes.

CORN & SMOKED COD CHOWDER ♥

Serves **4**
Preparation time **20 minutes**
Cooking temperature **high**
Cooking time **2¼ to 3¼ hours**

low-calorie cooking oil spray
1 **leek**, thinly sliced, white and green parts kept separate
2 oz **smoked Canadian bacon**, diced
1¼ cups finely diced **potato**
1 cup finely diced **celeriac**
½ cup **frozen kernel corn**
2 cups **fish stock**
1 **bay leaf**
8 oz **smoked cod fillet**
1 cup **skim milk**
¼ cup **reduced-fat cream cheese**
salt and **pepper**
chopped **parsley**, to garnish

Preheat the slow cooker if necessary. Spray a large
skillet with a little low-calorie cooking oil spray and
place over medium heat until hot. Add the white leek
slices and the bacon and cook for 3 to 4 minutes until
the leeks have softened and the bacon is just beginning
to brown.

Add the potato, celeriac, kernel corn, and stock. Bring
to a boil, stirring, then add the bay leaf and season
to taste. Transfer to the slow-cooker pot, arrange the
fish on top, and press the fish into the liquid. Cover
and cook on high for 2 to 3 hours until the potatoes
and celeriac are tender and the fish flakes easily when
pressed with a small knife. Transfer the fish to a plate,
remove the skin and bones, and break into pieces.

Stir the milk and cream cheese into the slow-cooker
pot, then stir in the reserved green leek slices and
the flaked fish. Cover again and cook for 15 minutes
until the leeks are tender. Ladle into bowls and serve
garnished with chopped parsley.

FOR SALMON & CRAB CHOWDER, follow the recipe
above, using an 8 oz salmon fillet instead of the smoked
cod. Cook as above, stirring in 1½ oz canned brown crab
meat for the last 15 minutes of cooking time.

OLD ENGLISH PEA & HAM SOUP

Serves **4 to 6**
Preparation time **15 minutes**
Cooking temperature **high**
Cooking time **5 to 6 hours**

1 cup **dried green split peas**, soaked
   overnight in cold water
2 **onions**, chopped
2 **celery stalks**, diced
1 **carrot**, diced
3 pints **water**
3 teaspoons **English mustard**
1 **bay leaf**
1 lb **unsmoked boneless ham**
¼ cup chopped **fresh parsley**
salt and **pepper**

Preheat the slow cooker if necessary. Drain the peas and add to a large saucepan with the onions, celery, carrot, and measurement water. Bring to a boil, skim off any scum that rises to the surface, and boil for 10 minutes.

Pour the mixture into the slow-cooker pot, then stir in the mustard, bay leaf, and some pepper. Rinse the ham in several changes of cold water, then add to the pot, and press below the surface of the liquid. Cover and cook on high for 5 to 6 hours or until the peas are soft and the ham cooked through and tender.

Lift the ham out of the slow-cooker pot with a carving fork, drain well, then cut off the rind and fat. Cut the meat into bite-sized pieces. Purée the soup with a hand-held stick blender or leave chunky, if preferred. Stir the ham back into the pot and mix in the parsley. Taste and adjust the seasoning, adding salt, if needed. Ladle the soup into bowls and serve with crusty bread, if liked.

FOR SPLIT PEA & PARSNIP SOUP, soak 1 cup dried yellow split peas as above. Drain and put into a saucepan with 1 chopped onion, 2¼ cups diced parsnips, and 3 pints chicken or vegetable stock. Boil for 10 minutes, then transfer to the slow-cooker pot. Cover and cook as above. Purée and adjust the seasoning, if needed. Beat ½ stick butter with 2 minced garlic cloves, 3 tablespoons chopped cilantro, and 1 teaspoon each coarsely crushed cumin seeds and coriander seeds. Ladle the soup into bowls and top with spoonfuls of the butter.

TOMATO & RED BELL PEPPER SOUP

Serves **4 to 6**
Preparation time **15 minutes**
Cooking temperature **high**
Cooking time **2½ to 3¼ hours**

2 tablespoons **olive oil**
1 **onion**, chopped
1 **red bell pepper**, cored, seeded,
    and diced
1½ lb **tomatoes**, coarsely chopped
1 **garlic clove**, minced
2½ cups **vegetable stock**
1 tablespoon **tomato paste**
2 teaspoons **superfine sugar**
1 tablespoon **balsamic vinegar**,
    plus extra to garnish
salt and **pepper**

Preheat the slow cooker if necessary. Heat the oil in a large skillet, add the onion, and fry until softened. Stir in the red bell pepper, tomatoes, and garlic and fry for 1 to 2 minutes.

Pour in the stock, add the tomato paste, sugar, balsamic vinegar, and a little salt and pepper and bring to a boil, stirring. Pour into the slow-cooker pot, cover with the lid, and cook on high for 2½ to 3 hours or until the vegetables are tender.

Purée the soup while still in the slow-cooker pot using a hand-held stick blender. Alternatively, transfer to a blender and purée, in batches if necessary, until smooth, then return to the slow-cooker pot and reheat on high for 15 minutes.

Taste and adjust the seasoning, if needed, then ladle the soup into bowls and garnish with a drizzle of extra balsamic vinegar or stir in spoonfuls of Scallion & Basil Pesto (*see* below).

FOR SCALLION & BASIL PESTO TO GARNISH THE SOUP, coarsely chop 4 scallions, then finely chop with a hand-held stick blender in a pitcher, or in a blender, with 4 basil sprigs, ¼ cup freshly shredded Parmesan cheese, ¼ cup olive oil, and a little pepper until it becomes a coarse paste. Spoon over the top of the soup just before serving.

THAI COCONUT & PUMPKIN SOUP

Serves **4 to 6**
Preparation time **20 minutes**
Cooking temperature **low** and **high**,
   if necessary
Cooking time **7 to 8¼ hours**

1 tablespoon **sunflower oil**
1 **onion**, chopped
4 teaspoons **Thai red curry paste**
1 teaspoon **galangal paste**
2 **garlic cloves**, minced
1 **butternut squash**, about 2 lb, peeled,
   seeded, and cut into ¾-inch chunks
1 cup **coconut cream**
3¼ cups **vegetable stock**
1 tablespoon **soy sauce**
small bunch of **cilantro**
salt and **pepper**

Preheat the slow cooker if necessary. Heat the oil in a large skillet, add the onion, and fry until softened. Stir in the curry paste, galangal paste, and garlic and cook for 1 minute, then mix in the squash.

Pour in the coconut cream and stock, then add the soy sauce and bring to a boil, stirring. Pour into the slow-cooker pot, cover with the lid, and cook on low for 7 to 8 hours or until the squash is tender. (You may find that the coconut cream separates slightly, but this will disappear after puréeing.)

Purée the soup while still in the slow-cooker pot using a hand-held stick blender. Alternatively, transfer to a blender and purée, in batches if necessary, until smooth, then return it to the slow-cooker pot and reheat on high for 15 minutes.

Reserve a few cilantro sprigs, chop the rest, and stir into the soup. Ladle the soup into bowls and garnish with the reserved cilantro sprigs.

FOR PUMPKIN & ORANGE SOUP, fry the onion in 2 tablespoons butter, then add the diced butternut squash with the grated zest and juice of 2 small oranges, 2 pints vegetable stock, and 3 whole star anise. Bring to a boil, stirring, add a little salt and pepper, and continue as above. Remove the star anise before puréeing and serve with swirls of heavy cream.

HADDOCK & BACON CHOWDER

Serves **4**
Preparation time **15 minutes**
Cooking temperature **high**
Cooking time **2½ to 3½ hours**

2 tablespoons **butter**
1 **onion**, finely chopped
2 cups diced **potatoes**
4 **slices smoked bacon**, diced
3¼ cups boiling **fish stock**
1 cup **frozen kernel corn**, defrosted
1 **bay leaf**
1 lb **smoked haddock fillet**, skinned
¾ cup **heavy cream**
salt and **pepper**
chopped **parsley**, to garnish

Preheat the slow cooker if necessary. Heat the butter in a large skillet, add the onion, potatoes, and bacon and fry gently, stirring, until just beginning to color.

Transfer the potato mixture to the slow-cooker pot. Pour in the boiling stock, then add the kernel corn, bay leaf, and a little salt and pepper. Cover with the lid and cook on high for 2 to 3 hours or until the potatoes are tender.

Add the fish and press it just below the surface of the stock, cutting the pieces in half, if needed. Replace the lid and cook on high for 30 minutes or until the fish flakes easily when pressed in the center with a knife.

Transfer the fish to a plate with a lifter and break it into flakes with a knife and fork, checking for and removing any bones. Stir the cream into the soup, then return the fish. Ladle the soup into bowls and scatter with the parsley.

FOR SALMON & CRAB CHOWDER, fry the onion and potatoes, omitting the bacon, and continue to cook for 2 to 3 hours as above. Replace the smoked haddock with a 1¾ oz canned dressed brown crab meat, stirred into the potato mixture, and 1 lb salmon fillet, skinned, cut into 4 strips and pressed below the surface of the stock. Cook for 30 to 40 minutes until the salmon flakes easily, then continue as above.

CHICKEN & TORTELLONI SOUP

Serves **4**
Preparation time **15 minutes**
Cooking temperature **high**
Cooking time **5 hours**
    20 minutes to 7½ hours

1 **chicken carcass**
1 **onion**, quartered
2 **celery stalks**, sliced
2 **carrots**, thinly sliced
2 **thyme** or **basil sprigs**
2½ pints boiling **water**
½ teaspoon **black peppercorns**,
    coarsely crushed
3 cups **spinach**, rinsed, drained,
    and coarsely torn
3 **tomatoes**, diced
8 oz **fresh spinach tortelloni**
salt
freshly shredded **Parmesan cheese**,
    to serve

Preheat the slow cooker if necessary. Put the chicken carcass into the slow-cooker pot, breaking it in half if necessary to make it fit. Add the vegetables, thyme or basil sprigs, and measurement boiling water, then add the peppercorns and salt to taste.

Cover with the lid and cook on high for 5 to 7 hours. Lift the carcass out of the slow-cooker pot and remove any meat; cut this into small pieces and reserve. Strain the stock, discarding the bones, vegetables, and herbs, then pour the hot stock back into the slow-cooker pot.

Add the shredded chicken, spinach, tomatoes, and tortelloni. Replace the lid and cook for 20 to 30 minutes, still on high, until piping hot. Ladle the soup into bowls and serve scattered with a little shredded Parmesan.

FOR PESTO & LEMON SOUP, cook the chicken carcass as above, then stir 2 teaspoons pesto sauce and the grated zest and juice of 1 lemon into the strained stock. Mix in 1½ cups finely chopped broccoli, 1 cup frozen peas, and ¼ lb rinsed, drained, and coarsely chopped spinach with the shredded chicken, omitting the tomatoes and tortelloni. Cook as above and serve topped with extra pesto and shredded Parmesan.

LAMB & BARLEY BROTH

Serves **4 to 6**
Preparation time **15 minutes**
Cooking temperature **low**
Cooking time **8 to 10 hours**

2 tablespoons **butter**
1 tablespoon **sunflower oil**
1 **lamb rump chop** or ¼ lb **lamb
    fillet**, diced
1 **onion**, chopped
1 small **leek**, chopped
1 lb mixed **parsnip**, **turnip** and **carrot**,
    cut into small dice
¼ cup **pearl barley**
2½ pints **lamb** or **chicken stock**
¼ teaspoon **ground allspice**
2 to 3 **rosemary sprigs**
salt and **pepper**
chopped **parsley** or **chives**,
    to garnish (optional)

Preheat the slow cooker if necessary. Heat the butter and oil in a large skillet, add the lamb, onion, and leek and fry, stirring, until the lamb is lightly browned.

Stir in the root vegetables and barley, then add the stock, allspice, rosemary, and plenty of salt and pepper and bring to a boil, stirring. Pour into the slow-cooker pot, cover with the lid, and cook on low for 8 to 10 hours or until the barley is tender.

Stir well, taste, and adjust the seasoning, if needed, then ladle the soup into bowls. Garnish with chopped herbs and serve with warm bread, if liked.

FOR HUNGARIAN CHORBA, fry the lamb and vegetables as above, omitting the pearl barley. Stir in 1 teaspoon smoked paprika, then add ¼ cup converted rice and a few dill sprigs. Stir in 2½ pints lamb stock, 2 tablespoons red wine vinegar, and 1 tablespoon light brown sugar. Add salt and pepper, bring to a boil, and continue as above. Garnish with extra chopped dill and serve with rye bread.

CARROT & CUMIN SOUP

Serves **4 to 6**
Preparation time **20 minutes**
Cooking temperature **low** and **high**,
    if necessary
Cooking time **7 to 8¼ hours**

1 tablespoon **sunflower oil**
1 large **onion**, chopped
1¼ lb **carrots**, thinly sliced
1½ teaspoons **cumin seeds**,
    coarsely crushed
1 teaspoon **ground turmeric**
¼ cup **converted rice**
2½ pints **vegetable stock**
salt and **pepper**

TO SERVE
¾ cup **plain yogurt**
mango chutney
poppadums (optional)

Preheat the slow cooker if necessary. Heat the oil in a large skillet, add the onion, and fry over medium heat, stirring, until softened. Stir in the carrots, crushed cumin seeds, and turmeric and fry for 2 to 3 minutes to release the cumin flavor and to color the onions.

Stir in the rice, then add the stock and a little salt and pepper and bring to a boil. Pour into the slow-cooker pot, cover with the lid, and cook on low for 7 to 8 hours or until the carrots are tender.

Purée the soup while still in the slow-cooker pot using a hand-held stick blender. Alternatively, transfer to a blender and purée, in batches if necessary, until smooth, then return to the slow-cooker pot and reheat on high for 15 minutes.

Taste and adjust the seasoning, if needed, then ladle the soup into bowls. Top with spoonfuls of the yogurt and a little mango chutney, and serve with poppadums, if liked.

FOR SPICED PARSNIP SOUP, fry the onion as above, replacing the carrots with 1¼ lb halved and thinly sliced parsnips and adding 1 teaspoon each ground turmeric, cumin, and coriander and a 1½-inch piece of peeled and finely chopped fresh ginger root. Continue as above.

MINESTRONE SOUP

Serves **4**
Preparation time **25 minutes**
Cooking temperature **low** and **high**
Cooking time **6¼ to 8½ hours**

1 tablespoon **olive oil**
1 **onion**, chopped
1 **carrot**, diced
2 **smoked bacon slices**, diced
2 **garlic cloves**, minced
4 **tomatoes**, skinned and chopped
2 **celery stalks**, diced
2 small **zucchini**, diced
3 teaspoons **pesto**, plus extra
  to serve
2½ pints **chicken** or **vegetable stock**
3 oz **broccoli raab**, stems and florets
  cut into small pieces
1½ oz **tiny dried soup pasta**
salt and **pepper**
freshly shredded **Parmesan cheese**,
  to serve

Preheat the slow cooker if necessary. Heat the oil in a large skillet, add the onion, carrot, and bacon and fry, stirring, until lightly browned.

Add the garlic, then stir in the tomatoes, celery, and zucchini and cook for 1 to 2 minutes. Stir in the pesto and stock, then add a little salt and pepper and bring to a boil, stirring.

Pour into the slow-cooker pot, cover, and cook on low for 6 to 8 hours or until the vegetables are tender. Add the broccoli and pasta, replace the lid, and cook on high for 15 to 30 minutes or until the pasta is tender.

Stir well, taste, and adjust the seasoning, if needed, then ladle the soup into bowls. Top with extra spoonfuls of pesto, to taste, and scatter with shredded Parmesan. Serve with crusty bread, if liked.

FOR CURRIED VEGETABLE & CHICKEN SOUP, omit the bacon and add the diced meat from 2 chicken thighs when frying the onion and carrot. Add the garlic, tomatoes, celery, and zucchini, then add 3 teaspoons mild curry paste instead of the pesto and ¼ cup basmati rice. Add 2½ pints chicken stock and continue as above, omitting the pasta. Garnish with chopped cilantro and serve with warmed naan bread.

CHUNKY CHICKPEA & CHORIZO SOUP

Serves **4**
Preparation time **20 minutes**
Cooking temperature **low**
Cooking time **6 to 8 hours**

2 tablespoons **olive oil**
1 **onion**, chopped
2 **garlic cloves**, minced
5 oz **chorizo sausage**, casing
    removed, diced
¾ teaspoon **smoked paprika**
2 to 3 **thyme sprigs**
2 pints **chicken stock**
1 tablespoon **tomato paste**
¾ lb **sweet potatoes**, diced
14 oz can **chickpeas**, drained
salt and **pepper**
chopped **parsley** or **thyme leaves**,
    to garnish

Preheat the slow cooker if necessary. Heat the oil in a skillet, add the onion, and fry, stirring, for 5 minutes or until just beginning to turn golden.

Stir in the garlic and chorizo and cook for 2 minutes. Mix in the paprika, add the thyme sprigs, stock, and tomato paste and bring to a boil, stirring, then add a little salt and pepper.

Add the sweet potatoes and chickpeas to the slow-cooker pot and pour in the hot stock mixture. Cover and cook on low for 6 to 8 hours until the sweet potatoes are tender.

Ladle into bowls, scatter with a little chopped parsley or thyme leaves, and serve with warmed pitta bread, if liked.

FOR TOMATO, CHICKPEA & CHORIZO SOUP, make the soup as above up to the point where the paprika and thyme have been added. Reduce the stock to 3¼ cups and add to the skillet with the tomato paste and 2 teaspoons brown sugar. Bring to a boil. Omit the sweet potatoes but add 1 lb skinned and diced tomatoes to the slow-cooker pot along with the chickpeas. Pour in the stock mixture and continue as above.

CRAB GUMBO

Serves **4**
Preparation time **25 minutes**
Cooking temperature **high**
Cooking time **3 hours**
    20 minutes to 4½ hours

1 tablespoon **sunflower oil**
1 **onion**, finely chopped
1 **garlic clove**, chopped
2 **celery stalks**, sliced
1 **carrot**, cut into small dice
14 oz can **diced tomatoes**
2½ cups **fish stock**
¼ cup **converted rice**
1 **bay leaf**
2 **thyme sprigs**
¼ teaspoon **crushed dried
    red chiles**
3 oz **okra**, sliced
1¾ oz can **dressed brown
    crab meat**
salt and **pepper**
5¾ oz can **white crab meat**,
    to serve (optional)

Preheat the slow cooker if necessary. Heat the oil in a large skillet, add the onion, and fry for 5 minutes or until softened.

Stir in the garlic, celery, and carrot, then mix in the tomatoes, stock, rice, thyme, and chiles. Add a little salt and pepper and bring to a boil. Pour into the slow-cooker pot, cover with the lid, and cook on high for 3 to 4 hours or until the vegetables and rice are tender.

Stir the soup, then add the okra and dressed brown crab meat. Replace the lid and cook on high for 20 to 30 minutes. Ladle the soup into bowls and top with the flaked white crab meat and serve with warm crusty bread, if liked.

FOR MIXED VEGETABLE GUMBO, make the soup as above, omitting the cans of brown and white crab meat. Garnish with croutons made by frying 2 slices of bread, cut into cubes, in 2 tablespoons butter, 3 tablespoons olive oil, and ¼ teaspoon crushed dried red chiles until golden.

LEEK, POTATO & STILTON SOUP

Serves **4 to 6**
Preparation time **25 minutes**
Cooking temperature **low**
Cooking time **5½ to 6½ hours**

2 tablespoons **butter**
1 tablespoon **sunflower oil**
1 lb **leeks**, thinly sliced, white and
   green parts kept separate
1 **slice smoked Canadian bacon**, diced,
   plus 4 **slices smoked bacon**, broiled
   and then chopped, to garnish
¾ lb **potatoes**, diced
2 pints **chicken** or **vegetable stock**
1¼ cups **milk**
¾ cup **heavy cream**
5 oz **aged Stilton** (rind
   removed), diced
salt and **pepper**

Preheat the slow cooker if necessary. Heat the butter and oil in a large skillet, then add the white leek slices, the diced bacon, and potatoes and fry over medium heat, stirring, until just beginning to turn golden.

Pour in the stock, add a little salt and pepper, and bring to a boil, stirring. Transfer to the slow-cooker pot, cover with the lid, and cook on low for 5 to 6 hours. Stir the reserved green leek slices and milk into the slow-cooker pot. Replace the lid and cook, still on low, for 30 minutes or until the leeks are tender. Coarsely purée the soup in the pot using a hand-held stick blender, or use a potato masher, if preferred.

Mix in the cream and two-thirds of the Stilton cheese and continue stirring until the cheese has melted. Taste and adjust the seasoning, if needed, then ladle the soup into bowls and sprinkle with the remaining cheese and chopped broiled bacon.

FOR COCK-A-LEEKIE SOUP, heat the butter and oil as above, then add 2 chicken thighs on the bone and fry until golden, remove them from the pan, and add to the slow-cooker pot. Fry the white leek slices, bacon, and potatoes as above, then mix in 2½ pints chicken stock, ¼ cup chopped ready-to-eat pitted prunes, and a thyme sprig. Season, bring to a boil, then transfer to the slow-cooker pot. Cover and cook on low for 8 to 10 hours. Take the chicken off of the bone, discarding the skin, then dice the meat and return it to the pot with the green leek slices. Cook for 30 minutes, then ladle into bowls, omitting the milk, cream, Stilton, and bacon garnish.

THAI BROTH WITH FISH DUMPLINGS

Serves **4**
Preparation time **30 minutes**
Cooking temperature **low** and **high**
Cooking time **2¼ to 3¼ hours**

2 pints boiling **fish stock**
2 teaspoons **Thai fish sauce**
1 tablespoon **Thai red curry paste**
1 tablespoon **soy sauce**
1 **carrot**, thinly sliced
2 **garlic cloves**, minced
bunch of **asparagus**, trimmed and stems cut into 4
2 **bok choy**, thickly sliced

DUMPLINGS
bunch of **scallions**, sliced
1 cup **cilantro leaves**
1½-inch piece of **fresh ginger root**,
  peeled and sliced
13 oz **cod fillet**, skinned
1 tablespoon **cornstarch**
1 **egg white**

Preheat the slow cooker if necessary. Make the dumplings. Put half the scallions into a food processor with the cilantro and ginger and chop finely. Add the cod, cornstarch, and egg white and process until the fish is finely chopped. With wetted hands, shape into 12 balls.

Pour the fish stock into the slow-cooker pot, add the fish sauce, curry paste, and soy sauce. Add the rest of the scallions, the carrot, and garlic, then add the dumplings. Cover with the lid and cook on low for 2 to 3 hours. When almost ready to serve, add the asparagus and bok choy to the broth. Replace the lid and cook on high for 15 minutes or until just tender. Ladle into bowls to serve.

FOR THAI BROTH WITH NOODLES & SHRIMP, prepare and cook the broth as above, omitting the dumplings. Add the asparagus, bok choy, and 7 oz cooked frozen shelled jumbo shrimp, fully defrosted, and cook for 15 minutes on high. Meanwhile, soak 3 oz dried rice noodles in boiling water following the package instructions. Drain and add to 4 soup bowls. Ladle the broth on top and garnish with chopped cilantro.

CAULIFLOWER & CHEESE SOUP

Serves **4**
Preparation time 20 minutes
Cooking temperature **low** and **high**
Cooking time 4¼ to 5¼ hours

2 tablespoons **butter**
1 tablespoon **olive oil**
1 **onion**, chopped
1 small **baking potato**, about 5 oz, cut into
  small dice
1 **cauliflower**, trimmed and cut into pieces
  (about 4 cups)
2½ cups **vegetable stock**
1 teaspoon **English mustard**
3 teaspoons **Worcestershire sauce**
1 cup shredded **Parmesan** or **sharp Cheddar cheese**
1 cup **milk**
grated **nutmeg**
salt and **pepper**

Preheat the slow cooker if necessary. Heat the butter and oil in a large skillet, add the onion and potato, and fry for 5 minutes or until softened but not colored.

Stir in the cauliflower, stock, mustard, Worcestershire sauce, cheese, and a little salt and pepper and bring to a boil. Pour into the slow-cooker pot, cover with the lid, and cook on low for 4 to 5 hours or until the vegetables are tender.

Purée the soup while still in the slow-cooker pot using a hand-held stick blender. Alternatively, transfer to a blender and purée, in batches if necessary, until smooth, then return to the slow-cooker pot.

Stir in the milk, replace the lid, and cook on high for 15 minutes until reheated. Stir and add nutmeg to taste. Ladle the soup into bowls and serve.

FOR PUMPKIN AND CHEESE SOUP, omit the cauliflower and add 1 lb peeled, seeded, and diced pumpkin or butternut squash to the fried onion and potato mixture. Continue as above.

FRAGRANT SPICED CHICKEN ♥

Serves **4**
Preparation time **15 minutes**
Cooking temperature **high**
Cooking time **5¼ to 6¼ hours**

3 lb **roasting chicken**
1 **onion**, chopped
1½ cups sliced **carrots**
3-inch piece of **fresh ginger root**, peeled and sliced
2 **garlic cloves**, sliced
1 large **mild red chile**, halved
3 large **star anise**
¼ cup **soy sauce**
¼ cup **rice vinegar**
1 tablespoon **light brown sugar**
2 pints boiling **water**
small bunch of **cilantro**
3 oz **snow peas**, thickly sliced
5 oz **bok choy**, thickly sliced
salt and **pepper**
7 oz **dried egg noodles**, to serve

Preheat the slow cooker if necessary. Place the chicken, breast-side down, in the slow-cooker pot. Add the onion, carrots, ginger, garlic, chile, and star anise and spoon over the soy sauce, vinegar, and sugar. Pour over the measurement boiling water.

Add the cilantro stems, reserving the leaves, and season to taste. Cover and cook on high for 5 to 6 hours or until the chicken is thoroughly cooked and the meat juices run clear when the thickest parts of the leg and breast are pierced with a sharp knife.

Transfer the chicken to a cutting board and keep warm. Add the snow peas and bok choy to the pot, cover again, and cook for about 10 minutes or until just wilted. Meanwhile, cook the noodles following the package instructions, drain well, and divide between 4 bowls.

Carve the chicken into bite-sized pieces and arrange on top of the noodles with the reserved cilantro leaves, then ladle over the hot broth and serve.

FOR ITALIAN-SPICED CHICKEN WITH PESTO, put the chicken into the pot with 1 chopped onion, 1¾ cups sliced carrots, 2 sliced garlic cloves, 1 sliced fennel bulb, and 1 sliced lemon. Pour over the boiling water as above and replace the cilantro with a small bunch of basil. Use 3 diced tomatoes, 5 oz chopped broccoli raab, and 2 tablespoons pesto sauce instead of the snow peas and bok choy. Cook 8 oz fresh tagliatelle in a large saucepan of lightly salted boiling water following the package instructions until just tender and serve with the chicken.

STEWS &
CASSEROLES

CHICKEN & SAGE HOTPOT

Serves **4**
Preparation time **30 minutes**
Cooking temperature **high**
Cooking time **4 to 5 hours**

1 tablespoon **sunflower oil**
6 **boneless, skinless chicken thighs**, about 1 lb 2 oz, each cut into 3 pieces
1 **onion**, sliced
4 **slices smoked bacon**, diced
2 tablespoons **all-purpose flour**
2½ cups **chicken stock** or a mixture of **stock** and **hard dry cider**
2 to 3 **sage sprigs**
4 oz **blood sausage**, casing removed, diced (optional)
1½ cups diced **carrots**
1½ cups diced **turnips**
1¼ lb **potatoes**, thinly sliced
2 tablespoons **butter**
salt and **pepper**

Preheat the slow cooker if necessary. Heat the oil in a large skillet, add the chicken a few pieces at a time until all the meat is in the pan, then add the onion and bacon and fry, stirring, until the chicken is golden.

Stir in the flour, then gradually mix in the stock or stock and hard cider. Add the sage sprigs and a little salt and pepper and bring to a boil, stirring.

Add the blood sausage, if using, carrots, and turnips to the slow-cooker pot. Pour in the hot chicken mixture, then arrange the potatoes overlapping on the top and press below the surface of the liquid. Season with a little extra salt and pepper, then cover with the lid, and cook on high for 4 to 5 hours or until the potatoes are tender and the chicken is cooked through.

Lift the pot out of the housing using oven mitts, dot the potatoes with butter, and brown under a preheated hot broiler. Spoon the hotpot into shallow dishes to serve.

FOR BEEF HOTPOT WITH MUSTARD, replace the chicken with 1½ lb trimmed and diced beef chuck. Fry the beef in the oil and transfer to the slow-cooker pot, then fry the onion, omitting the bacon. Stir in the flour, then mix in 2½ cups beef stock, 2 teaspoons English mustard, 1 tablespoon Worcestershire sauce, 1 tablespoon tomato paste, and salt and pepper and bring to a boil. Omit the blood sausage and continue as above.

PORK STEW WITH SWEET POTATOES

Serves **4**
Preparation time **20 minutes**
Cooking temperature **low** and **high**
Cooking time **8¼ to 9¼ hours**

low-calorie cooking oil spray
1 lb **lean pork**, cubed
1 **onion**, chopped
1¾ cups sliced **white mushrooms**
2 cups **chicken stock**
2 tablespoons **tomato paste**
2 tablespoons **soy sauce**
¼ teaspoon **chili powder**
½ teaspoon **ground allspice**
¼ teaspoon **ground cinnamon**
1 teaspoon **granulated sweetener**
1 cup thinly sliced **carrots**
2 **celery stalks**, thickly sliced
¾ lb **sweet potatoes**, cut into
   1-inch chunks
¼ lb shredded **curly kale**

Preheat the slow cooker if necessary. Spray a large skillet with a little low-calorie cooking oil spray and place over high heat until hot. Add the pork a few pieces at a time until all the pork is in the pan and cook for 3 minutes, stirring. Add the onion and cook for a further 2 to 3 minutes until the pork is golden.

Stir in the mushrooms, then add the stock, tomato paste, and soy sauce. Add the chili powder, allspice, cinnamon, and sweetener, season to taste, and bring to a boil, stirring.

Place the carrots, celery, and sweet potatoes in the slow-cooker pot, then pour over the pork and sauce. Press the meat into the liquid, cover, and cook on low for 8 to 9 hours until the pork is tender.

Stir the stew, then add the kale. Cover again and cook on high for 15 minutes, then spoon into bowls and serve immediately.

FOR FRAGRANT SAUSAGE & SWEET POTATO STEW, place 1 lb reduced-fat pork sausages under a preheated hot broiler until browned but not cooked through. Transfer to the slow-cooker pot. Continue with the recipe above, omitting the pork.

BLACK BEAN CHILI

Serves **4 to 6**
Preparation time **30 minutes, plus
 overnight soaking**
Cooking temperature **low**
Cooking time **8 to 10 hours**

1¼ cups **dried black beans**, soaked
 overnight in cold water
2 tablespoons **olive oil**
1 large **onion**, chopped
2 **carrots**, diced
2 **celery stalks**, sliced
2 to 3 **garlic cloves**, chopped
1 teaspoon **fennel seeds**, crushed
1 teaspoon **cumin seeds**, crushed
2 teaspoons **coriander
 seeds**, crushed
1 teaspoon **chili powder** or
 smoked paprika
14 oz can **diced tomatoes**
1¼ cups **vegetable stock**
1 tablespoon **brown sugar**
¾ cup **sour cream** or **plain
 yogurt** (optional)
salt and **pepper**
boiled **rice** or **crusty bread**, to serve

Preheat the slow cooker if necessary. Drain and rinse the soaked beans, then drain again. Place them in a saucepan, add fresh water to cover, and bring to a boil. Boil vigorously for 10 minutes, then drain into a sieve.

Meanwhile, heat the oil in a saucepan, add the onion, and fry, stirring, for 5 minutes or until softened. Add the carrots, celery, and garlic and fry for 2 to 3 minutes. Stir the crushed fennel, cumin, and coriander seeds into the vegetables along with the chili powder or paprika and cook for 1 minute.

Add the tomatoes, stock, sugar, and a little pepper. Bring to a boil, then pour into the slow-cooker pot. Mix in the beans, pressing them under the liquid, then cover with the lid, and cook on low for 8 to 10 hours.

Season the cooked beans to taste with salt. Top with spoonfuls of sour cream or plain yogurt, if liked, and Avocado Salsa (*see* below), and serve accompanied by boiled rice or crusty bread.

FOR AVOCADO SALSA TO ACCOMPANY THE CHILI, halve, seed, and peel 1 avocado. Dice the flesh and toss with the grated zest and juice of 1 lime. Mix with ½ finely chopped red onion, 2 diced tomatoes, and 2 tablespoons chopped cilantro leaves. Make the salsa about 10 minutes before serving the stew.

SPICED BEEF & RED BELL PEPPER STEW

Serves 4
Preparation time 20 minutes
Cooking temperature low
Cooking time 8 to 10 hours

low-calorie cooking oil spray
1 lb **beef chuck**, trimmed of fat
   and cubed
2 **red onions**, cut into wedges
2 **celery stalks**, thickly sliced
2 **red bell peppers**, cored, seeded,
   and cut into chunks
2 **garlic cloves**, minced
1 teaspoon **cumin seeds**,
   coarsely crushed
1 teaspoon **chili powder**
2 teaspoons **all-purpose flour**
2 cups **beef stock**
1 tablespoon **tomato paste**
salt and **pepper**

TO SERVE
¼ cup chopped **cilantro**
1¼ cups **long-grain rice**, boiled

Preheat the slow cooker if necessary. Spray a large skillet with a little low-calorie cooking oil spray and place over high heat until hot. Add the beef a few pieces at a time until all the beef is in the pan and cook for 5 minutes, stirring, until browned. Use a slotted spoon to transfer the beef to the slow-cooker pot.

Add a little more low-calorie cooking oil spray to the pan, add the onion wedges, and cook for 2 to 3 minutes, stirring. Add the celery and red bell peppers, then stir in the garlic, crushed cumin seeds, and chili powder and cook for 1 minute.

Stir in the flour, then add the stock and tomato paste, season to taste, and bring to a boil, stirring. Spoon it onto the beef, cover, and cook on low for 8 to 10 hours until the beef is tender.

Stir the chopped cilantro into the cooked rice and spoon into shallow bowls. Stir the beef casserole, spoon over the rice, and serve.

FOR CHINESE BEEF WITH GINGER ROOT, follow the recipe above, replacing the cumin seeds and chili powder with 2 tablespoons soy sauce and 2 tablespoons finely chopped fresh ginger root. Serve with 8 oz dried egg noodles, cooked following the package instructions.

TURKEY & SAUSAGE STEW

Serves **4**
Preparation time **30 minutes**
Cooking temperature **high**
Cooking time **5½ to 6¾ hours**

1 **turkey drumstick**, about 1 lb 6 oz
2 tablespoons **sunflower oil**
4 **slices smoked bacon**, diced
3 large **pork and herb sausages**,
    about 7 oz in total, each cut into
    4 pieces
1 **onion**, sliced
1 **leek**, sliced, white and green parts
    kept separate
2 tablespoons **all-purpose flour**
2½ cups **chicken stock**
small bunch of **mixed herbs**
10 oz **baby carrots**, halved if large
2 **celery stalks**, sliced
½ cup fresh **cranberries**
salt and **pepper**

PARSLEY DUMPLINGS
1¼ cups **all-purpose flour** sifted with
    1¼ teaspoons **baking powder**
½ cup **vegetable**
    shortening, shredded
¼ cup chopped **parsley**
5 to 7 tablespoons **water**

Preheat the slow cooker if necessary. If the turkey drumstick does not fit into the slow-cooker pot, sever the knuckle end with a large heavy knife, hitting it with a rolling pin.

Heat the oil in a large skillet, add the drumstick, bacon, and sausage pieces and fry until browned all over. Transfer to the slow-cooker pot. Add the onion and white leek slices to the skillet and fry until softened. Stir in the flour, then mix in the stock. Add the herbs and salt and pepper and bring to a boil. Add the carrots, celery, and cranberries to the pot and pour in the hot onion mixture.

Cover and cook on high for 5 to 6 hours or until the turkey is almost falling off of the bone. Lift the turkey out of the slow-cooker pot. Remove and discard the skin, then cut the meat into pieces, discarding the bones and tendons. Return the meat to the pot with the reserved green leek slices.

Make the dumplings. Add the flour and baking powder mixture, shortening, parsley, and salt and pepper to a bowl. Stir in enough of the measurement water to make a soft dough. Knead, then shape into 12 small balls. Arrange over the turkey, replace the lid, and cook, still on high, for 30 to 45 minutes or until the dumplings are cooked. Spoon into shallow bowls to serve.

FOR TURKEY & CRANBERRY PUFF PIE, make the stew as above. Roll out 1 lb ready-made puff pastry, defrosted if frozen, trim to an oval a little larger than the top of the slow-cooker pot and put on an oiled cookie sheet. Brush the top with beaten egg, then bake in a preheated oven, 400°F, for about 25 minutes until golden. Spoon the stew onto plates and top with wedges of the pastry.

POLISH SAUSAGE STEW

Serves **4**
Preparation time **20 minutes**
Cooking temperature **low**
Cooking time **8 to 10 hours**

low-calorie cooking oil spray
¾ lb **boneless, skinless chicken thighs**, cubed
1 **onion**, chopped
2 teaspoons **mild paprika**
1 teaspoon **caraway seeds**
1 **apple**, quartered, cored, and thinly sliced
½ lb **tomatoes**, diced
1 tablespoon **granulated sweetener**
¾ lb **sauerkraut**, drained
7 oz **smoked pork sausage**, sliced
¾ cup sliced **gherkins**
2 cups hot **chicken stock**
salt and **pepper**

TO GARNISH
3 tablespoons chopped **dill**
3 tablespoons chopped **parsley**

Preheat the slow cooker if necessary. Spray a large skillet with a little low-calorie cooking oil spray and place over high heat until hot. Add the chicken a few pieces at a time until all the chicken is in the pan, then add the onion and cook for 5 minutes, stirring, until the chicken is golden.

Add the paprika, caraway, apple, tomatoes, and sweetener to the skillet and heat through. Place the sauerkraut in the slow-cooker pot and pour the chicken mixture on top, then add the sliced sausage and gherkins.

Pour in the hot stock and season to taste. Stir well, cover, and cook on low for 8 to 10 hours until the chicken is cooked through and tender. Serve in bowls, garnished with the chopped dill and parsley.

FOR POLISH PORK STEW, follow the recipe above, using 1 lb diced lean pork instead of the chicken. Use 1 teaspoon mild paprika and 1 teaspoon smoked hot paprika or chili powder instead of 2 teaspoons mild paprika, and continue with the recipe, omitting the smoked sausage.

ALL-IN-ONE CHICKEN CASSEROLE

Serves **4**
Preparation time **20 minutes**
Cooking temperature **low**
Cooking time **8¼ to 10¼ hours**

low-calorie cooking oil spray
4 **skinless chicken legs**, 2 lb in total
2 oz **smoked Canadian bacon**, diced
10 oz **baby new potatoes**, scrubbed
   and thickly sliced
2 small **leeks**, thickly sliced, white
   and green parts kept separate
2 **celery stalks**, thickly sliced
2 **carrots**, sliced
2 teaspoons **all-purpose flour**
1 teaspoon **dried mixed herbs**
1 teaspoon **mustard powder**
2 cups **chicken stock**
3 cups **curly kale**, sliced
salt and **pepper**

Spray a large skillet with a little low-calorie cooking oil spray and place over high heat until hot. Add the chicken and cook for 5 minutes, turning, until browned all over. Transfer to the slow-cooker pot.

Add the bacon and potatoes to the skillet with a little extra low-calorie cooking oil spray and cook for 4 to 5 minutes, stirring, until the bacon is beginning to brown. Stir in the white leek slices, celery, and carrots. Add the flour, herbs, and mustard and stir well.

Pour in the stock, season to taste, and bring to a boil, stirring. Spoon over the chicken, cover, and cook on low for 8 to 10 hours or until the chicken is tender and cooked through.

Add the reserved green leek slices and the kale to the slow-cooker pot, cover, and cook for 15 minutes, still on low, until the vegetables are just tender. Serve in shallow bowls.

FOR CHICKEN HOTPOT, follow the main recipe to make the chicken mixture, omitting the new potatoes and carrots. Transfer to the slow-cooker pot and cover with 10 oz scrubbed and thinly sliced baking potatoes and 2 thinly sliced carrots, arranging the slices alternately overlapping. Spray with low-calorie cooking oil spray, season to taste, then cook as above. Brown the top under a preheated hot broiler, if liked.

CHUNKY CHICKEN & BASIL STEW

Serves **4**
Preparation time **20 minutes**
Cooking temperature **low** and **high**
Cooking time **8½ to 10¾ hours**

low-calorie cooking oil spray
1¼ lb **boneless, skinless chicken
  thighs**, each cut into 3 pieces
1 **onion**, chopped
2 small **carrots**, finely diced
2 teaspoons **all-purpose flour**
1½ cups **chicken stock**
¾ cup **basil leaves**, torn, plus extra
  to garnish
¾ cup **frozen peas**, defrosted
7 oz **broccolini, (long-stem broccoli)**,
  stems cut into 3 or 4 pieces
5 oz **fine green snap beans**,
  thickly sliced
salt and **pepper**

Preheat the slow cooker if necessary. Spray a large skillet with a little low-calorie cooking oil spray and place over high heat until hot. Add the chicken a few pieces at a time until all the chicken is in the pan and cook for 5 minutes, stirring, until golden. Transfer to the slow-cooker pot using a slotted spoon.

Add a little more low-calorie cooking oil spray to the pan if necessary, then cook the onion for 4 to 5 minutes until just beginning to soften. Stir in the carrots and flour, then add the stock and bring to a boil, stirring. Add the basil, season to taste, and pour over the chicken. Cover and cook on low for 8 to 10 hours until the chicken is tender and cooked through.

Add the peas, broccolini, and green snap beans, cover again, and cook on high for 15 to 30 minutes until the vegetables are tender. Serve in bowls, garnished with extra basil.

FOR CHUNKY CHICKEN WITH 30 GARLIC CLOVES, brown 1¼ lb boneless, skinless chicken thighs, each cut into 3 pieces, in a skillet and place in the slow-cooker pot with 30 unpeeled garlic cloves. Follow the recipe above, using ½ lb small peeled shallots instead of the onion and carrot, and 3 thyme sprigs and 2 teaspoons Dijon mustard instead of the basil. Cook as above, omitting the green vegetables, and serve scattered with chopped parsley.

IRISH STEW

Serves **4**
Preparation time **20 minutes**
Cooking temperature **high**
Cooking time **6 to 7 hours**

2 tablespoons **sunflower oil**
2¼ lb **stewing lamb** or **budget
    lamb chops** of different sizes
1 **onion**, coarsely chopped
3 **carrots**, sliced
2 cups diced **turnips**
2 cups diced **parsnips**
2 tablespoons **all-purpose flour**
2½ cups **potato chunks**, cut no
    bigger than 1½ inches
3½ cups **lamb** or **chicken stock**
3 **rosemary sprigs**
salt and **pepper**
¼ cup mixed snipped **chives** and
    chopped **rosemary**, to garnish

Preheat the slow cooker if necessary. Heat the oil in a large skillet, add the lamb, and fry until browned on both sides. Scoop out of the pan with a slotted spoon and transfer to a plate.

Add the onion to the skillet and fry for 5 minutes or until softened. Add the carrots, turnips, and parsnips and cook for 1 to 2 minutes, then stir in the flour. Add the potatoes, stock, rosemary sprigs, and plenty of salt and pepper and bring to a boil, stirring.

Pour into the slow-cooker pot, add the lamb, and press below the surface of the liquid. Cover with the lid and cook on high for 6 to 7 hours or until the lamb is falling off the bones and the potatoes are tender.

Spoon into shallow bowls, removing the lamb bones if liked, and scatter with the snipped chives and chopped rosemary. Serve with a spoon and fork and crusty bread, if liked.

FOR LAMB STEW WITH DUMPLINGS, make the stew as above. About 35 to 50 minutes before the end of cooking, sift 1¼ cups all-purpose flour with 1¼ teaspoons baking powder, add to a bowl with ½ cup shredded vegetable shortening, 2 teaspoons chopped rosemary leaves, and a little salt and pepper and stir to combine. Add 5 to 7 tablespoons water to make a soft but not sticky dough. Shape into 12 balls, add to the slow-cooker pot, cover, and cook on high for 30 to 45 minutes until well risen.

BALSAMIC BEEF HOTPOT

Serves **4**
Preparation time **30 minutes**
Cooking temperature **high**
Cooking time **7 to 8 hours**

low-calorie cooking oil spray
1¼ lb **beef chuck**, trimmed of fat
    and cubed
1 **onion**, chopped
2 cups **turnip cubes**, cut no larger
    than ¾ inch
2½ cups sliced **carrots**
2 cups sliced **mushrooms**
2 teaspoons **all-purpose flour**
2 cups **beef stock**
2 tablespoons **balsamic vinegar**
1 teaspoon **mustard powder**
1 lb **potatoes**, sliced
salt and **pepper**
1 tablespoon chopped **parsley**,
    to garnish

TO SERVE
2¼ cups **broccoli florets**, steamed
7 oz **sugar snap peas**, steamed

Preheat the slow cooker if necessary. Spray a large skillet with a little low-calorie cooking oil spray and place over high heat until hot. Add the beef a few pieces at a time until all the beef is in the pan. Cook for 5 minutes, stirring, until browned. Use a slotted spoon to transfer the beef to the slow-cooker pot.

Add a little more low-calorie cooking oil spray to the skillet, add the onion, and cook for 4 to 5 minutes until beginning to brown. Add the turnips, carrots, and mushrooms and cook for 2 minutes. Add the flour and stir well.

Stir in the stock, vinegar, and mustard, season to taste, and bring to a boil. Pour over the beef in the slow-cooker pot. Arrange the potato slices on top, slightly overlapping. Season lightly, then press the potatoes into the stock. Cover with the lid and cook on high for 7 to 8 hours until the potatoes and beef are tender.

Lift the pot out of the housing using oven mitts. Spray the potatoes with a little extra low-calorie cooking oil spray, then place under a preheated hot broiler until the potatoes are golden. Scatter with the parsley and serve with the steamed vegetables.

FOR MUSTARD BEEF HOTPOT, follow the recipe above, using 1 tablespoon wholegrain mustard in place of the balsamic vinegar and mustard powder.

CHICKEN & NAVY BEAN STEW

Serves **4**
Preparation time **20 minutes**
Cooking temperature **low**
Cooking time **8 to 9 hours**

2 tablespoons **olive oil**
1 lb 6 oz **boneless, skinless chicken thighs**, cubed
1 **onion**, sliced
2 **garlic cloves**, minced
2 tablespoons **all-purpose flour**
2½ cups **chicken stock**
1 **red bell pepper**, cored, seeded, and sliced
7 oz can **kernel corn**, drained
14 oz can **navy beans**, drained
10 oz small **new potatoes**, scrubbed and thinly sliced
2 **thyme sprigs**, plus extra leaves to garnish (optional)
salt and **pepper**

Preheat the slow cooker if necessary. Heat the oil in a large skillet, add the chicken and onion, and fry, stirring, until lightly browned.

Stir in the garlic and flour, then gradually mix in the stock. Add the red bell pepper, corn, navy beans, and new potatoes. Add the thyme and a little salt and pepper and bring to a boil, stirring.

Transfer the mixture to the slow-cooker pot and press the chicken and potatoes below the surface of the liquid. Cover with the lid and cook on low for 8 to 9 hours or until the chicken is cooked through and the potatoes are tender.

Stir well, then spoon into shallow bowls and scatter with a few extra thyme leaves, if using. Serve with hot garlic bread, if liked.

FOR SPANISH CHICKEN WITH CHORIZO, fry the chicken and onion as above with 3 oz ready-diced chorizo sausage until well colored, then mix in 1 teaspoon smoked paprika, the garlic, and flour. Continue as above, replacing the thyme sprigs with 2 rosemary sprigs. Serve scattered with chopped parsley.

HEARTY WINTER SAUSAGE STEW ♥

Serves **4**
Preparation time **20 minutes**
Cooking temperature **high**
Cooking time **5 to 6 hours**

low-calorie cooking oil spray
2 oz **smoked Canadian bacon**, chopped
1 **red onion**, chopped
½ teaspoon **smoked hot paprika** or **chili powder**
1¼ cups **chicken stock**
14 oz can **reduced-sugar baked beans**
14½ oz **extra-lean sausages**
1 **red bell pepper**, cored, seeded, and chopped
3½ cups diced **pumpkin**, skin and seeds discarded
2 **celery stalks**, thickly sliced
2 **sage sprigs** or ½ teaspoon **dried sage**
salt and **pepper**

Preheat the slow cooker if necessary. Spray a large skillet with a little low-calorie cooking oil spray and place over high heat until hot. Add the bacon and onion and fry for 4 to 5 minutes, stirring, until just beginning to brown. Stir in the paprika or chili powder, then pour in the stock and baked beans. Season to taste, then bring to a boil, stirring.

Arrange the sausages in a single layer in the bottom of the slow-cooker pot, top with the red bell pepper, pumpkin, celery, and sage, then pour over the hot stock and beans. Cover and cook on high for 5 to 6 hours. Stir the stew, spoon into shallow bowls, and serve.

FOR HEARTY WINTER CHICKEN STEW, follow the recipe above, using 1 lb 6 oz boneless, skinless chicken thighs instead of the sausages, and browning it with the bacon and onion. Add to the slow-cooker pot with the vegetables, pour over the hot stock and beans, cover, and cook on low for 7 to 8 hours.

HAM & CIDER HOTPOT ♥

Serves **4**
Preparation time **25 minutes**
Cooking temperature **high**
Cooking time **6 to 7 hours**

1 lb **unsmoked ham**, trimmed of fat
1 lb 6 oz **baking potatoes**, cut into ¾-inch chunks
7 oz small **shallots**, peeled
3 **carrots**, thickly sliced
2 **celery stalks**, thickly sliced
1 large **leek**, thickly sliced
2 **bay leaves**
1 cup **hard dry cider**
1 cup hot **chicken stock**
¼ teaspoon **cloves**
1 teaspoon **mustard powder**
pepper
3 tablespoons snipped **chives**, to garnish

Preheat the slow cooker if necessary. Rinse the ham with cold water, drain, and place in the slow-cooker pot with the potatoes. Arrange the shallots, carrots, celery, and leek slices around the ham, then tuck in the bay leaves.

Pour the hard cider and stock into a saucepan, add the cloves and mustard powder, then season with pepper (hams can be salty, so don't be tempted to add salt). Bring to a boil, then pour the mixture around the ham. Cover and cook on high for 6 to 7 hours until the ham is cooked through.

Cut the ham into pieces and serve in bowls with the vegetables and stock, garnished with snipped chives.

FOR HAM IN COLA, follow the recipe above, using 2 cups diet cola instead of the hard cider and stock and omitting the potatoes. Serve with 1 lb 6 oz boiled baby new potatoes and 5 oz steamed green snap beans.

SKINNY CASSOULET

Serves **4**
Preparation time **20 minutes**
Cooking temperature **low**
Cooking time **8 to 10 hours**

low-calorie cooking oil spray
1 lb **lean pork**, diced
3 oz **chorizo sausage**, sliced
1 **onion**, chopped
3 **garlic cloves**, minced
1 **red bell pepper**, cored, seeded,
   and diced
2 **celery stalks**, sliced
1 **carrot**, diced
2 cups **tomato purée**
1 teaspoon **dried
   Mediterranean herbs**
2 x 14 oz cans **cannellini
   beans**, drained
3 tablespoons **fresh bread crumbs**
salt and **pepper**

Preheat the slow cooker if necessary. Spray a large skillet with a little low-calorie cooking oil spray and place over high heat until hot. Add the pork a few pieces at a time until all the meat is in the pan and cook for 5 minutes, stirring, until browned. Use a slotted spoon to transfer the pork to the slow-cooker pot.

Add the chorizo and onion to the skillet and cook for 4 to 5 minutes until the onion has softened. Stir in the garlic, red bell pepper, celery, carrot, tomato purée, and herbs. Season to taste and bring to a boil, stirring.

Place the beans in the slow-cooker pot, pour in the tomato purée mixture, and stir well. Level the surface with the back of a spoon, then scatter the bread crumbs evenly over the top. Cover and cook on low for 8 to 10 hours until the pork is tender. Spoon into shallow bowls and serve with a salad, if liked.

FOR CHICKEN CASSOULET, follow the recipe above, using 1 lb boneless, skinless chicken thighs, diced, instead of the pork. Mix the bread crumbs with 2 tablespoons chopped rosemary and 2 tablespoons chopped parsley, then spoon over the cassoulet and cook as above.

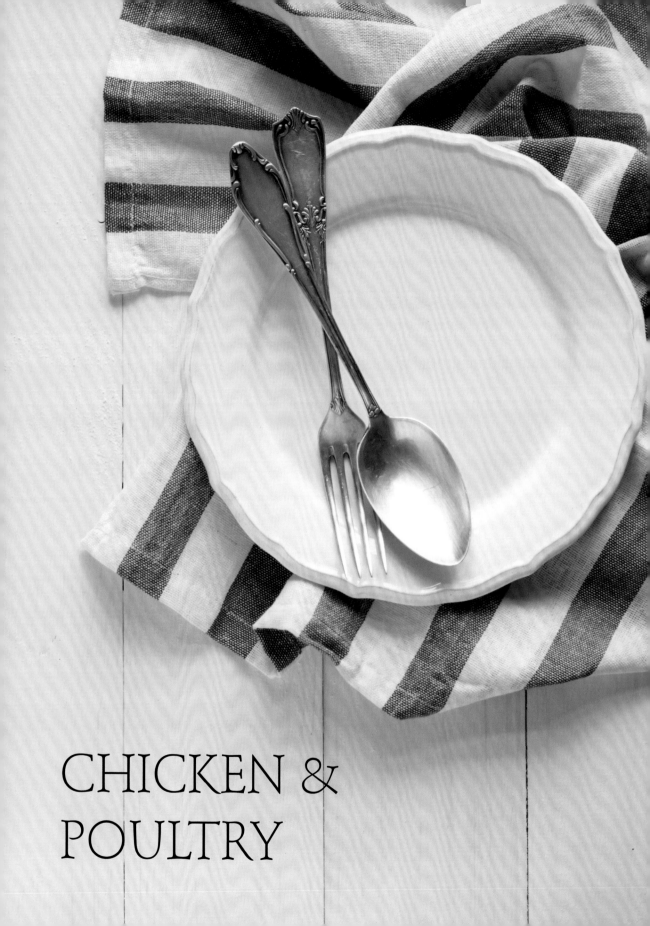

CHICKEN &
POULTRY

LEMON CHICKEN

Serves **4**
Preparation time **20 minutes**
Cooking temperature **high**
Cooking time **3¼ to 4¼ hours**

1 tablespoon **olive oil**
4 **boneless, skinless chicken breasts**,
   about 1¼ lb in total
1 **onion**, chopped
2 **garlic cloves**, minced
2 tablespoons **all-purpose flour**
2 cups **chicken stock**
½ **lemon** (cut in half lengthwise), cut
   into 4 wedges
2 **bok choy**, thickly sliced
4 oz **sugar snap peas**,
   halved lengthwise
¼ cup **crème fraîche**
2 tablespoons mixed chopped **mint**
   and **parsley**
salt and **pepper**

TO SERVE
couscous mixed with finely chopped
   tomato, **red onion**, and **red
   bell pepper**

Preheat the slow cooker if necessary. Heat the oil in a large skillet, add the chicken breasts, and fry over high heat until browned on both sides. Remove from the skillet and transfer to a plate. Add the onion to the skillet and fry, stirring, for 5 minutes or until lightly browned.

Stir in the garlic and flour, then mix in the stock and lemon wedges. Season with salt and pepper and bring to a boil.

Put the chicken breasts in the slow-cooker pot, pour the hot stock mixture over them, and press the chicken below the surface of the liquid. Cover and cook on high for 3 to 4 hours until tender and cooked through.

Add the bok choy and sugar snap peas and cook, still on high, for 15 minutes or until just tender. Lift out the chicken, slice the pieces, and arrange them on plates. Stir the crème fraîche and herbs into the sauce, then spoon it and the vegetables over the chicken. Serve with couscous mixed with finely chopped tomato, red onion, and red bell pepper.

FOR LEMON CHICKEN WITH HARISSA, add 4 teaspoons harissa to the skillet with the chicken stock and wedges cut from ½ lemon. Continue as above. Omit the bok choy at the end, adding instead ¼ lb broccoli, the florets cut into small pieces and stems sliced, and ½ sliced zucchini. Reduce the sugar snap peas to just 2 oz.

TARRAGON CHICKEN WITH MUSHROOMS

Serves **4**
Preparation time **20 minutes**
Cooking temperature **low** and **high**
Cooking time **8¼ to 9½ hours**

low-calorie cooking oil spray
4 **skinless chicken legs**, 2¼ lb in total
2 **leeks**, sliced, white and green
   parts kept separate
2½ cups sliced **white mushrooms**
1 tablespoon **all-purpose flour**
1 teaspoon **mustard powder**
2 cups **chicken stock**
2 tablespoons chopped **tarragon**,
   plus extra to garnish
3 tablespoons **sherry** (optional)
4 oz **fine green snap beans**
salt and **pepper**

Preheat the slow cooker if necessary. Spray a large skillet with a little low-calorie cooking oil spray and place over high heat until hot. Add the chicken legs and cook for 4 to 5 minutes, turning once, until golden. Transfer to the slow-cooker pot.

Add a little extra low-calorie cooking oil spray to the pan if necessary, then add the white leek slices and the mushrooms and cook for 2 to 3 minutes. Stir in the flour, then add the mustard powder, stock, tarragon, and sherry, if using. Season to taste and bring to a boil, stirring.

Pour the liquid and vegetables over the chicken, cover, and cook on low for 8 to 9 hours until the chicken is tender and cooked through.

Stir the casserole, then add the reserved green leek slices and the green snap beans. Cover again and cook on high for 15 to 30 minutes until the vegetables are tender. Spoon into shallow bowls and serve garnished with a little extra tarragon, accompanied by Low-cal Garlicky Mashed Potatoes (*see* below), if liked.

FOR LOW-CAL GARLICKY MASHED POTATOES TO ACCOMPANY THE TARRAGON CHICKEN, cut 1 lb 6 oz potatoes into chunks, then cook in a saucepan of lightly salted boiling water for about 15 minutes until tender. Drain and mash with 3 tablespoons chicken stock, 2 crushed garlic cloves, and a little salt and pepper.

FRENCH-STYLE CHICKEN POT ROAST

Serves **4**
Preparation time **20 minutes**
Cooking temperature **high**
Cooking time **5 to 6 hours**

2 lb 10 oz **roasting chicken**
½ lb **baby new potatoes**, scrubbed
   and halved
1 **red bell pepper**, cored, seeded,
   and diced
1 **yellow bell pepper**, cored, seeded,
   and diced
4 **garlic cloves**, halved
½ lb **cherry tomatoes**, halved
½ **lemon**, sliced
small bunch of **basil**, divided
1¼ cups hot **chicken stock**
1 tablespoon **tomato paste**
3 teaspoons **granulated sweetener**
¼ cup **pitted green olives in brine**,
   drained and halved
salt and **pepper**

Preheat the slow cooker if necessary. Put the chicken into the slow-cooker pot, then tuck the potatoes, bell peppers, garlic, and tomatoes around it. Season the chicken, then arrange the lemon slices over the breast. Tear half the basil into pieces and scatter them over the chicken and vegetables.

Mix the hot stock with the tomato paste and sweetener, then pour into the slow-cooker pot and add the olives. Cover with the lid and cook on high for 5 to 6 hours or until the chicken is thoroughly cooked and the meat juices run clear when the thickest parts of the leg and breast are pierced with a sharp knife.

Lift the pot out of the housing wearing oven mitts and place under a preheated hot broiler until the chicken is golden. Cut the meat off of the bones and arrange it in shallow bowls with the vegetables and stock, garnished with the remaining basil. If you prefer a thicker sauce, drain the stock into a small saucepan and boil rapidly to reduce by half.

FOR LEMON & TARRAGON POT-ROASTED CHICKEN, place the chicken in the slow-cooker pot and tuck ½ lb halved, scrubbed baby new potatoes, 3 chopped carrots, 3 chopped celery stalks, and 2 tarragon sprigs around it. Season the chicken and cover the breast with ½ sliced lemon. Mix 1¼ cups hot chicken stock with 1 tablespoon tomato paste and 3 teaspoons Dijon mustard and pour over the chicken. Cook as above and serve garnished with extra tarragon.

POT-ROASTED CHICKEN WITH LEMON

Serves **4 to 5**
Preparation time **25 minutes**
Cooking temperature **high**
Cooking time **5 to 6 hours**

2 tablespoons **olive oil**
3 lb **roasting chicken**
1 large **onion**, cut into 6 wedges
2 cups **hard dry cider**
3 teaspoons **Dijon mustard**
2 teaspoons **superfine sugar**
3¾ cups hot **chicken stock**
3 **carrots**, cut into chunks
3 **celery stalks**, thickly sliced
1 **lemon**, cut into 6 wedges, plus
    extra to garnish (optional)
½ cup **tarragon sprigs**
3 tablespoons **crème fraîche**
salt and **pepper**

Preheat the slow cooker if necessary. Heat the oil in a large skillet, add the chicken, breast-side down, and fry for 10 minutes, turning the chicken several times until browned all over.

Put the chicken, breast-side down, in the slow-cooker pot. Fry the onion wedges in the remaining oil in the skillet until lightly browned. Add the hard cider, mustard, and sugar and season with salt and pepper. Bring to a boil, then pour over the chicken. Add the hot stock, then the vegetables, lemon wedges, and 3 sprigs of the tarragon, making sure that the chicken and all the vegetables are well below the level of the stock so that they cook evenly and thoroughly.

Cover with the lid and cook on high for 5 to 6 hours or until the chicken is thoroughly cooked and the meat juices run clear when the thickest parts of the leg and breast are pierced with a sharp knife. Turn the chicken after 4 hours, if liked.

Lift the chicken out of the stock, drain well, and transfer to a large serving plate. Remove the vegetables with a slotted spoon and arrange them around the chicken. Measure 2½ cups of the hot cooking stock from the slow-cooker pot into a pitcher. Reserve a few tarragon sprigs to garnish, pick the leaves from the remainder, chop them, and beat them into the pitcher along with the crème fraîche to make a gravy. Adjust the seasoning to taste. Carve the chicken in the usual way and serve with the gravy and vegetables. Garnish with extra lemon wedges, if liked, and the leaves of the reserved tarragon sprigs, coarsely torn.

CARIBBEAN CHICKEN WITH RICE & PEAS

Serves **4**
Preparation time **20 minutes**
Cooking temperature **low** and **high**
Cooking time **7 to 9 hours**

8 **chicken thighs**, about 2¼ lb in total
3 tablespoons **Jerk Marinade**
   (*see* below)
2 tablespoons **sunflower oil**
2 large **onions**, chopped
2 **garlic cloves**, minced
14 fl oz can **full-fat coconut milk**
1¼ cups **chicken stock**
14 oz can **red kidney beans**, drained
1 cup **converted white long-grain rice**
¾ cup **frozen peas**
salt and **pepper**

TO GARNISH
lime wedges
cilantro sprigs

Preheat the slow cooker if necessary. Remove the skin from the chicken thighs, slash each thigh 2 to 3 times, and rub with the jerk marinade.

Heat 1 tablespoon of the oil in a large skillet, add the chicken, and fry over high heat until browned on both sides. Lift out with a slotted spoon and transfer to a plate. Add the remaining oil, the onions, and garlic, reduce the heat, and fry for 5 minutes or until softened and lightly browned. Pour in the coconut milk and stock, season to taste, and bring to a boil.

Transfer half the mixture to the slow-cooker pot, add half the chicken pieces, all the beans, and then the remaining chicken, onions, and coconut mixture. Cover and cook on low for 6 to 8 hours until the chicken is tender and cooked through.

Stir in the rice, replace the lid and cook on high for 45 minutes. Add the frozen peas (no need to defrost) and cook for a further 15 minutes. Spoon onto plates and serve garnished with lime wedges and cilantro sprigs.

FOR JERK MARINADE, wearing disposable gloves, halve 1 to 2 Scotch bonnet chiles, depending on their size, discard the seeds, and chop finely. Add to a sterilized screw-top jar with 1 tablespoon finely chopped thyme leaves, 1 teaspoon each ground allspice and cinnamon, ½ teaspoon grated nutmeg, ½ teaspoon salt, ½ teaspoon ground black pepper, 3 teaspoons brown sugar, 2 tablespoons sunflower oil, and ¼ cup apple cider vinegar. Screw the lid on securely and shake to mix. Use 3 tablespoons of the marinade and store the remainder in the refrigerator for up to 2 weeks.

THAI GREEN CHICKEN CURRY

Serves **4**
Preparation time **20 minutes**
Cooking temperature **low** and **high**
Cooking time **8¼ to 10¼ hours**

1 tablespoon **sunflower oil**
2 tablespoons **Thai green curry paste**
2 teaspoons **galangal paste**
2 **Thai green chiles**, seeded and thinly sliced
1 **onion**, finely chopped
8 **chicken thighs**, about 2¼ lb in total, skinned, boned, and cubed
14 fl oz can **full-fat coconut milk**
¾ cup **chicken stock**
4 dried **kaffir lime leaves**
2 teaspoons **light brown sugar**
2 teaspoons **fish sauce**
3½ oz **sugar snap peas**
3½ oz **green snap beans**, halved
small bunch of **cilantro**
boiled **rice**, to serve

Preheat the slow cooker if necessary. Heat the oil in a skillet, add the curry paste, galangal paste, and green chiles and cook for 1 minute.

Stir in the onion and chicken and cook, stirring, until the chicken is just beginning to turn golden. Pour in the coconut milk and stock, then add the lime leaves, sugar, and fish sauce. Bring to a boil, stirring.

Transfer the mixture to the slow-cooker pot, cover with the lid, and cook on low for 8 to 10 hours or until the chicken is tender.

Stir in the peas and beans and cook on high for 15 minutes or until they are just tender. Tear the cilantro leaves and scatter them over the top, then spoon into bowls and serve with rice.

FOR THAI RED CHICKEN CURRY, make the curry as above but omit the green curry paste and green chiles and instead add 2 tablespoons red curry paste and 2 minced garlic cloves. Cook for 8 to 10 hours as above but omit the peas and beans, then spoon into bowls and scatter with some torn cilantro leaves.

TURKEY WITH PUMPKIN & CRANBERRIES ♥

Serves **4**
Preparation time **20 minutes**
Cooking temperature **low**
Cooking time **6 to 8 hours**

low-calorie cooking oil spray
1 lb **turkey breast**, diced
1 **onion**, chopped
2 teaspoons **all-purpose flour**
1¼ cups **chicken stock**
juice of 1 large **orange**
½ teaspoon **ground mixed spice**
¼ cup **dried cranberries**
4 cups cubed **pumpkin**, skin and seeds discarded,
   cut into 1-inch cubes
salt and **pepper**

Preheat the slow cooker if necessary. Spray a large skillet with a little low-calorie cooking oil spray and place over high heat until hot. Add the turkey a few pieces at a time until all the turkey is in the pan. Add the onion and cook for 5 minutes, stirring and turning the turkey pieces, until golden all over.

Sprinkle in the flour and stir well. Add the stock, orange juice, mixed spice, and cranberries and season to taste. Bring to a boil, stirring.

Place the pumpkin in the slow-cooker pot and pour the turkey mixture on top, pushing the turkey pieces into the liquid. Cover and cook on low for 6 to 8 hours until the turkey is tender and cooked through. Spoon into shallow dishes and serve with steamed green snap beans and broccoli, if liked.

FOR TURKEY CURRY WITH GOLDEN RAISINS & PUMPKIN, follow the recipe above but omit the mixed spice and cranberries and add 3 teaspoons medium-hot curry powder and ¼ cup golden raisins instead.

ASIAN TURKEY WITH RAINBOW CHARD ♥

Serves **4**
Preparation time **20 minutes**
Cooking temperature **low** and **high**
Cooking time **8¼ to 9½ hours**

low-calorie cooking oil spray
1 lb **turkey breast**, diced
1 **onion**, chopped
2 **garlic cloves**, minced
3 cups sliced **white mushrooms**
2 cups **chicken stock**
1-inch piece of **fresh ginger root**,
   peeled and chopped
2 tablespoons **soy sauce**
1 tablespoon **tamarind paste**
1 tablespoon **tomato paste**
1 tablespoon **cornstarch**
7 oz **rainbow chard**, thickly sliced
salt and **pepper**

Preheat the slow cooker if necessary. Spray a large skillet with a little low-calorie cooking oil spray and place over high heat until hot. Gradually add the turkey to the skillet and cook for 5 minutes, stirring, until golden. Transfer to the slow-cooker pot using a slotted spoon.

Add a little extra low-calorie cooking oil spray to the skillet, if necessary, and cook the onion for 4 to 5 minutes until softened. Stir in the garlic and mushrooms and cook for 2 to 3 minutes more. Add the stock, ginger, soy sauce, tamarind paste, and tomato paste, season to taste, and bring to a boil, stirring. Pour over the turkey, cover, and cook on low for 8 to 9 hours until the turkey is cooked through.

Mix the cornstarch to a smooth paste with a little cold water and stir into the turkey mixture. Arrange the chard on top, cover again, and cook on high for 15 to 30 minutes until tender. Spoon into bowls and serve with rice, if liked.

FOR BLACK BEAN TURKEY, follow the recipe above, adding the mushrooms to the skillet with a 1 lb jar of black bean sauce, then bring to a boil. Transfer to the slow-cooker pot and cook as above. Stir-fry 9 oz ready-prepared stir-fry vegetables in a little low-calorie cooking oil spray and serve.

CREAMY TARRAGON CHICKEN

Serves **4**
Preparation time **15 minutes**
Cooking temperature **high**
Cooking time **3 to 4 hours**

1 tablespoon **olive oil**
1 tablespoon **butter**
4 **boneless, skinless chicken breasts**,
  about 1 lb 7 oz in total
7 oz **shallots**, halved
1 tablespoon **all-purpose flour**
1¼ cups **chicken stock**
¼ cup **dry vermouth**
2 **tarragon sprigs**, plus
  1 tablespoon chopped
3 tablespoons **heavy cream**
2 tablespoons snipped **chives**
salt and **pepper**
coarsely mashed **potatoes** mixed
  with **peas**, to serve

Preheat the slow cooker if necessary. Heat the oil and butter in a skillet, add the chicken, and fry over high heat until golden on both sides but not cooked through. Drain and put into the slow-cooker pot in a single layer.

Add the shallots to the skillet and cook, stirring, for 4 to 5 minutes or until just beginning to turn golden. Stir in the flour, then gradually mix in the stock and vermouth. Add the tarragon sprigs and a little salt and pepper and bring to a boil, stirring.

Pour the sauce over the chicken breasts, cover, and cook on high for 3 to 4 hours or until the chicken is tender and cooked through to the center.

Stir the cream into the sauce and scatter the chopped tarragon and chives all over the chicken. Serve with coarsely mashed potatoes mixed with peas.

FOR CREAMY PESTO CHICKEN, prepare the dish as above, but replace the vermouth with ¼ cup white wine and the tarragon with 1 tablespoon pesto. Sprinkle the chicken with some tiny basil leaves and a little freshly shredded Parmesan cheese instead of the chives. Serve the chicken sliced, if liked, and mixed with cooked penne and drizzled with the creamy sauce.

TANGY TURKEY TAGINE

Serves **4**
Preparation time **25 minutes**
Cooking temperature **low**
Cooking time **8 to 9 hours**

low-calorie cooking oil spray
14 oz **turkey breast**, diced
1 **onion**, chopped
2 **garlic cloves**, minced
1 tablespoon **all-purpose flour**
2 cups **chicken stock**
2 pinches of **saffron threads** or
   1 teaspoon **ground turmeric**
2-inch **cinnamon stick**
finely grated zest of 1 **lemon**
14 oz can **chickpeas**, drained
¼ cup **golden raisins**
salt and **pepper**

TO SERVE
1 cup **couscous**
2 cups boiling **water**
¼ cup chopped **mint** or mixed **mint**
   and **parsley**

Preheat the slow cooker if necessary. Spray a large skillet with a little low-calorie cooking oil spray and place over high heat until hot. Add the turkey a few pieces at a time until all the turkey is in the pan and cook for 5 minutes, stirring, until golden. Use a slotted spoon to transfer the turkey to a plate.

Add the onion to the skillet and cook for 4 to 5 minutes until softened. Stir in the garlic and flour, then add the stock and mix well. Add the saffron or turmeric, cinnamon, and lemon zest, then the chickpeas and golden raisins. Season to taste and bring to a boil, stirring.

Pour into the slow-cooker pot, add the turkey pieces, and press into the liquid. Cover and cook on low for 8 to 9 hours until the turkey is tender and cooked through.

Meanwhile, place the couscous in a mixing bowl, pour over the boiling water, cover with a plate, and let soak for 5 minutes until tender. Stir in the chopped herbs, season to taste, and fluff up with a fork.

Divide the couscous between 4 plates and top with the tagine. Serve with warmed naan bread, if liked.

FOR HARISSA-BAKED TURKEY, follow the recipe above, using 1¼ cups chicken stock and 1½ cups diced tomatoes instead of 2 cups chicken stock. Omit the saffron, cinnamon, and lemon, and add 2 teaspoons harissa and a 1-inch piece of fresh ginger root, peeled and chopped, instead. Cook as above and serve with the couscous and herbs.

CREAMY CHICKEN KORMA

Serves **4**
Preparation time **15 minutes**
Cooking temperature **low**
Cooking time **6¼ to 7¼ hours**

2 tablespoons **butter**
4 **boneless, skinless chicken breasts**,
    about 5 oz each
1 **onion**, finely chopped
2 **garlic cloves**, minced
1-inch piece of **fresh ginger root**,
    peeled and finely chopped
3 tablespoons **korma curry paste**
¼ cup **ground almonds**
1 cup **chicken stock**
3 tablespoons **heavy cream**
3 tablespoons chopped **cilantro**
salt and **pepper**
3 tablespoons toasted **flaked**
    almonds, to garnish
boiled **rice**, to serve

Preheat the slow cooker if necessary. Heat the butter in a large skillet, add the chicken, and fry on both sides until browned but not cooked through. Lift out of the pan with a slotted spoon and transfer to the slow-cooker pot.

Add the onion, garlic, and ginger to the pan and fry for 2 to 3 minutes, then stir in the curry paste and cook for 1 minute. Stir in the ground almonds, stock, and salt and pepper and bring to a boil.

Pour the sauce over the chicken. Cover with the lid and cook on low for 6 to 7 hours or until the chicken is tender and cooked through.

Stir in the cream and chopped cilantro, replace the lid, and cook, still on low, for 15 minutes. Slice the chicken. Spoon onto rice-lined plates and scatter with the almonds.

FOR CREAMY PANEER KORMA, omit the chicken and fry 2 small, very finely chopped onions in 2 tablespoons butter until softened. Add the garlic, ginger, and curry paste, then stir in the ground almonds and stock and bring to a boil as above. Drain and cut 14½ oz paneer (Indian cheese) into ¾-inch cubes, then add to the slow-cooker pot with the sauce. Continue as above.

SWEET & SOUR CHICKEN

Serves **4**
Preparation time **20 minutes**
Cooking temperature **low**
Cooking time **6¼ to 8¼ hours**

1 tablespoon **sunflower oil**
8 small **chicken thighs**, about 2¼ lb in total, skinned, boned, and cubed
4 **scallions**, thickly sliced, white and green parts kept separate
2 **carrots**, halved lengthwise and thinly sliced
1-inch piece of **fresh ginger root**, peeled and finely chopped
14 oz can **pineapple chunks in 100% pineapple juice**
1¼ cups **chicken stock**
1 tablespoon **cornstarch**
1 tablespoon **tomato paste**
2 tablespoons **superfine sugar**
2 tablespoons **soy sauce**
2 tablespoons **malt vinegar**
8 oz can **bamboo shoots**, drained
1¼ cups **bean sprouts**
3½ oz **snow peas**, thinly sliced
rice, to serve

Preheat the slow cooker if necessary. Heat the oil in a skillet, add the chicken thighs, and fry, stirring, until browned on all sides. Mix in the white scallion slices, carrots, and ginger and cook for 2 minutes.

Stir in the pineapple chunks and their juice and the stock. Put the cornstarch, tomato paste, and sugar into a small bowl, then gradually mix in the soy sauce and vinegar to make a smooth paste. Stir into the skillet and bring to a boil, stirring.

Tip the chicken and sauce into the slow-cooker pot, add the bamboo shoots, and press the chicken beneath the surface of the sauce. Cover with the lid and cook on low for 6 to 8 hours.

When almost ready to serve, add the green scallion slices, bean sprouts, and snow peas to the slow-cooker pot and mix well. Replace the lid and cook, still on low, for 15 minutes or until the vegetables are just tender. Spoon into rice-filled bowls.

FOR LEMON CHICKEN, follow the recipe as above up until the addition of the chicken stock. Gradually mix the juice of 1 lemon into the cornstarch to make a smooth paste, then stir into the stock with 2 tablespoons dry sherry and 4 teaspoons superfine sugar. Bring to a boil, stirring, then add to the slow-cooker pot and cook as above, adding the green scallion slices, bean sprouts, and snow peas at the end.

TANGY BRAISED CHICKEN, FENNEL & LEEKS

Serves **4**
Preparation time **20 minutes**
Cooking temperature **low**
Cooking time **8½ to 9½ hours**

low-calorie cooking oil spray
1 lb 6 oz **boneless, skinless chicken thighs**, halved
1 **fennel bulb**, cored and sliced, green fronds reserved
2 **leeks**, thinly sliced, white and green parts kept separate
1½ cups **chicken stock**
finely grated zest and juice of ½ **orange**
2 teaspoons **cornstarch**
salt and **pepper**

Preheat the slow cooker if necessary. Spray a large skillet with a little low-calorie cooking oil spray and place over high heat until hot. Add the chicken and cook for 3 to 4 minutes, turning once, until browned on both sides. Use a slotted spoon to transfer to a plate.

Add the fennel and white leek slices to the skillet and cook for 2 to 3 minutes until just beginning to soften, then add the stock and orange zest and juice. Mix the cornstarch to a smooth paste with a little cold water and stir into the pan. Season to taste and bring to a boil, stirring.

Transfer the mixture to the slow-cooker pot, arrange the chicken pieces on top in a single layer, and press into the liquid. Cover and cook on low for 8 to 9 hours until the chicken is cooked through.

Add the reserved green leek slices, stir into the sauce, cover again, and cook, still on low, for 30 minutes. Serve garnished with the reserved fennel fronds.

FOR BRAISED MUSTARD CHICKEN & LEEKS, follow the recipe above, using 3 oz diced Canadian bacon instead of the fennel. Use 1 teaspoon Dijon mustard instead of the orange zest and juice and cook as above. Garnish with chopped parsley.

KASHMIRI BUTTER CHICKEN ♥

Serves **4**
Preparation time **30 minutes**
Cooking temperature **low**
Cooking time **5 to 7 hours**

2 **onions**, quartered
3 **garlic cloves**
1½-inch piece of **fresh ginger root**, peeled
1 large **red chile**, seeded
8 **boneless, skinless chicken thighs**
1 tablespoon **sunflower oil**
2 tablespoons **butter**
1 teaspoon **cumin seeds**, crushed
1 teaspoon **fennel seeds**, crushed
4 **cardamom pods**, crushed
1 teaspoon **paprika**
1 teaspoon **ground turmeric**
¼ teaspoon **ground cinnamon**
1¼ cups **chicken stock**
1 tablespoon **brown sugar**
2 tablespoons **tomato paste**
⅓ cup **heavy cream**
salt

TO GARNISH
toasted **sliced almonds**
cilantro sprigs
boiled **rice**, to serve

Preheat the slow cooker if necessary. Blend the onions, garlic, ginger, and chile in a food processor or blender, or chop finely.

Cut each chicken thigh into 4 pieces. Heat the oil in a large skillet and add the chicken a few pieces at a time until all the meat has been added. Cook over high heat until browned. Drain and transfer to a plate.

Reduce the heat and add the butter to the skillet. When it has melted, add the onion paste and cook until it is just beginning to color. Stir in the crushed cumin and fennel seeds, the cardamom pods and their black seeds, and the ground spices. Cook for 1 minute, then mix in the stock, sugar, tomato paste, and salt. Bring to a boil, stirring.

Transfer the chicken to the slow-cooker pot, pour the onion mixture and sauce over the top, and press the pieces of chicken below the surface of the liquid. Cover with the lid and cook on low for 5 to 7 hours.

Stir in the cream. Garnish with toasted sliced almonds and cilantro sprigs and serve with boiled rice and Cilantro Flat Breads (*see* below), if liked.

FOR CILANTRO FLAT BREADS TO ACCOMPANY THE CURRY, sift together 1½ cups all-purpose flour, and 2 teaspoons baking powder, then mix it in a bowl with 3 tablespoons coarsely chopped cilantro leaves and a little salt. Add 2 tablespoons sunflower oil, then gradually mix in 6 to 7 tablespoons water to make a soft dough. Cut the dough into 4 pieces and roll out each piece thinly on a lightly floured surface to form a rough oval. Cook on a preheated ridged grill pan for 3 to 4 minutes on each side until singed and puffed up.

BRAISED DUCK WITH ORANGE SAUCE

Serves **4**
Preparation time **15 minutes**
Cooking temperature **high**
Cooking time **4 to 5 hours**

4 **duck legs**, about 6 oz each
1 **onion**, sliced
2 tablespoons **all-purpose flour**
¾ cup **chicken stock**
¾ cup **dry white wine**
1 large **orange**, ½ squeezed juice, ½ sliced
1 **bay leaf**
1 teaspoon **Dijon mustard**
½ teaspoon **black peppercorns**, coarsely crushed
salt

Preheat the slow cooker if necessary. Dry-fry the duck in a large skillet over low heat until the fat begins to run, then increase the heat until the duck is browned on both sides. Lift out of the pan with a slotted spoon and transfer to the slow-cooker pot.

Pour off any excess fat to leave about 1 tablespoon. Fry the onion until softened. Stir in the flour, then mix in the stock, wine, orange juice, bay leaf, a little salt, and the crushed peppercorns and bring to a boil, stirring. Add the orange slices.

Pour the sauce over the duck, cover with the lid, and cook on high for 4 to 5 hours or until the duck is tender and almost falling off the bones. Serve with rice and steamed green snap beans, if liked.

FOR BRAISED DUCK WITH CRANBERRIES & PORT, fry the duck and onions as above. Mix in the flour and stock, then replace the wine with ¾ cup ruby port and 1 cup fresh cranberries. Add the orange slices and juice and continue as above.

MUSTARD CHICKEN & BACON

Serves **4**
Preparation time **15 minutes**
Cooking temperature **low**
Cooking time **8¼ to 10¼ hours**

1 tablespoon **butter**
1 tablespoon **sunflower oil**
4 **chicken thighs** and 4 **chicken drumsticks**
4 slices smoked Canadian **bacon**, diced
¾ lb **leeks**, thinly sliced, white and green parts kept separate
2 tablespoons **all-purpose flour**
2½ cups **chicken stock**
3 teaspoons **wholegrain mustard**
salt and **pepper**
mashed **potatoes**, to serve

Preheat the slow cooker if necessary. Heat the butter and oil in a skillet, add the chicken, and fry over high heat until browned on all sides. Transfer to the slow-cooker pot with a slotted spoon.

Add the bacon and white leek slices to the skillet and fry, stirring, for 5 minutes or until just beginning to turn golden. Stir in the flour, then gradually mix in the stock, mustard, and a little salt and pepper. Bring to a boil. Pour into the slow-cooker pot, cover with the lid, and cook on low for 8 to 10 hours.

Add the green leek slices and stir into the sauce, then replace the lid and cook, still on low, for 15 minutes or until the green leeks are just softened. Spoon into shallow serving bowls and serve with mashed potatoes.

FOR MUSTARD CHICKEN & FRANKFURTER CASSEROLE, fry the chicken as above, then drain and add to the slow-cooker pot. Add 1 chopped onion to the pan, then mix in 4 chilled, sliced frankfurters and fry for 5 minutes. Stir in the flour, then mix in the stock, mustard, and seasoning as above. Add 1 cup canned kernel corn, drained, transfer to the slow-cooker pot and cook on low for 8 to 10 hours.

TURKEY KEEMA MUTTER ♥

Serves **4**
Preparation time **20 minutes**
Cooking temperature **low** and **high**
Cooking time **8¼ to 10¼ hours**

low-calorie cooking oil spray
1 lb **ground turkey breast**
1 **onion**, chopped
2 **garlic cloves**, minced
1-inch piece of **fresh ginger root**, peeled
    and finely chopped
1 teaspoon **cumin seeds**, crushed
4 teaspoons **medium-hot curry powder**
2 cups **tomato purée**
2 teaspoons **granulated sweetener**
1 cup **frozen peas**
¼ cup chopped **cilantro**, divided
salt and **pepper**
½ **red onion**, thinly sliced, to garnish
4 small **chapatis**, 2 oz each, to serve

Preheat the slow cooker if necessary. Spray a large
skillet with a little low-calorie cooking oil spray and
place over high heat until hot. Add the ground turkey
and onion and fry for 4 to 5 minutes, stirring and
breaking up the meat with a wooden spoon, until it is
just beginning to brown.

Stir in the garlic, ginger, cumin, and curry powder and
cook for 1 minute, then add the tomato purée and
sweetener. Season to taste and bring to a boil, stirring.
Transfer to the slow-cooker pot, cover with the lid,
and cook on low for 8 to 10 hours until the turkey is
cooked through.

Add the frozen peas to the slow-cooker pot with
half the cilantro. Cover again and cook on high for
15 minutes. Scatter with the remaining cilantro and
the red onion and serve with the chapatis.

FOR KEEMA MUTTER IN BAKED POTATOES, follow
the recipe above to make and cook the turkey and pea
mixture. Scrub and prick 4 baking potatoes, 6 oz each,
place in the microwave rolled up in a piece of paper
towel, and cook on full power for about 20 minutes
until tender. Transfer to serving plates, cut in half,
and top with the keema mutter, remaining cilantro,
and red onion.

POT-ROAST PHEASANT WITH CHESTNUTS

Serves **2 to 3**
Preparation time **15 minutes**
Cooking temperature **high**
Cooking time **3 to 4 hours**

2 tablespoons **butter**
1 tablespoon **olive oil**
1½ lb **oven-ready pheasant**
7 oz **shallots**, halved
2 oz **sliced smoked bacon**, diced,
    or **ready-diced pancetta**
2 **celery stalks**, thickly sliced
1 tablespoon **all-purpose flour**
1¼ cups **chicken stock**
¼ cup **dry sherry**
3½ oz **vacuum-packed prepared chestnuts**
2 to 3 **thyme sprigs**
salt and **pepper**

Preheat the slow cooker if necessary. Heat the butter
and oil in a skillet, add the pheasant, breast-side down,
the shallots, bacon or pancetta, and celery and fry until
golden brown, turning the pheasant and stirring the
other ingredients. Transfer the pheasant to the slow-
cooker pot, placing it breast-side down.

Stir the flour into the onion mixture. Gradually add the
stock and sherry, then add the chestnuts, thyme, and
a little salt and pepper. Bring to a boil, stirring, then
spoon over the pheasant. Cover with the lid and cook
on high for 3 to 4 hours until tender. Test with a knife
through the thickest part of the pheasant leg and breast
to make sure that the juices run clear. To serve, carve
the pheasant breast into thick slices and cut the legs
off of the carcass.

FOR POT-ROAST GUINEA FOWL WITH PRUNES, fry
a guinea fowl, weighing about 2¼ lb, instead of the
pheasant as above. Transfer the fowl to the slow
cooker, mix in 2 tablespoons all-purpose flour, then add
2 cups chicken stock and the sherry. Omit the chestnuts
and add ¼ cup halved ready-to-eat pitted prunes
instead. Continue as above, but cook for 5 to 6 hours.

SUN-DRIED TOMATO & CHICKEN PILAF

Serves **4**
Preparation time **25 minutes**
Cooking temperature **high**
Cooking time **3 to 4 hours**

1 tablespoon **olive oil**
4 **boneless, skinless chicken breasts**
1 large **onion**, coarsely chopped
2 **garlic cloves**, chopped (optional)
14 oz can **diced tomatoes**
½ cup **sun-dried tomatoes in oil**,
   drained and sliced
2 teaspoons **pesto**
2½ cups hot **chicken stock**
1 cup **converted brown
   long-grain rice**
⅓ cup **wild rice**
salt and **pepper**

TO SERVE
arugula
olive oil and lemon dressing

Preheat the slow cooker if necessary. Heat the oil in a skillet and fry the chicken breasts on one side only until browned. Remove from the pan with a slotted spoon, transfer to a plate, and set aside.

Fry the onion and garlic, if using, in the pan, stirring, for 5 minutes or until lightly browned. Add the diced tomatoes, sun-dried tomatoes, and pesto, season with salt and pepper, and bring to a boil. Pour into the slow-cooker pot, then stir in the stock.

Rinse the brown rice well in a sieve under cold running water, then stir into the slow-cooker pot with the wild rice. Arrange the chicken breasts on top of the rice, browned-side up, pressing them just below the level of the liquid so they don't dry out during cooking. Cover with the lid and cook on high for 3 to 4 hours or until the chicken is cooked and the rice is tender.

Spoon onto serving plates and serve with a salad of arugula tossed in an olive oil and lemon dressing.

FOR RED BELL PEPPER, LEMON & CHICKEN PILAF, fry 4 boneless, skinless chicken breasts as above and transfer to a plate. In the pan, fry 1 large, coarsely chopped onion and 1 cored, seeded, and diced red bell pepper until the onion is just turning golden. Add a 14-oz can diced tomatoes, 2 tablespoons finely chopped lemon thyme leaves, and the grated zest and juice of 1 lemon. Bring to a boil and add to the slow cooker with the hot chicken stock and rice, as above, with the chicken. Continue as above.

MOROCCAN MEATBALLS

Serves **4**
Preparation time **30 minutes**
Cooking temperature **low**
Cooking time **6 to 8 hours**

1 lb **ground turkey**
½ cup drained **canned green lentils**
1 **egg yolk**
1 tablespoon **olive oil**
1 **onion**, sliced
2 **garlic cloves**, finely chopped
1 teaspoon **ground turmeric**
1 teaspoon **ground coriander**
½ teaspoon **ground cumin**
½ teaspoon **ground cinnamon**
1-inch piece of **fresh ginger root**,
    peeled and finely chopped
14 oz can **diced tomatoes**
¾ cup **chicken stock**
salt and **pepper**

Preheat the slow cooker if necessary. Mix together the ground turkey, green lentils, a little salt and pepper, and the egg yolk in a bowl or food processor. Divide into 20 pieces, then shape into small balls with wetted hands.

Heat the oil in a large skillet, add the meatballs, and fry, stirring, until browned but not cooked through. Lift out of the pan with a slotted spoon and put into the slow-cooker pot. Add the onion and fry until softened, then stir in the garlic, spices, and ginger and cook for 1 minute.

Stir in the tomatoes, stock, and a little salt and pepper and bring to a boil, stirring. Pour over the meatballs, cover with the lid, and cook on low for 6 to 8 hours or until cooked through. Stir, then spoon onto couscous-lined plates (*see* below).

FOR LEMON COUSCOUS TO ACCOMPANY THE MEATBALLS, put 1 cup couscous into a bowl and pour over 2 cups boiling water. Add the grated zest and juice of 1 lemon, 2 tablespoons olive oil, and some salt and pepper. Cover and let stand for 5 minutes. Fluff up with a fork and stir in a small bunch of chopped cilantro.

FISH &
SEAFOOD

FISH PIE

Serves **4 to 5**
Preparation time **20 minutes**
Cooking temperature **low**
Cooking time **2 to 3 hours**

1 tablespoon **sunflower oil**
1 **leek**, thinly sliced
½ stick **butter**
½ cup **all-purpose flour**
2 cups **milk**
¾ cup **fish stock**
¾ cup shredded **Cheddar cheese**
1 **bay leaf**
1¾ lb mixed **salmon** and **smoked** and
  unsmoked haddock fillet, skinned
  and cut into large cubes
salt and **pepper**

TOPPING
¼ cup chopped **parsley**
4 cups hot **homemade** or **store-bought**
  mashed potatoes
2 tablespoons **butter**
2 tablespoons shredded
  Cheddar cheese

Preheat the slow cooker if necessary. Heat the oil in a saucepan, add the leek, and fry, stirring, for 4 to 5 minutes or until softened. Scoop out of the pan with a slotted spoon and transfer to a plate.

Add the butter, flour, and milk to the pan and bring to a boil, whisking constantly until thickened and smooth. Mix in the stock, cheese, bay leaf, and a little salt and pepper.

Arrange the cubed fish in the slow-cooker pot so that it is in an even layer, then pour over the hot sauce. Cover and cook on low for 2 to 3 hours or until the fish flakes easily when pressed in the center with a knife.

When almost ready to serve, stir the parsley into the hot mashed potatoes. Stir the fish, then spoon into individual baking dishes, if liked. Spoon the potato over the top, dot with the butter, and scatter with the cheese. If not using separate dishes, lift the pot out of the housing using oven mitts and place under a preheated medium broiler until golden. Serve with steamed asparagus, if liked.

FOR MIXED FISH & SPINACH GRATIN, wash ¾ lb baby spinach in cold water, drain, and place in a large saucepan. Cover and cook until just wilted. Transfer to a sieve and squeeze out as much water as possible. Spoon into the bottom of a 2-inch deep baking dish. Make the fish pie mixture as above and spoon out of the slow-cooker pot onto the spinach, then sprinkle with ½ cup shredded Cheddar cheese and ¼ cup fresh bread crumbs. Broil as above.

TUNA ARRABIATA ♥

Serves **4**
Preparation time **20 minutes**
Cooking temperature **low**
Cooking time **4 to 5 hours**

1 tablespoon **olive oil**
1 **onion**, chopped
2 **garlic cloves**, minced
1 **red bell pepper**, cored, seeded,
    and diced
1 teaspoon **smoked paprika**
¼ to ½ teaspoon **crushed dried
    red chiles**
14 oz can **diced tomatoes**
¾ cup **vegetable** or **fish stock**
7 oz can **tuna in water**, drained
salt and **pepper**

TO SERVE
¾ lb **dried spaghetti**
¼ cup freshly shredded
    Parmesan cheese
small handful of **basil leaves**

Preheat the slow cooker if necessary. Heat the oil in a large skillet over medium heat, add the onion, and cook, stirring, for 5 minutes or until just browning around the edges. Add the garlic, red bell pepper, paprika, and chiles and cook for 2 minutes.

Add the tomatoes and stock and season to taste. Bring to a boil, then transfer to the slow-cooker pot. Break the tuna into large pieces and stir into the tomato mixture. Cover and cook on low for 4 to 5 hours.

Meanwhile, cook the spaghetti in a saucepan of lightly salted boiling water following the package instructions until just tender. Drain and stir into the tomato sauce.

Spoon into 4 shallow bowls and scatter with the shredded Parmesan and basil leaves.

FOR DOUBLE TOMATO ARRABIATA, follow the recipe above using ¾ cup sliced, drained sun-dried tomatoes in oil and 1½ cups sliced baby mushrooms instead of the tuna. Cook and serve as above.

MACARONI WITH SMOKED HADDOCK

Serves **4**
Preparation time **15 minutes**
Cooking temperature **low**
Cooking time **2¼ to 3¼ hours**

2 cups **dried macaroni**
1 tablespoon **olive oil**
1 **onion**, chopped
½ stick **butter**
½ cup **all-purpose flour**
2 cups **milk**
2 cups **fish stock**
1½ cups shredded **Cheddar cheese**, divided
¼ teaspoon grated **nutmeg**
1 lb **smoked haddock fillet**, skinned and cut into 1-inch cubes
1 cup canned **kernel corn**, drained
4 oz **spinach**, rinsed, drained, and coarsely torn
salt and **pepper**

Preheat the slow cooker if necessary. Tip the macaroni into a bowl, cover with plenty of boiling water, and let soak for 10 minutes while preparing the rest of the dish.

Heat the oil in a saucepan, add the onion, and fry gently, stirring, for 5 minutes or until softened. Add the butter and, when melted, stir in the flour. Gradually mix in the milk and bring to a boil, stirring until smooth. Stir in the stock, 1 cup of the cheese, the nutmeg, and the salt and pepper and bring back to a boil, stirring.

Drain the macaroni and add to the slow-cooker pot with the haddock and corn. Pour over the sauce and gently stir together. Cover with the lid and cook on low for 2 to 3 hours.

Stir the spinach into the macaroni, replace the lid, and cook on low for 15 minutes. Lift the pot out of the housing using oven mitts and stir once more. Scatter the remaining cheese over the macaroni, then place under a preheated hot broiler until the top is golden. Serve with broiled cherry tomatoes on the vine, if liked.

FOR STILTON & MACARONI WITH BACON, soak the macaroni as above. Make the cheese sauce with the milk, adding vegetable stock in place of fish stock and replacing the Cheddar cheese with Stilton cheese. Omit the fish and cook as above with the kernel corn. Stir in the spinach and 6 slices broiled smoked Canadian bacon, diced. Cook for 15 minutes, then finish with a little extra Stilton and brown under the broiler as above.

CHERMOULA POACHED SALMON

Serves **4**
Preparation time **15 minutes**
Cooking temperature **low**
Cooking time **1¾ to 2¼ hours**

6 **scallions**
½ cup **parsley**
1½ cups **cilantro**
grated zest and juice of 1 **lemon**
¼ cup **olive oil**
½ teaspoon **cumin seeds**,
    coarsely crushed
1 lb **thick-end salmon fillet** no longer
    than **7** inches, skinned
1 cup **fish stock**
⅓ cup **mayonnaise**
4 oz **mixed salad greens**
salt and **pepper**

Preheat the slow cooker if necessary. Finely chop the scallions and herbs with a large knife, or in a food processor if you have one. Mix with the lemon zest and juice, the oil, cumin, and a little salt and pepper.

Rinse the salmon with cold water, drain well, and place on a long piece of foil the width of the salmon. Press half the herb mixture over both sides of the salmon then use the foil to lower the fish into the slow-cooker pot.

Bring the stock to a boil in a small saucepan, pour it over the salmon, and tuck the ends of the foil down if needed. Cover with the lid and cook on low for 1¾ to 2¼ hours or until the fish flakes into opaque pieces when pressed in the center with a knife.

Lift the salmon out of the slow-cooker pot using the foil and transfer to a plate. Mix the remaining herb mixture with the mayonnaise. Arrange the salad greens on 4 plates. Cut the salmon into 4 pieces and place on the salad. Serve with spoonfuls of the herb mayonnaise.

FOR CLASSIC POACHED SALMON, omit the chermoula herb mixture. Rinse the salmon as above, then lower into the slow-cooker pot on a piece of foil. Add ½ sliced lemon, ½ sliced onion, 2 tarragon sprigs, and a little salt and pepper. Bring 1 cup fish stock and ¼ cup white wine to a boil in a small saucepan, pour it over the fish, and cook as above. Drain and serve hot or cold with a salad and spoonfuls of plain mayonnaise.

SQUID IN PUTTANESCA SAUCE

Serves **4**
Preparation time **25 minutes**
Cooking temperature **low**
Cooking time **3½ to 4½ hours**

1 lb **prepared squid tubes**
1 tablespoon **olive oil**
1 **onion**, chopped
2 **garlic cloves**, minced
14 oz can **diced tomatoes**
¾ cup **fish stock**
4 teaspoons drained **capers**
½ cup **pitted black olives**
2 to 3 **thyme sprigs**, plus extra leaves
    to garnish (optional)
1 teaspoon **fennel seeds**,
    coarsely crushed
1 teaspoon **superfine sugar**
salt and **pepper**
cooked **linguine**, to serve

Preheat the slow cooker if necessary. Take the tentacles out of the squid tubes and rinse inside the tubes with cold water. Put them in a sieve and rinse the outside of the tubes and the tentacles. Drain well, put the tentacles in a small bowl, cover, and return to the refrigerator. Thickly slice the squid tubes.

Heat the oil in a large skillet, add the onion and fry, stirring, for 5 minutes or until golden. Add the garlic and cook for 2 minutes. Stir in the tomatoes, stock, capers, olives, thyme, crushed fennel seeds, sugar, and salt and pepper and bring to a boil.

Pour the sauce into the slow-cooker pot, add the sliced squid, and press the pieces below the surface of the sauce. Cover with the lid and cook on low for 3 to 4 hours.

Stir the squid mixture and add the tentacles, pressing them below the surface of the sauce. Cook on low for another 30 minutes. Serve tossed with linguine and garnished with extra thyme leaves, if liked.

FOR SQUID IN RED WINE & TOMATO SAUCE, replace the stock, capers, olives, and fennel seeds with ¾ cup red wine. Cook as above, then garnish with chopped parsley and serve with warm crusty bread.

BRAISED TROUT WITH WARM PUY LENTILS

Serves **4**
Preparation time **20 minutes**
Cooking temperature **low**
Cooking time **2½ to 3 hours**

14 oz can **Puy lentils**, drained
2 tablespoons **balsamic vinegar**
4 **scallions**, chopped
3 **tomatoes**, diced
4 **thick trout steaks**, 5 oz each
finely grated zest and juice of
   ½ **lemon**
leaves from 2 to 3 **thyme sprigs**
large pinch of **crushed dried
   red chiles**
¾ cup hot **fish stock**
salt and **pepper**
2½ cups **arugula**, to serve

Preheat the slow cooker if necessary. Place the lentils in the slow-cooker pot, then stir in the balsamic vinegar, scallions, and tomatoes.

Arrange the trout steaks on top in a single layer, then sprinkle with the lemon zest and juice, thyme leaves, and chiles and season to taste. Pour the stock around the trout steaks, then cover and cook on low for 2½ to 3 hours or until the trout is cooked through and flakes easily when pressed in the center with a small knife.

Divide the arugula between 4 serving plates. Arrange the trout and lentils on top and spoon over a little of the stock. Serve immediately.

FOR SMOKED COD & SPINACH SALAD, follow the recipe above, using 1½ cups sliced button mushrooms instead of the tomatoes and 4 thick smoked cod loin steaks, 5 oz each, instead of the trout. After cooking, stir 2 cups baby spinach, rinsed and drained, into the lentil mixture and serve each portion topped with a poached egg.

SALMON IN HOT MISO BROTH

Serves **6**
Preparation time **15 minutes**
Cooking temperature **low** and **high**
Cooking time **1 hour 40 minutes to 2 hours 10 minutes**

4 **salmon steaks**, about 4 oz each
1 **carrot**, thinly sliced
4 **scallions**, thinly sliced
2 cups thinly sliced **mushrooms**
1 large **red chile**, halved, seeded, and finely chopped
¾-inch piece of **fresh ginger root**, peeled and finely chopped
3 tablespoons **miso**
1 tablespoon **dark soy sauce**
2 tablespoons **mirin** (optional)
2½ pints hot **fish stock**
3 oz **snow peas**, thinly sliced
cilantro leaves, to garnish

Preheat the slow cooker if necessary. Rinse the salmon in cold water, drain, and place in the slow-cooker pot. Arrange the carrot, scallions, mushrooms, chile, and ginger on top of the fish.

Add the miso, soy sauce, and mirin, if using, to the hot stock and stir until the miso has dissolved. Pour the stock mixture over the salmon and vegetables. Cover with the lid and cook on low for 1½ to 2 hours or until the fish is tender and the soup is piping hot.

Transfer the fish to a plate using a lifter. Flake it into chunky pieces, discarding the skin and any bones. Return the fish to the slow-cooker pot and add the snow peas. Cook on high for 10 minutes or until the snow peas are just tender, then ladle the soup into bowls and garnish with cilantro leaves.

FOR SALMON IN AROMATIC THAI BROTH, follow the recipe as above, adding 3 teaspoons Thai red curry paste, 3 small dried kaffir lime leaves, and 2 teaspoons fish sauce instead of the miso and mirin.

TAPENADE-TOPPED COD ♥

Serves **4**
Preparation time **15 minutes**
Cooking temperature **low**
Cooking time **3½ to 4 hours**

1 cup **tomato purée**
7 oz **spinach**, rinsed and drained
1 cup coarsely chopped **tomatoes**
2 oz **chorizo sausage**, casing removed, diced
4 **skinless cod steaks**, 5 oz each
½ cup **green olives stuffed with hot pimento**
small handful of **basil leaves**, plus extra to garnish
salt and **pepper**

Preheat the slow cooker if necessary. Spoon the tomato purée over the bottom of the slow-cooker pot, then arrange the spinach, tomatoes, and chorizo in an even layer on top. Season to taste and place the fish steaks on top in a single layer, then season again.

Place the olives and basil in a food processor and blend until finely chopped, or chop with a knife. Spread the mixture over the cod steaks, then cover and cook on low for 3½ to 4 hours until the fish is bright white and flakes easily when pressed in the center with a small knife. Serve garnished with extra basil.

FOR HERB-TOPPED COD, mix ½ cup finely chopped parsley and ½ cup finely chopped basil with ½ teaspoon crushed cumin seeds and the grated zest of 1 lemon. Follow the recipe above, using this herb mixture to spread over the cod steaks before cooking instead of the olives and basil.

MACKEREL WITH HARISSA POTATOES

Serves **4**
Preparation time **20 minutes**
Cooking temperature **low**
Cooking time **5 to 7 hours**

1 lb **new potatoes**, scrubbed and thickly sliced
1 tablespoon **olive oil**
1 **onion**, chopped
½ **red bell pepper**, cored, seeded, and diced
½ **yellow bell pepper**, cored, seeded, and diced
1 **garlic clove**, minced
2 teaspoons **harissa**
1 cup coarsely chopped **tomatoes**
1 tablespoon **tomato paste**
1¼ cups **fish stock**
4 small **mackerel**, about 10 oz each, gutted
    and heads removed
salt and **pepper**

Preheat the slow cooker if necessary. Bring a saucepan
of water to a boil, add the potatoes, and cook for 4 to
5 minutes or until almost tender. Drain and reserve.

Heat the oil in a skillet, add the onion, and fry,
stirring, for 5 minutes or until softened and just
beginning to turn golden. Stir in the bell peppers
and garlic and fry for 2 to 3 minutes. Mix in the
harissa, tomatoes, tomato paste, stock, and a little
salt and pepper and bring to a boil.

Tip the potatoes into the bottom of the slow-cooker
pot. Rinse the fish well, drain, and arrange in a single
layer on top of the potatoes, then cover with the hot
tomato mixture. Cover with the lid and cook on low for
5 to 7 hours or until the potatoes are tender and the fish
flakes when pressed in the center with a small knife.

Spoon into shallow bowls and serve with warmed pitta
bread, if liked.

FOR HARISSA-SPICED POTATOES WITH FETA, follow
the recipe as above but omit the fish and instead scatter
the top of the tomato mixture with ¾ cup crumbled feta
cheese and ½ cup pitted black olives. Cook as above
and scatter with torn parsley just before serving.

HOT SOUSED HERRINGS

Serves **4**
Preparation time **15 minutes**
Cooking temperature **high**
Cooking time **1½ to 2 hours**

1 large **red onion**, thinly sliced
1 large **carrot**, cut into matchsticks
1 large **celery stalk**, thinly sliced
6 small **herrings**, gutted, filleted, rinsed, and drained
2 **tarragon sprigs**, plus extra to garnish
1 **bay leaf**
¾ cup **apple cider vinegar**
2 tablespoons **superfine sugar**
2½ cups boiling **water**
½ teaspoon **mixed peppercorns**
salt

Preheat the slow cooker if necessary. Put half the onion,
carrot, and celery in the bottom of the slow-cooker pot.
Arrange the herring fillets on top, then cover with the
remaining vegetables.

Add the tarragon, bay leaf, vinegar, and sugar, then
pour over the measurement boiling water. Add the
peppercorns and a little salt. Cover with the lid and
cook on high for 1½ to 2 hours.

Spoon the fish, vegetables, and a little of the cooking
liquid into shallow bowls, halving the fish fillets if liked.
Garnish with tarragon sprigs. Serve with pickled beets,
dill pickles, and bread and butter, if liked.

FOR SWEDISH BAKED HERRINGS, make as above,
adding 2 dill sprigs instead of the tarragon and
increasing the amount of sugar to ¼ cup. Let cool once
cooked and serve with ½ cup sour cream mixed with
1 teaspoon hot horseradish and dill pickles on the side.

SALMON & ASPARAGUS RISOTTO

Serves **4**
Preparation time **15 minutes**
Cooking temperature **high**
Cooking time **1¾ to 2 hours**

2 tablespoons **butter**
1 tablespoon **olive oil**
1 **onion**, chopped
grated zest of 1 **lemon**
1 cup **risotto rice**
¾ cup **dry white wine**
3¾ cups **fish** or **vegetable stock**
4 **salmon steaks**, about 5 oz each
bunch of **asparagus**, trimmed and
    thickly sliced
salt and **pepper**
snipped **chives**, to garnish
½ cup **crème fraîche**, to serve

Preheat the slow cooker if necessary. Heat the butter and oil in a large skillet, add the onion, and fry for 5 minutes or until softened. Stir in the lemon zest and rice and cook for 1 minute. Mix in the wine, stock, and a little salt and pepper, and bring to a boil, stirring.

Pour into the slow-cooker pot. Arrange the salmon steaks in a single layer on the rice, turning on their sides, if needed, so they are just below the surface of the stock. Cover with the lid and cook on low for 1¾ to 2 hours or until the rice is tender and the salmon flakes into opaque pieces when pressed in the center with a knife.

When almost ready to serve, bring a saucepan of water to a boil, add the asparagus, and cook for 5 minutes or until just tender. Spoon the rice into shallow bowls and top with spoonfuls of the crème fraîche, the drained asparagus, and salmon steaks, broken into pieces. Scatter with snipped chives and a little extra pepper.

FOR SMOKED FISH KEDGEREE, add ½ teaspoon ground turmeric and 1 bay leaf to the fried onion instead of the lemon zest. Add 2 pints stock and bring to a boil, then transfer to the slow-cooker pot. Replace the salmon with 1¼ lb smoked haddock fillet, cut into 2 pieces, then cook as above. Skin and flake the fish. Discard the bay leaf, then return the fish to the pot and stir in ¼ cup heavy cream and ½ cup lightly cooked frozen peas. Spoon into bowls and top with 4 hard-cooked eggs, cut into wedges. Scatter with snipped chives and season with a little extra pepper.

POACHED SALMON WITH BEURRE BLANC

Serves **4**
Preparation time **25 minutes**
Cooking temperature **low**
Cooking time **1¾ to 2¼ hours**

1 stick **butter**
1 large **onion**, thinly sliced
1 **lemon**, sliced, plus extra to garnish
1 lb piece of **thick-end salmon fillet**, no
longer than 7 inches
1 **bay leaf**
1 cup **dry white wine**
¾ cup **fish stock**
3 tablespoons finely snipped **chives**,
plus extra to garnish
salt and **pepper**

Preheat the slow cooker if necessary. Brush the inside of the slow-cooker pot with a little of the butter. Fold a large piece of foil into 3, then place it in the bottom of the pot with the ends sticking up to use as a strap. Arrange the onion slices and half the lemon slices on the foil. Place the salmon, flesh-side up, on top. Season with salt and pepper, then add the bay leaf and remaining lemon slices.

Pour the wine and stock into a saucepan, bring to a boil, then pour over the salmon. Fold the foil down if necessary to fit the cooker lid, then cook on low for 1¾ to 2¼ hours until the fish is opaque and flakes easily when pressed in the center with a knife.

Lift the salmon carefully out of the pot using the foil strap, draining off as much liquid as possible. Transfer to a serving plate, discard the bay leaf and lemon and onion slices, and keep warm. Strain the cooking liquid into a saucepan and boil rapidly for 4 to 5 minutes or until reduced to about ¼ cup.

Reduce the heat and gradually beat in small pieces of the remaining butter, little by little, until the sauce thickens and becomes creamy. (Don't be tempted to hurry making the sauce either by adding the butter at once or by increasing the heat to the sauce, or you may find that it separates.) Stir in the snipped chives and adjust the seasoning if needed.

Cut the salmon into 4 portions, discard the skin, and transfer to individual plates. Spoon a little of the sauce around the fish. Garnish with extra lemon slices and chives.

BAKED SEAFOOD WITH SAFFRON

Serves **4**
Preparation time **15 minutes**
Cooking temperature **low** and **high**
Cooking time **5½ to 7½ hours**

1 **onion**, finely chopped

1 **red bell pepper**, cored, seeded, and diced

2 **garlic cloves**, minced

14 oz can **diced tomatoes**

¾ cup **dry white wine** or **fish stock**

large pinch of **saffron threads**

2 **thyme sprigs**

1 tablespoon **olive oil**

14 oz package **frozen seafood** (shrimp, mussels, squid), thawed

10 oz **dried tagliatelle**

salt and **pepper**

chopped **parsley**, to serve

Preheat the slow cooker if necessary. Put the onion, red bell pepper, garlic, and tomatoes into the slow-cooker pot, then add the wine or stock, saffron, thyme, oil, and a little salt and pepper.

Cover with the lid and cook on low for 5 to 7 hours. Rinse the seafood with cold water, drain, and then stir into the slow-cooker pot. Replace the lid and cook on high for 30 minutes or until piping hot.

When almost ready to serve, cook the tagliatelle in a large saucepan of lightly salted boiling water following the package instructions until just tender. Drain and toss with chopped parsley. Spoon into shallow bowls and top with the seafood sauce.

FOR BAKED SALMON WITH PESTO, omit the seafood and drain a 14 oz can red salmon, remove the skin and bones, and break the fish into large flakes. Put the onion, red bell pepper, and garlic into the slow-cooker pot. Heat the tomatoes and wine or stock in a small saucepan or the microwave, then add to the pot with 2 teaspoons pesto and the oil, omitting the saffron and thyme. Mix in the salmon and continue as above.

SMOKED COD WITH MASHED BEANS

Serves **4**
Preparation time **15 minutes**
Cooking temperature **low**
Cooking time **1½ to 2 hours**

2 x 14 oz cans **cannellini
    beans**, drained
bunch of **scallions**, thinly
    sliced; white and green parts
    kept separate
1¾ cups boiling **fish stock**
1 teaspoon **wholegrain mustard**
grated zest and juice of 1 **lemon**
4 **smoked cod loins**, about
    1¼ lb in total
¼ cup **crème fraîche**
small bunch of **parsley**, **watercress**,
    or **arugula**, coarsely chopped
salt and **pepper**

Preheat the slow cooker if necessary. Put the drained beans into the slow-cooker pot with the white scallion slices. Mix the fish stock with the mustard, lemon zest and juice, and a little salt and pepper, then pour into the pot.

Arrange the fish on top and season with a little extra pepper. Cover with the lid and cook on low for 1½ to 2 hours or until the fish flakes easily when pressed in the center with a knife.

Transfer the fish to a plate using a lifter. Pour off nearly all the cooking liquid, then mash the beans coarsely. Stir in the crème fraîche, the green scallion slices, and the parsley, watercress, or arugula. Taste and adjust the seasoning, if needed. Spoon the mashed beans onto plates and top with the fish.

FOR BAKED SALMON WITH MASHED BEANS AND BASIL, add the beans to the slow-cooker pot with the ingredients as above, omitting the mustard. Arrange 4 salmon steaks, about 5 oz each, on top, season, and cook as above. Mash the beans with the crème fraîche, green scallion slices, and a small bunch of coarsely torn basil and serve with the fish as above.

BAKED MACKEREL WITH BEETS

Serves **4**
Preparation time **20 minutes**
Cooking temperature **high**
Cooking time **1½ to 2 hours**

2 tablespoons **olive oil**
1 **onion**, sliced
1 **celery stalk**, sliced
1 **carrot**, thinly sliced
2 tablespoons **light brown sugar**
¼ cup **apple cider vinegar**
1 cup **fish stock**
2 **bay leaves**
4 **cloves**
8 oz package **cooked beets in natural juice**, drained and sliced
1 **apple**, peeled, cored, and sliced
4 **mackerel**, about 7 oz each, gutted, heads removed, rinsed, and drained
salt and **pepper**

MUSTARD CREAM
2 teaspoons **wholegrain mustard**
⅓ cup **crème fraîche**
2 tablespoons snipped **chives**, plus extra to garnish

Preheat the slow cooker if necessary. Heat the oil in a skillet, add the onion, celery, and carrot and fry for about 5 minutes or until softened.

Add the sugar, vinegar, stock, bay leaves, cloves, and a little salt and pepper and bring to a boil. Arrange the beets in the bottom of the slow-cooker pot, then top with the apple. Slash the fish 2 or 3 times on each side, then arrange in a single layer on top of the apple.

Pour over the hot stock and vegetables, cover with the lid, and cook on high for 1½ to 2 hours or until the fish flakes easily when pressed in the center with a knife.

When almost ready to serve, mix together the ingredients for the mustard cream in a small bowl and season to taste. Carefully transfer the fish, vegetables, and some of the stock to shallow bowls, then garnish with snipped chives. Serve with spoonfuls of the mustard cream and crusty sliced bread, if liked.

FOR BAKED MACKEREL WITH HOT POTATO SALAD, make the recipe as above, omitting the beets. When the fish is almost ready, cook ¾ lb scrubbed baby new potatoes in a saucepan of boiling water for 15 minutes or until just tender. Make the mustard cream as above and toss with the hot potatoes. Serve with the drained mackerel and sliced dill pickles.

TROUT SPIRALS WITH LEMON FOAM

Serves **4**
Preparation time **30 minutes**
Cooking temperature **low**
Cooking time **1½ to 2 hours**

½ stick **butter**, at room temperature
grated zest and juice of 1 **lemon**
4 **trout fillets**, skinned, about 1 lb 5 oz in total
1 **plaice**, filleted into 4, skinned
1 cup boiling **fish stock**
3 **egg yolks**
salt and **pepper**

Preheat the slow cooker if necessary. Beat the butter with the lemon zest and a little salt and pepper.

Lay the trout fillets on a cutting board so that the skinned sides are uppermost. Trim the edges to neaten, if needed, and spread with half the lemon butter. Top with the plaice fillets, skinned-side uppermost, and spread with the remaining butter. Roll up each fish stack, starting at the tapered end. Secure each spiral with 2 wooden toothpicks at right angles to each other and arrange in the bottom of the slow-cooker pot.

Pour the lemon juice and boiling stock over the fish and add a little salt and pepper. Cover with the lid and cook on low for 1½ to 2 hours or until the fish flakes easily when pressed in the center with a knife.

Lift the fish spirals out of the slow-cooker pot with a slotted spoon, put onto a serving plate, and remove the toothpicks. Strain the cooking juices into a bowl. Put the egg yolks in a saucepan and gradually beat in the strained stock until smooth. Cook over medium heat, beating constantly without boiling, for 3 to 4 minutes or until lightly thickened and foamy. Pour into a pitcher. Serve the fish with a generous drizzle of the sauce with a salad and a separate bowl of tiny new potatoes, if liked.

FOR SALMON STEAKS WITH LEMON & TARRAGON FOAM, put 4 salmon steaks, about 5 oz each and spread with the lemon butter, in the bottom of the slow-cooker pot and continue as above. Make the sauce as above, then beat in 2 teaspoons chopped tarragon to serve.

SMOKED MACKEREL KEDGEREE

Serves **4**
Preparation time **15 minutes**
Cooking temperature **low**
Cooking time **3¼ to 4¼ hours**

1 tablespoon **sunflower oil**
1 **onion**, chopped
1 teaspoon **ground turmeric**
2 tablespoons **mango chutney**
3¼ to 3¾ cups **vegetable stock**
1 **bay leaf**
1 cup **converted long-grain brown rice**
3 **smoked mackerel fillets**, about 8 oz in total, skinned
¾ cup **frozen peas**
1 cup **watercress** or **arugula**
4 **hard-cooked eggs**, cut into wedges
salt and **pepper**

Preheat the slow cooker if necessary. Heat the oil in a skillet, add the onion, and fry, stirring, for 5 minutes or until softened and just beginning to turn golden.

Stir in the turmeric, chutney, stock, bay leaf, and a little salt and pepper and bring to a boil. Pour into the slow-cooker pot and add the rice. Add the smoked mackerel to the pot in a single layer. Cover with the lid and cook on low for 3 to 4 hours or until the rice is tender and has absorbed almost all the stock.

Stir in the peas, breaking up the fish into chunky pieces. Add extra hot stock if needed. Cook, still on low, for 15 minutes more. Stir in the watercress or arugula, spoon onto plates, and garnish with the wedges of egg.

FOR SMOKED HADDOCK KEDGEREE WITH CARDAMOM, make the recipe as above but omit the mango chutney and instead add 4 crushed cardamom pods with their black seeds. Replace the smoked mackerel with 13 oz skinned smoked haddock fillet, cut into 2 pieces. Continue as above, adding the peas and egg wedges at the end but omitting the watercress or arugula. Drizzle with ¼ cup heavy cream.

SALMON-WRAPPED COD WITH LEEKS

Serves **4**
Preparation time **30 minutes**
Cooking temperature **low**
Cooking time **1½ to 2 hours**

2 **cod loins**, about 1½ lb in total
juice of 1 **lemon**
4 **dill sprigs**, plus extra
    to garnish (optional)
4 slices of **smoked salmon**, about
    6 oz in total
1 **leek**, thinly sliced, white and green
    parts kept separate
¼ cup **Noilly Prat**
1 cup boiling **fish stock**
2 teaspoons drained
    capers (optional)
¾ stick **butter**, diced
2 tablespoons chopped **chives**
    or **parsley**
salt and **pepper**

Preheat the slow cooker if necessary. Cut each cod loin in half to yield 4 portions, then drizzle with the lemon juice and season with salt and pepper. Place a dill sprig on top of each portion, then wrap in a slice of smoked salmon.

Put the white leek slices into the bottom of the slow-cooker pot and arrange the fish on top in a single layer, tilting them at an angle, if needed, to fit. Add the Noilly Prat and hot stock, then cover and cook on low for 1½ to 2 hours or until the fish flakes easily when pressed in the center with a knife.

Transfer the fish to a serving plate using a lifter, cover with foil, and keep hot. Pour the white leeks and cooking juices from the slow-cooker pot into a saucepan, add the reserved green leek slices and the capers, if using, and boil rapidly for about 5 minutes or until the liquid is reduced to a generous ¼ cup. Scoop out and reserve the leeks as soon as the green slices have softened.

Beat in the butter, one dice at a time until melted, and continue until all the butter has been added and the sauce is smooth and glossy. Return the cooked leeks to the sauce with the chopped herbs and taste and adjust the seasoning. Arrange the fish on plates, then spoon the sauce around. Sprinkle with extra dill and serve with baby new potatoes, if liked.

FOR SMOKED COD WITH BUTTERED LEEKS, make the recipe as above, with smoked cod loins, omitting the smoked salmon and dill and replacing the Noilly Prat with dry white wine.

THREE-FISH GRATIN

Serves **4**
Preparation time **20 minutes**
Cooking temperature **low**
Cooking time **2 to 3 hours**

2 tablespoons **cornstarch**
1¾ cups **skim milk**
½ cup shredded **sharp**
   Cheddar cheese
3 tablespoons chopped **parsley**
1 **leek**, thinly sliced
1 **bay leaf**
1 lb mixed **skinless fish fillets**
   (such as salmon, cod, and
   smoked haddock), diced
salt and **pepper**

TOPPING
¼ cup **fresh bread crumbs**
¼ cup shredded **sharp**
   Cheddar cheese

TO SERVE
2¼ cups steamed **peas**
¾ lb steamed **snow peas**

Preheat the slow cooker if necessary. Place the cornstarch in a saucepan with a little of the milk and mix to a smooth paste. Stir in the rest of the milk, then add the cheese, parsley, leek, and bay leaf. Season to taste and bring to a boil, stirring until thickened.

Place the fish in the slow-cooker pot. Pour over the hot leek sauce, cover, and cook on low for 2 to 3 hours until the fish is cooked through.

Transfer the fish mixture to a shallow baking dish, scatter the bread crumbs and cheese on top, then place under a preheated hot broiler for 4 to 5 minutes until golden brown. Serve immediately with the steamed peas and snow peas.

FOR FISH PIES, follow the recipe above, omitting the bread crumb and cheese topping. Cut 1¼ lb potatoes into chunks and cook in a saucepan of lightly salted boiling water for 15 minutes or until tender. Drain and mash with ¼ cup skim milk, then season and stir in ¼ cup shredded sharp Cheddar cheese. Divide the cooked fish mixture between 4 individual pie dishes, spoon the mashed potatoes on top, rough up the surface of the potatoes with a fork, then brush with 1 beaten egg. Cook under a preheated medium broiler until golden.

SALMON BOURRIDE

Serves **4**
Preparation time **20 minutes**
Cooking temperature **low**
Cooking time **3 to 3½ hours**

low-calorie cooking oil spray
1 **onion**, chopped
2 **garlic cloves**, minced
½ **red bell pepper**, cored, seeded,
   and very thinly sliced
½ **orange bell pepper**, cored, seeded,
   and very thinly sliced
14 oz can **diced tomatoes**
¾ cup **vegetable stock**
1 teaspoon **granulated sweetener**
1 teaspoon **cornstarch**
14 oz can **artichoke hearts**, drained
4 **salmon steaks**, 4½ oz each
finely grated zest of 1 **lemon**
½ teaspoon **dried**
   Mediterranean herbs
salt and **pepper**
7 oz steamed **green snap**
   beans, to serve

Preheat the slow cooker if necessary. Spray a large skillet with a little low-calorie cooking oil spray and place over high heat until hot. Add the onion, garlic, and bell peppers and cook for 4 to 5 minutes until softened.

Stir in the tomatoes, stock, and sweetener. Mix the cornstarch to a smooth paste with a little cold water and stir into the pan. Season to taste and bring to a boil, stirring.

Transfer the mixture to the slow-cooker pot, stir in the artichoke hearts, then arrange the salmon steaks in a single layer on top, pressing them down into the liquid. Sprinkle the lemon zest and herbs over the salmon and season lightly.

Cover and cook on low for 3 to 3½ hours until the salmon steaks are cooked and flake easily when pressed in the center with a small knife. Spoon into shallow bowls and serve with the steamed green snap beans.

FOR SQUID BOURRIDE, rinse 1¼ lb prepared squid tubes and take the tentacles out of the tubes. Slice the squid tubes and drain well. Follow the recipe above, using the sliced squid tubes instead of the salmon and cooking on low for 4 to 5 hours. Add the squid tentacles and continue cooking for a further 30 minutes until tender, then serve with the steamed green snap beans.

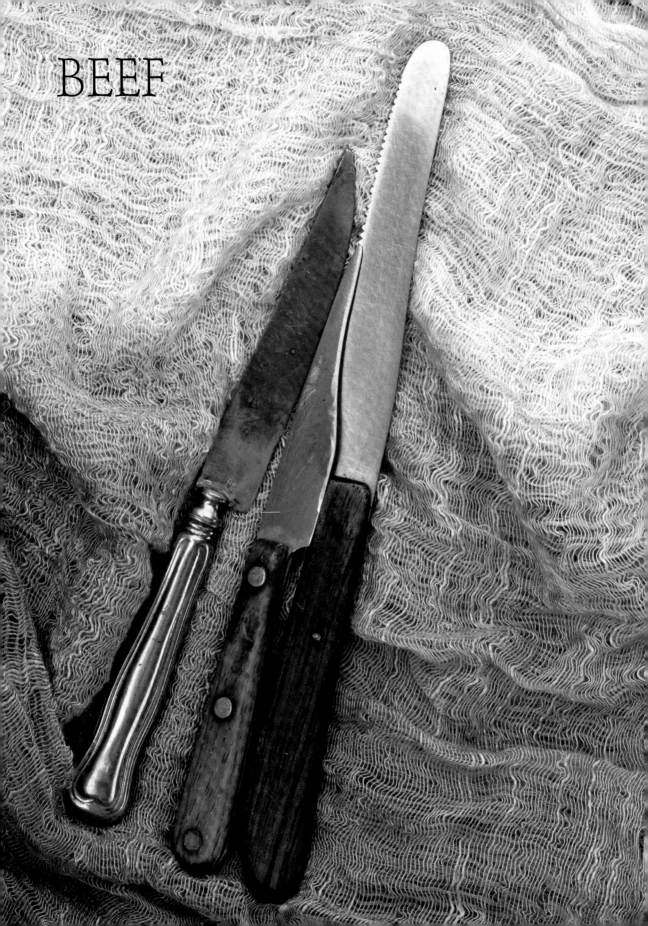

BEEF

JUMBO BURGER WITH TOMATO SAUCE

Serves **4**
Preparation time **25 minutes**
Cooking temperature **high**
Cooking time **3 to 4 hours**

vegetable oil, for oiling
bunch of **scallions**, chopped, divided
½ lb **lean ground beef**
½ lb **lean sausages flavored with
    herbs**, casing split and removed
¼ cup **fresh bread crumbs**
2 tablespoons **Worcestershire sauce**
14 oz can **diced tomatoes**
½ cup **vegetable stock**
1 teaspoon **English mustard**
1 tablespoon **light brown sugar**
1 **green** or **red bell pepper**, cored,
    seeded, and diced
salt and **pepper**

TO SERVE
4 **burger buns**
shredded **lettuce**

Preheat the slow cooker if necessary. Lightly oil the inside of 2 soufflé dishes 4 inches in diameter, 2½ inches deep, and with a capacity of 12 fl oz. Line the bottom with disks of nonstick parchment paper, checking first that they will fit in the slow-cooker pot.

Add half the scallions, the beef, sausagemeat, and bread crumbs to a bowl or food processor. Add 1 tablespoon of the Worcestershire sauce, season with salt and pepper, and mix together. Divide between the 2 dishes and press down well to level off the surface. Cover with foil and put the dishes side by side in the slow-cooker pot.

Add the tomatoes, stock, remaining Worcestershire sauce, mustard, and sugar to a small saucepan. Season with salt and pepper and bring to a boil. Stir in the remaining scallions and the green or red bell pepper and spoon the mixture into the gaps around the dishes.

Cover with the lid and cook on high for 3 to 4 hours until the burgers are cooked. Test with a skewer to make sure the juices do not run pink. Lift the burger dishes out of the slow cooker with a dish towel, pour the excess fat out of the dishes, then turn the burgers out.

Split the burger buns and add shredded lettuce to the bottom halves. Cut the burgers in half horizontally. Place 1 half on each bun, then top with spoonfuls of the tomato sauce and serve the remaining sauce in a small bowl. Accompany with microwave or oven fries, if liked.

FOR TURKEY BURGER & TOMATO SAUCE, omit the ground beef and add ½ lb ground turkey leg meat. Make and cook as above.

BEEF BOURGUIGNON ♥

Serves **4**
Preparation time **20 minutes**
Cooking temperature **low**
Cooking time **10 to 11 hours**

low-calorie cooking oil spray
1¼ lb **beef chuck**, trimmed of fat
    and cubed
3½ oz diced **bacon**
10 oz small **shallots**, peeled
3 **garlic cloves**, minced
1 tablespoon **all-purpose flour**
¾ cup **red wine**
1¼ cups **beef stock**
1 tablespoon **tomato paste**
small bunch of **mixed herbs** or
    a **dried bouquet garni**
salt and **pepper**
chopped **parsley**, to garnish

Preheat the slow cooker if necessary. Spray a large skillet with a little low-calorie cooking oil spray and place over high heat until hot. Add the beef a few pieces at a time until all the meat is in the pan and cook for 5 minutes, stirring, until browned. Use a slotted spoon to transfer the beef to the slow-cooker pot.

Add the bacon and shallots to the skillet and cook over medium heat for 2 to 3 minutes until the bacon is just beginning to brown. Stir in the garlic and flour, then add the wine, stock, tomato paste, and herbs. Season to taste and bring to a boil, stirring.

Pour the sauce over the beef, cover, and cook on low for 10 to 11 hours until the beef is tender. Stir the bourguignon, garnish with chopped parsley, and serve with rice, if liked.

FOR BEEF GOULASH, follow the recipe above, adding 2 teaspoons mild paprika, 1 teaspoon caraway seeds, ¼ teaspoon ground cinnamon, and ¼ teaspoon ground allspice instead of the herbs.

BEEF STEW WITH DUMPLINGS

Serves **4**
Preparation time **35 minutes**
Cooking temperature **low** and **high**
Cooking time **8 to 10½ hours**

2 tablespoons **olive oil**
1½ lb **beef chuck**, trimmed of fat
   and cubed
1 large **onion**, chopped
2 to 3 **garlic cloves**, chopped
2 tablespoons **all-purpose flour**
1¼ cups **Burgundy red wine**
1¼ cups **beef stock**
1 tablespoon **tomato paste**
2 **bay leaves**
5 oz **baby carrots**, larger ones halved
½ lb **leeks**, thinly sliced
salt and **pepper**

HORSERADISH DUMPLINGS
1¼ cups **all-purpose flour**, sifted with
   1¼ teaspooons **baking powder**,
   plus extra flour for dusting
⅓ cup shredded **shortening**
2 teaspoons **horseradish sauce**
3 tablespoons snipped **chives**
5 to 7 tablespoons **water**

Preheat the slow cooker if necessary. Heat the oil in a skillet and add the beef a few pieces at a time until all the meat is in the pan. Fry over high heat until just beginning to brown, then add the onion and fry, stirring, for 5 minutes.

Stir in the garlic and flour, then gradually mix in the wine and stock. Add the tomato paste and bay leaves and season with salt and pepper. Bring to a boil, then transfer the mixture to the slow-cooker pot. Cover with the lid and cook on low for 7 to 9 hours.

Stir the stew, then add the carrots, replace the lid, and cook on high for 30 to 45 minutes.

Meanwhile, make the dumplings. Mix the flour, shortening, horseradish, chives, and salt and pepper together in a bowl. Stir in enough of the measurement water to make a soft but not sticky dough. With floured hands, shape into 8 balls.

Stir the leeks into the stew, then add the dumplings, replace the lid and cook, still on high, for another 30 to 45 minutes or until the dumplings are light and fluffy. Spoon into shallow dishes and serve, remembering to remove the bay leaves.

FOR GUINNESS BEEF STEW WITH MUSTARD DUMPLINGS, make the stew as above, replacing the red wine with 1¼ cups Guinness or stout. Top with dumplings made with 3 teaspoons wholegrain mustard instead of the horseradish sauce and chives.

BEEF & ROOT VEGETABLE HOTPOT

Serves **4**
Preparation time **25 minutes**
Cooking temperature **high**
Cooking time **7 to 8 hours**

1 tablespoon **sunflower oil**
1½ lb **beef chuck**, trimmed of fat
   and cubed
1 **onion**, chopped
2 tablespoons **all-purpose flour**
2½ cups **beef stock**
2 tablespoons **Worcestershire sauce**
1 tablespoon **tomato paste**
2 teaspoons **English mustard**
3 **rosemary sprigs**, divided
1 cup diced **carrots**
1 cup diced **turnips**
1 cup diced **parsnips**
1 lb 6 oz **potatoes**, thinly sliced
2 tablespoons **butter**
salt and **pepper**

Preheat the slow cooker if necessary. Heat the oil in a skillet, add the beef a few pieces at a time until all the meat is in the pan, and fry over high heat, stirring, until browned. Scoop the beef out of pan with a slotted spoon and transfer to the slow-cooker pot.

Add the onion to the skillet and fry, stirring, for 5 minutes or until softened and just beginning to turn golden. Stir in the flour, then gradually mix in the stock. Add the Worcestershire sauce, tomato paste, mustard, and leaves from 2 sprigs of the rosemary. Season and bring to a boil, stirring.

Add the diced vegetables to the slow-cooker pot. Pour the onions and sauce over them, then cover with the potato slices, arranging them so that they overlap, and pressing them down into the stock. Scatter with the leaves torn from the remaining rosemary sprig and season with a little salt and pepper.

Cover and cook on high for 7 to 8 hours until the potatoes are tender. Lift the pot out of the housing using oven mitts, dot the potatoes with the butter, and brown under a preheated hot broiler, if liked.

FOR CHICKEN & BLOOD SAUSAGE HOTPOT, replace the beef with 1¼ lb chicken thighs that have been skinned, boned, and diced. Continue as above, adding 3½ oz diced blood sausage (casing removed) along with the root vegetables. Cover with the potatoes and cook as above.

STEAK & MUSHROOM PUDDING

Serves **4**
Preparation time **40 minutes**
Cooking temperature **high**
Cooking time **5 to 6 hours**

2 tablespoons **butter**, plus extra
    for greasing
1 tablespoon **sunflower oil**
2 large **onions**, coarsely chopped
2 teaspoons **superfine sugar**
1½ cups **white mushrooms**, sliced
1 tablespoon **all-purpose flour**
¾ cup hot **beef stock**
1 teaspoon **Dijon mustard**
1 tablespoon **Worcestershire sauce**
1 lb 6 oz **beef rump**, trimmed of fat
    and thinly sliced
salt and **pepper**

PASTRY
2½ cups **all-purpose flour**, sifted with
    2½ teaspoons **baking powder**, plus
    extra flour for dusting
½ teaspoon **salt**
¼ lb **suet**, shredded
about 1 cup **water**

Preheat the slow cooker if necessary. Heat the butter and oil in a skillet, add the onions, and fry for 5 minutes or until softened. Sprinkle the sugar over the onions and fry for 5 more minutes or until browned. Add the mushrooms and fry for 2 to 3 minutes. Stir in the flour.

Mix the stock, mustard, Worcestershire sauce, and salt and pepper together in a pitcher.

Make the suet pastry. Put the flour and baking powder mixture, salt, and suet in a bowl and mix well. Gradually stir in enough of the measurement water to make a soft but not sticky dough. Knead the dough lightly, then roll out on a floured surface to a disk 13 inches in diameter. Cut out a one-quarter segment and reserve. Press the remaining dough into a 3-pint buttered pudding bowl, butting the edges together.

Layer the fried onions, mushrooms, and sliced steak in the bowl. Pour the stock over the top. Pat the reserved pastry into a disk the same size as the top of the bowl. Fold the top edges of the pastry in the bowl over the filling, brush with a little water and cover with the pastry lid.

Cover the pudding with a large domed circle of buttered foil so that there is room for the pastry to rise. Tie with string to use a handle for lifting the bowl at the end of cooking. Stand the bowl in the slow-cooker pot on top of an upturned saucer. Pour boiling water into the pot to come halfway up the sides of the bowl. Cover with the lid and cook on high for 5 to 6 hours.

Remove the bowl from the slow cooker using a dish towel and remove the string and foil. The pastry should have risen and feel dry to the touch.

BEEF ADOBO

Serves **4**
Preparation time **25 minutes**
Cooking temperature **low**
Cooking time **8 to 10 hours**

1 tablespoon **sunflower oil**
1½ lb **beef chuck**, trimmed of fat
  and cubed
1 large **onion**, sliced
2 **garlic cloves**, minced
2 tablespoons **all-purpose flour**
2 cups **beef stock**
¼ cup **soy sauce**
¼ cup **wine vinegar**
1 tablespoon **superfine sugar**
2 **bay leaves**
juice of 1 **lime**
salt and **pepper**
boiled **long-grain rice**, to serve

TO GARNISH
1 **carrot**, cut into thin sticks
½ bunch of **scallions**, cut into shreds
cilantro leaves

Preheat the slow cooker if necessary. Heat the oil in a large skillet and add the beef a few pieces at a time until all the meat is in the pan. Fry over high heat, turning, until evenly browned all over, lift out of the pan using a slotted spoon, and transfer to a plate.

Add the onion to the pan and fry for 5 minutes or until it is just beginning to brown. Mix in the garlic and cook for 2 minutes. Stir in the flour, then gradually mix in the stock. Add the soy sauce, vinegar, sugar, bay leaves, and salt and pepper and bring to a boil, stirring.

Transfer the beef to the slow-cooker pot, pour over the onion and stock mixture, cover with the lid, and cook on low for 8 to 10 hours.

Stir in lime juice to taste and garnish with the carrot sticks, shredded scallions, and cilantro leaves. Serve in shallow bowls lined with rice.

FOR HOISIN BEEF, combine 3 tablespoons each soy sauce and rice or wine vinegar with 2 tablespoons hoisin sauce and 1-inch piece of peeled and finely chopped fresh ginger root. Add this mixture to the beef stock with the sugar. Omit the bay leaves. Bring the mixture to a boil, then continue as above, adding the lime juice just before serving.

OLIVE & LEMON MEATBALLS

Serves **4**
Preparation time **30 minutes**
Cooking temperature **low**
Cooking time **6 to 8 hours**

MEATBALLS
½ cup **pitted black olives**, chopped
grated zest of ½ **lemon**
1 lb **extra-lean ground beef**
1 **egg yolk**
1 tablespoon **olive oil**

SAUCE
1 **onion**, chopped
2 **garlic cloves**, minced
14 oz can **diced tomatoes**
1 teaspoon **superfine sugar**
¾ cup **chicken stock**
salt and **pepper**
small **basil leaves**, to garnish
cooked **tagliatelle** tossed with
  chopped **basil** and melted
  butter, to serve

Preheat the slow cooker if necessary. Put all the ingredients for the meatballs except for the oil in a bowl and mix with a wooden spoon. Wet your hands and shape the mixture into 20 balls.

Heat the oil in a large skillet, add the meatballs, and cook over high heat, turning them until browned on all sides. Transfer to a plate with a slotted spoon and set aside.

Make the sauce. Add the onion to the pan and fry, stirring, for 5 minutes or until lightly browned. Add the garlic, tomatoes, sugar, stock, and salt and pepper and bring to a boil, stirring.

Add the meatballs to the slow-cooker pot, pour over the hot sauce, cover, and cook on low for 6 to 8 hours. Garnish with basil leaves and serve with tagliatelle tossed with chopped basil and melted butter.

FOR HERB & GARLIC MEATBALLS, replace the olives and lemon zest with 2 minced garlic cloves and 3 tablespoons chopped basil leaves. Mix, shape, and cook the meatballs with the sauce as above, adding a small handful of basil leaves to the sauce to serve.

INDIAN-SPICED COTTAGE PIE

Serves **4**
Preparation time **30 minutes**
Cooking temperature **low**
Cooking time **8 to 10 hours**

1 tablespoon **sunflower oil**
1 lb **lean ground beef**
1 **onion**, chopped
¼ cup **korma curry paste**
1 teaspoon **ground turmeric**
2 **carrots**, diced
2 tablespoons **all-purpose flour**
½ cup **dried red lentils**, rinsed
and drained
¼ cup packed **golden raisins**
1 tablespoon **tomato paste**
2 pints **beef stock**
salt and **pepper**

TOPPING
1¾ lb **potatoes**, cut into chunks
½ stick **butter**, divided
3 tablespoons **milk**
1 tablespoon **sunflower oil**
bunch of **scallions**, chopped
½ teaspoon **ground turmeric**

Preheat the slow cooker if necessary. Heat the oil in a large skillet, add the ground beef and onion, and cook, stirring and breaking up the meat, until it is evenly browned. Stir in the curry paste and turmeric and cook for 1 minute. Stir in the carrots and flour, then add the lentils, golden raisins, tomato paste, stock, and salt and pepper. Bring to a boil, stirring, then pour into the slow-cooker pot. Cover with the lid and cook on low for 8 to 10 hours or until the lentils are soft and the beef is tender.

When almost ready to serve, put the potatoes in a saucepan of boiling water and simmer for 15 minutes or until tender. Drain and mash with half the butter, the milk, and salt and pepper. Heat the oil in a skillet, add the scallions, and fry for 2 to 3 minutes or until softened. Add the turmeric and cook for 1 minute, then mix into the mashed potatoes.

Stir the beef mixture and lift the pot out of the housing using oven mitts. Transfer to a serving dish, if liked. Spoon the mashed potatoes on top, dot with remaining butter, then place under a preheated medium broiler until golden. Serve with cooked peas, if liked.

FOR TRADITIONAL COTTAGE PIE, fry the beef and onion as above. Omit the curry paste and turmeric. Add the carrots and flour, then replace the lentils and golden raisins with a 14 oz can baked beans, 1 tablespoon each tomato paste and Worcestershire sauce, 1¼ cups beef stock, and 1 teaspoon dried mixed herbs. Transfer to the slow-cooker pot and continue as above. Top with the mashed potatoes, omitting the scallions and turmeric. Scatter evenly with ½ cup shredded Cheddar cheese and place under a preheated hot broiler until browned.

STIFADO

Serves **4**

Preparation time **25 minutes, plus overnight marinating**

Cooking temperature **high** and **low**

Cooking time **10 to 11 hours**

1 cup **red wine**

1 tablespoon **tomato paste**

2 tablespoons **olive oil**

2 to 3 **thyme sprigs** or **bay leaves**

4 **cloves**

¼ teaspoon **ground allspice**

10 oz **shallots**, halved if large

2 **garlic cloves**, minced

1½ lb **beef chuck**, trimmed of fat and cut into large chunks

4 teaspoons **cornstarch**

¾ cup cold **water**

½ **beef stock cube**

salt and **pepper**

Mix the wine, tomato paste, and oil in a shallow nonmetallic dish. Add the herbs, spices, and a little salt and pepper and mix together. Mix in the shallots and garlic, then add the beef and toss in the marinade. Cover with plastic wrap and let marinate in the refrigerator overnight.

Preheat the slow cooker if necessary. Put the cornstarch into a saucepan, mix in a little of the measurement water to make a smooth paste, then mix in the remaining water. Drain the marinade from the beef into the pan and crumble in the stock cube. Bring to a boil, stirring.

Tip the beef, shallots, and flavorings into the slow-cooker pot and pour over the hot stock. Cover with the lid and cook on high for 30 minutes. Reduce the heat and cook on low for 9½ to 10½ hours, or set to auto for 10 to 11 hours, until the meat is cooked through and tender. Spoon into bowls and serve with toasted French bread and herb butter, if liked.

FOR LAMB STIFADO, mix together 1 cup white wine, 1 tablespoon tomato paste, 2 tablespoons olive oil, 2 bay leaves, 2 teaspoons coarsely crushed coriander seeds, and ½ sliced lemon. Add the shallots and garlic and stir in 1½ lb diced lamb shoulder or shank. Let marinate in the refrigerator overnight, then continue as above.

TAMARIND BEEF WITH GINGER BEER

Serves **4**
Preparation time **20 minutes**
Cooking temperature **low**
Cooking time **8 to 10 hours**

2 tablespoons **sunflower oil**
1½ lb **lean beef chuck**, cubed
1 **onion**, chopped
2 **garlic cloves**, minced
2 tablespoons **all-purpose flour**
12 fl oz can **ginger beer**
6 teaspoons **tamarind paste**
½ teaspoon **crushed dried red chiles**
1 teaspoon **ground mixed spice**
1 tablespoon **dark brown sugar**
salt and **pepper**

Preheat the slow cooker if necessary. Heat the oil in a large skillet, add the beef a few pieces at a time until all the meat is in the pan, then add the onion and fry over medium heat, stirring, until the meat is browned.

Stir in the garlic and flour. Gradually mix in the ginger beer, then stir in the tamarind paste, chiles, mixed spice, sugar, and a little salt and pepper and bring to a boil, stirring.

Transfer to the slow-cooker pot and press the beef below the surface of the liquid. Cover with the lid and cook on low for 8 to 10 hours or until the meat is cooked through and tender.

Stir the beef, then ladle into bowls, top with Ginger & Cilantro Croutes (*see* below), and serve with steamed broccoli, if liked.

FOR GINGER & CILANTRO CROUTES TO ACCOMPANY THE CASSEROLE, beat a ¾-inch piece of peeled and grated fresh root ginger with 2 minced garlic cloves and ½ stick butter, stir in ½ mild, seeded, finely chopped red chile or a large pinch of crushed dried red chiles, 3 tablespoons chopped cilantro leaves, and a little salt and pepper. Toast 8 slices of French bread on both sides and spread with the butter while hot. Arrange the croutes on top of the casserole and serve immediately.

RANCHEROS PIE

Serves **4**
Preparation time **25 minutes**
Cooking temperature **low**
Cooking time **7 to 8 hours**

1 tablespoon **sunflower oil**
1 lb **ground beef**
1 **onion**, chopped
2 **garlic cloves**, minced
1 teaspoon **cumin seeds**,
    coarsely crushed
¼ to ½ teaspoon **crushed dried red
    chiles**, plus extra for scattering
¼ teaspoon **ground allspice**
2 **oregano sprigs**, coarsely chopped
3 tablespoons **golden raisins**
14 oz can **diced tomatoes**
1 cup **beef stock**
salt and **pepper**

TOPPING
1 lb **sweet potatoes**, peeled and
    thinly sliced
2 tablespoons **butter**

Preheat the slow cooker if necessary. Heat the oil in a skillet, add the ground beef and onion, and fry, stirring and breaking up the beef with a wooden spoon, until it is evenly browned.

Stir in the garlic, spices, oregano, golden raisins, tomatoes, and stock. Add a little salt and pepper and bring to a boil, stirring. Spoon into the slow-cooker pot, cover with the overlapping slices of sweet potato, dot with the butter, scatter with some crushed dried red chiles, and season with salt and pepper.

Cover with the lid and cook on low for 7 to 8 hours until the potato topping is tender. Lift the pot out of the housing using oven mitts and brown under a preheated hot broiler, if liked.

FOR COWBOY PIE, fry the ground beef and onion as above, then omit the garlic, spices, oregano, golden raisins, and tomatoes but add 2 tablespoons Worcestershire sauce, a 14 oz can baked beans, 1 bay leaf, and 1 cup beef stock. Cook the beef base as above. Top with 1½ lb potatoes, cooked and mashed with butter and salt and pepper. Scatter evenly with ½ cup shredded Cheddar cheese and brown under a preheated hot broiler.

BEEF & GUINNESS PUFF PIE

Serves **4 to 5**
Preparation time **50 minutes**
Cooking temperature **low**
Cooking time **8 to 10 hours**

2 tablespoons **sunflower oil**, plus
    extra for oiling
1½ lb **lean beef chuck**, cubed
1 **onion**, chopped
2 tablespoons **all-purpose flour**, plus
    extra for dusting
1¼ cups **Guinness**
¾ cup **beef stock**
2 teaspoons **hot horseradish sauce**
1 tablespoon **tomato paste**
1 **bay leaf**
3 cups sliced **white mushrooms**
salt and **pepper**

PASTRY
beaten **egg**, to glaze
1 lb **puff pastry**, defrosted if frozen
3½ oz **Stilton cheese** (rind
    removed), crumbled

Preheat the slow cooker if necessary. Heat the oil in a large skillet, add the beef a few pieces at a time until all the meat is in the pan, then add the onion and fry over medium heat, stirring, until the meat is browned.

Stir in the flour, then gradually mix in the Guinness and the stock. Stir in the horseradish sauce, tomato paste, and a little salt and pepper, then add the bay leaf and bring to a boil. Transfer to the slow-cooker pot and press the meat below the surface of the liquid. Cover with the lid and cook on low for 8 to 10 hours or until the meat is cooked through and very tender.

When almost ready to serve, discard the bay leaf and divide the beef mixture between 4 baking dishes, each about 1 pint in size. Mix in the mushrooms, then brush the top edge of the dishes with a little egg. Cut the pastry into 4 and roll each piece out on a floured surface until a little larger than the dishes, then press onto the dishes. Trim off the excess pastry and crimp the edges. Mark diagonal lines on top and brush with beaten egg. Put on an oiled baking pan and cook in a preheated oven, 400°F, for 30 minutes or until golden. Sprinkle with the Stilton and let melt for 1 to 2 minutes. Serve with green snap beans and curly kale, if liked.

FOR BEEF & BEER HOTPOT, make the meat base as above, omitting the mushrooms and adding 2 diced carrots. Spoon into the slow-cooker pot, then cover with 1 lb 6 oz thinly sliced potatoes, pressing them just below the stock. Cook as above. Dot 2 tablespoons butter over the potatoes, lift the pot out of the housing using oven mitts, and brown under a preheated hot broiler.

BEEF WITH CHOCOLATE & CHILES

Serves **4**
Preparation time **15 minutes**
Cooking temperature **low**
Cooking time **8 to 10 hours**

1 tablespoon **sunflower oil**
1 lb **ground beef**
1 **onion**, chopped
3 **garlic cloves**, minced
1 teaspoon **ground cinnamon**
1 teaspoon **ground cumin**
½ to 1 teaspoon **smoked** or **hot paprika**,
   plus extra to garnish
¼ to ½ teaspoon **crushed dried**
   red chiles
1 **bay leaf**
14 oz can **diced tomatoes**
14 oz can **red kidney beans**, drained
2 tablespoons **dark brown sugar**
1¼ cups **beef stock**
1 oz **semisweet chocolate**
salt and **pepper**

TO SERVE
sour cream
boiled **rice**

Preheat the slow cooker if necessary. Heat the oil in a skillet, add the ground beef and onion, and fry, stirring and breaking up the ground beef with a wooden spoon, until it is evenly browned.

Stir in the garlic, ground spices, chiles, and bay leaf and cook for 1 minute. Mix in the tomatoes, beans, sugar, and stock, then add the chocolate and a little salt and pepper and bring to a boil, stirring.

Pour into the slow-cooker pot, cover with the lid, and cook on low for 8 to 10 hours or until cooked through. Stir, spoon onto plates, and top with a little sour cream, salsa (*see* below), if liked, and extra paprika. Serve with rice.

FOR AVOCADO & RED ONION SALSA TO ACCOMPANY THE BEEF WITH CHOCOLATE AND CHILES, halve, seed, and peel 1 large ripe avocado. Dice the flesh, then toss in the grated zest and juice of 2 limes. Mix with 1 small, finely chopped red onion, 1 chopped tomato, and a small bunch of chopped cilantro.

BARLEY & BEEF WITH BEER

Serves **4**
Preparation time **15 minutes**
Cooking temperature **low**
Cooking time **9 to 10 hours**

1 tablespoon **sunflower oil**
1¼ lb **lean beef chuck**, cubed
1 **onion**, chopped
1 tablespoon **all-purpose flour**
1 cups diced **carrots**
2 cups diced **parsnips** or 1 ½ cups diced **potatoes**
1¼ cups **light ale**
3¼ cups **beef stock**
small bunch of **mixed herbs** or **dried bouquet garni**
½ cup **pearl barley**
salt and **pepper**

Preheat the slow cooker if necessary. Heat the oil in a skillet, add the beef a few pieces at a time until all the meat is in the pan, then fry over high heat, stirring, until browned. Remove the beef with a slotted spoon and transfer to the slow-cooker pot.

Add the onion to the skillet and fry, stirring, for 5 minutes or until lightly browned. Mix in the flour, then add the root vegetables and beer and bring to a boil, stirring. Pour into the slow-cooker pot.

Add the stock to the skillet with the herbs and a little salt and pepper, bring to a boil, then pour into the slow-cooker pot. Add the pearl barley, cover with the lid, and cook on low for 9 to 10 hours until the beef is tender. Serve with Herb Croutons (*see* below), if liked.

FOR HERB CROUTONS TO ACCOMPANY THE BEEF,
beat 2 tablespoons each chopped parsley and chives, 1 tablespoon chopped tarragon, and a little pepper into ¾ stick softened butter. Thickly slice ½ French baguette, toast lightly on both sides under a preheated hot broiler, then spread with the herb butter.

BEEF CHEEKS WITH BEER ♥

Serves **4**
Preparation time **20 minutes**
Cooking temperature **high**
Cooking time **5 to 6 hours**

1 tablespoon **sunflower oil**
1¼ lb **beef cheeks**, cut into slices 1½ inch thick
2 **red onions**, cut into wedges
1 cup **brown ale**
¾ cup **beef stock**
1 tablespoon **tomato paste**
2 teaspoons **cornstarch**
2 **rosemary sprigs**
2 **bay leaves**
10 oz small **Chantenay carrots**, halved lengthwise
2 **celery stalks**, thickly sliced
salt and **pepper**

Heat the oil in a large skillet over high heat until hot. Add the beef a few pieces at a time until all the meat is in the pan and cook for 5 minutes, stirring, until browned. Use a slotted spoon to transfer the beef to the slow-cooker pot, arranging it in a single layer.

Add the onions to the skillet and cook for 3 to 4 minutes until softened. Add the brown ale, stock, and tomato paste. Mix the cornstarch to a smooth paste with a little cold water and stir into the pan with the herbs. Season to taste and bring to a boil, stirring.

Place the carrots and celery on top of the beef, then pour in the hot beer mixture. Cover and cook on high for 5 to 6 hours until the beef is very tender. Spoon into shallow bowls and serve with snow peas, if liked.

FOR BEERY CHESTNUTS & MUSHROOMS, follow the recipe above, using 1 lb whole mixed small mushrooms instead of the beef, and adding a 6 oz can of whole chestnuts at the same time as the herbs.

GOURMET BOLOGNESE

Serves **4**
Preparation time **20 minutes**
Cooking temperature **low**
Cooking time **8 to 10 hours**

1 tablespoon **olive oil**
1 lb **lean ground beef**
1 **onion**, chopped
7½ oz **chicken livers**, defrosted
    if frozen
2 **garlic cloves**, minced
2 oz **pancetta** or **smoked Canadian
    bacon**, diced
2 cups **white mushrooms**, sliced
1 tablespoon **all-purpose flour**
¾ cup **red wine**
¾ cup **beef stock**
14 oz can **diced tomatoes**
2 tablespoons **tomato paste**
1 **bouquet garni**
salt and **pepper**
10 oz **dried tagliatelle**

TO SERVE
Parmesan cheese shavings
basil leaves

Preheat the slow cooker if necessary. Heat the oil in a skillet, add the ground beef and onion, and fry, stirring and breaking up the beef with a wooden spoon, until it is evenly browned.

Meanwhile, rinse the chicken livers in a sieve, drain, and then chop coarsely, discarding any white cores. Add to the skillet with the garlic, pancetta or bacon, and mushrooms. Cook for 2 to 3 minutes or until the chicken livers are browned all over.

Stir in the flour, then mix in the wine, stock, tomatoes, tomato paste, bouquet garni, and seasoning. Bring to a boil, stirring. Spoon into the slow-cooker pot, cover with the lid, and cook on low for 8 to 10 hours.

When almost ready to serve, cook the tagliatelle in a large saucepan of lightly salted boiling water following the package instructions until just tender. Drain and stir into the Bolognese sauce. Spoon into shallow bowls and scatter with Parmesan shavings and some basil leaves.

FOR BUDGET BOLOGNESE, omit the chicken livers and pancetta or bacon and add 1 diced carrot and 1 diced zucchini along with the garlic and mushrooms. Replace the wine with extra stock and continue as above.

LAMB

SLOW-COOKED GREEK LAMB

Serves **4**
Preparation time **20 minutes**
Cooking temperature **low** and **high**
Cooking time **9¼ to 10½ hours**

low-calorie cooking oil spray
4 **lean lamb leg steaks**, about
    ¼ lb each
1 large **onion**, thinly sliced
2 **garlic cloves**, minced
1 **lemon**, diced
1½ cups coarsely chopped **tomatoes**
2 teaspoons **coriander seeds**,
    coarsely crushed
1 **bay leaf**
1 teaspoon **granulated sweetener**
1 tablespoon **sun-dried tomato paste**
1¼ cups **lamb stock**
10 oz **baby new potatoes**, scrubbed
    and thickly sliced
2½ cups **zucchini**, diced
salt and **pepper**
2 tablespoons chopped **parsley**,
    to garnish

Preheat the slow cooker if necessary. Spray a large skillet with a little low-calorie cooking oil spray and place over high heat until hot. Add the lamb steaks and cook for 4 to 5 minutes, turning once, until browned on both sides. Transfer to a plate.

Add the onion to the skillet and cook for 4 to 5 minutes until softened, then add the garlic, lemon, and tomatoes. Add the coriander seeds, bay leaf, sweetener, tomato paste, and stock. Season to taste and bring to a boil.

Arrange the potatoes over the bottom of the slow-cooker pot, then place the lamb steaks in a single layer on top. Pour in the hot stock mixture, cover with the lid, and cook on low for 9 to 10 hours until the lamb and potatoes are tender.

Add the zucchini, cover again, and cook on high for 15 to 30 minutes until tender. Spoon into shallow bowls, scatter with the parsley, and serve.

FOR SLOW-COOKED LAMB WITH ROSEMARY, follow the recipe above, adding 3 rosemary sprigs instead of the lemon, crushed coriander seeds, and bay leaf. Cook as above, adding the zucchini at the end. Serve garnished with the parsley.

POT-ROAST LAMB WITH ROSEMARY

Serves **4**
Preparation time **5 minutes**
Cooking temperature **high**
Cooking time **7 to 8 hours**

½ **lamb shoulder on the bone**,
   about 2 to 2½ lb
3 **rosemary sprigs**
1 **red onion**, cut into wedges
2 tablespoons **redcurrant jelly**
1 cup **red wine**
1 cup **lamb stock**
salt and **pepper**

Preheat the slow cooker if necessary. Put the lamb into the slow-cooker pot, set the rosemary on top, and tuck the onion wedges around the sides of the meat.

Add the redcurrant jelly to a small saucepan and pour in the wine, and stock. Season with a little salt and pepper. Bring to a boil, stirring so that the jelly melts, then pour the mixture over the lamb. Cover with the lid and cook on high for 7 to 8 hours or until a knife goes into the center of the lamb easily and the meat is almost falling off of the bone.

Lift the meat out of the slow-cooker pot and put it onto a serving plate along with the onions. Discard the rosemary sprigs and pour the wine and stock mixture into a pitcher to serve as gravy. Carve the lamb onto plates and serve with steamed green vegetables and baby potatoes or Crushed New Potatoes with Rosemary Cream (*see* below), if liked.

FOR CRUSHED NEW POTATOES WITH ROSEMARY CREAM TO ACCOMPANY THE LAMB, bring a pan of water to a boil, add 1 lb scrubbed baby new potatoes, and cook for 15 minutes. Add 7 oz broccolini, thickly sliced, for the last 5 minutes. Drain and then coarsely break up with a fork. Stir in 1 tablespoon finely chopped rosemary, ¼ cup crème fraîche, and a little salt and pepper. Spoon a mound of potatoes into the center of 4 serving plates, then top with the carved pot roast lamb and drizzle the gravy around the edges of the potatoes.

SPICED LAMB WRAPS

Serves **4**
Preparation time **20 minutes**
Cooking temperature **low**
Cooking time **8 to 9 hours**

1 tablespoon **olive oil**
1 lb **ground lamb**
1 **red onion**, minced
2 teaspoons **ground cumin**
1 teaspoon **ground cinnamon**
½ teaspoon **chili powder**
1 teaspoon **dried oregano**
1 tablespoon **tomato paste**
½ cup **bulgur wheat**
2½ cups boiling **beef stock**
salt and **pepper**

TO SERVE
8 large **soft flour wraps**
1¾ cups **hummus**
1 **romaine lettuce**, shredded
small handful of **mint**, finely chopped
½ **cucumber**, cut into strips

Preheat the slow cooker if necessary. Heat the oil in a skillet, add the ground lamb and onion, and fry, stirring and breaking up the ground lamb with a wooden spoon, until it is evenly browned.

Stir in the ground spices, oregano, and tomato paste, then season with a little salt and pepper.

Spoon the mixture into the slow-cooker pot, add the bulgur wheat, then stir in the boiling stock. Cover with the lid and cook on low for 8 to 9 hours until the lamb is tender.

When ready to serve, warm the wraps in a dry skillet or in the microwave following the package instructions, then spread each one with a little hummus. Stir the lamb mixture. Spoon it over the wraps, then top with the lettuce, mint, and cucumber. Fold in the top and bottom of each wrap, then roll it up tightly to enclose the filling. Cut the wraps in half and serve.

FOR BEEF AND CHILE WRAPS, omit the lamb and fry 1 lb ground beef with the onion as above. Stir in the spices, oregano, and tomato paste as above, adding ¼ to ½ teaspoon crushed dried red chiles to taste. Cook and serve as above.

SLOW-COOKED LAMB SHANKS

Serves **4**
Preparation time **20 minutes**
Cooking temperature **high**
Cooking time **5 to 7 hours**

2 tablespoons **olive oil**
4 **lamb shanks**, about ¾ lb each
1¼ lb **new potatoes**, scrubbed
   and thickly sliced
2 **onions**, sliced
3 to 4 **garlic cloves**, minced
1¼ cups **white wine**
¾ cup **lamb stock**
1 tablespoon **liquid honey**
1 teaspoon **dried oregano**
3 oz **preserved lemons**, cut
   into chunks
½ cup **green olives** (optional)
salt and **pepper**
chopped **parsley**, to garnish

Preheat the slow cooker if necessary. Heat the oil in a large skillet, add the lamb, and fry, turning, until browned on all sides. Arrange the potatoes in the bottom of the slow-cooker pot, then put the lamb on top.

Add the onions to the pan and fry until softened, then mix in the garlic. Add the wine, stock, honey, oregano, and a little salt and pepper and bring to a boil. Pour evenly over the lamb, then add the lemon and olives, if using.

Cover with the lid and cook on high for 5 to 7 hours or until the potatoes are tender and the lamb is almost falling off the bone. Spoon into shallow bowls and scatter with parsley. Serve with a green salad, if liked.

FOR SLOW-COOKED LAMB SHANKS WITH PRUNES, fry the lamb as above and add to the potatoes. Fry the onion and garlic with 3 diced slices bacon, then mix in 1¼ cups red wine, ¾ cup lamb stock, 1 tablespoon tomato paste, ¼ cup ready-to-eat pitted prunes, and a small bunch of mixed herbs. Season with salt and pepper, cover, and cook as above.

WARMING LAMB POT ROAST

Serves **4**
Preparation time **20 minutes**
Cooking temperature **high**
Cooking time **5 to 6 hours**

low-calorie cooking oil spray
1¾ lb **leg of lamb on the bone**
1 **leek**, thickly sliced, white and green
    parts kept separate
2 teaspoons **all-purpose flour**
2 cups **lamb stock**
1 tablespoon **redcurrant jelly**
¼ cup **mint leaves**, chopped,
    plus extra to garnish
1¼ cups cubed **celeriac**, cut into
    ¾-inch pieces
1½ cups cubed **turnip**, cut into
    ¾-inch pieces
10 oz **baby Chantenay carrots**,
    halved lengthwise
salt and **pepper**

Preheat the slow cooker if necessary. Spray a large skillet with a little low-calorie cooking oil spray and place over high heat until hot. Season the lamb and seal in the hot pan for 5 to 10 minutes, turning, until browned on all sides. Transfer to the slow-cooker pot.

Add the white leek slices to the skillet with a little extra low-calorie cooking oil spray, cook for 2 to 3 minutes, then sprinkle in the flour and stir well. Add the stock, redcurrant jelly, and mint, then bring to a boil, stirring.

Arrange the celeriac, turnip, and carrots around the lamb, then pour in the leek and stock mixture. Cover and cook on high for 5 to 6 hours until the lamb starts to fall off of the bone and the vegetables are tender, adding the reserved green leek slices for the last 15 minutes of cooking.

Serve the lamb in shallow bowls with the hot vegetables and stock, garnished with extra mint. If you prefer a thicker sauce, drain the stock into a small saucepan and boil rapidly to reduce by half.

FOR LAMB POT ROAST WITH FLAGEOLET BEANS, follow the recipe above, adding a 14 oz can flageolet beans, drained, 2 rosemary sprigs, and 2 minced garlic cloves instead of the mint, turnip, and celeriac.

LAMB STEAKS WITH CUMBERLAND SAUCE

Serves **4**
Preparation time **20 minutes**
Cooking temperature **low**
Cooking time **8 to 10 hours**

1 tablespoon **sunflower oil**
1½ lb **lamb rump steaks**, trimmed of fat
1 **onion**, sliced
2 teaspoons **all-purpose flour**
½ cup **red wine**
½ cup **lamb stock**
finely shredded zest and juice of
   1 **orange**
finely shredded zest and juice of
   1 **lemon**
1-inch piece of **fresh ginger**
   root, peeled and finely chopped
1 tablespoon **tomato paste**
1 tablespoon **redcurrant jelly**
1 tablespoon **granulated sweetener**
salt and **pepper**
1½ lb **celeriac**, peeled and diced,
   to serve

Preheat the slow cooker if necessary. Heat the oil in a large skillet over high heat until hot. Add the lamb and cook for 2 to 3 minutes, turning once, until browned on both sides. Use a slotted spoon to transfer the lamb to the slow-cooker pot.

Add the onion to the pan and cook, stirring, over medium heat for 4 to 5 minutes, until softened. Stir in the flour, then add the wine, stock, half the orange and lemon zest, the orange and lemon juice, ginger, tomato paste, redcurrant jelly, and sweetener. Season to taste with salt and pepper and bring to a boil, stirring. Pour the mixture over the lamb, cover, and cook on low for 8 to 10 hours.

When almost ready to serve, cook the celeriac in a saucepan of lightly salted boiling water for 10 to 15 minutes until tender. Drain and mash with a little of the cooking water until smooth, then season to taste. Serve with the lamb in bowls, garnished with the remaining orange and lemon zest.

FOR LAMB STEAKS WITH CRANBERRY SAUCE, follow the recipe above, using ¼ cup dried cranberries and 1 tablespoon cranberry sauce instead of the ginger and redcurrant jelly. Cook and serve as above.

LAMB TAGINE WITH FIGS & ALMONDS

Serves **4**
Preparation time **15 minutes**
Cooking temperature **low**
Cooking time **8 to 10 hours**

1 tablespoon **olive oil**
1½ lb **diced lamb**
1 **onion**, sliced
2 **garlic cloves**, minced
1-inch piece of **fresh ginger root**,
   peeled and finely chopped
2 tablespoons **all-purpose flour**
2½ cups **lamb stock**
1 teaspoon **ground cinnamon**
2 large pinches of **saffron threads**
½ cup **dried figs**, stalks trimmed
   and diced
½ cup toasted **sliced almonds**
salt and **pepper**

Preheat the slow cooker if necessary. Heat the oil in a skillet, add the lamb a few pieces at a time until all the meat is in the pan, then fry over high heat, stirring, until browned. Remove from the pan with a slotted spoon and transfer to the slow-cooker pot.

Add the onion and fry, stirring, for 5 minutes or until softened and just beginning to turn golden. Stir in the garlic and ginger, then mix in the flour. Gradually stir in the stock. Add the spices, figs, and a little salt and pepper, and bring to a boil, stirring.

Spoon into the slow-cooker pot, cover, and cook on low for 8 to 10 hours or until the lamb is tender. Stir, then scatter with the toasted flaked almonds. Serve with Lemon & Chickpea Couscous (*see* below), if liked.

FOR LEMON & CHICKPEA COUSCOUS TO ACCOMPANY THE TAGINE,
put 1 cup couscous into a bowl, add the grated zest and juice of 1 lemon, 2 tablespoons olive oil, a 14 oz can chickpeas, drained, and some salt and pepper. Add 2 cups boiling water, then cover the bowl with a plate and let stand for 5 minutes. Remove the plate, add ¼ cup chopped parsley or cilantro, and fluff up with a fork.

EASY LAMB & BARLEY RISOTTO

Serves **4**
Preparation time **10 minutes**
Cooking temperature **low**
Cooking time **7 to 8 hours**

¾ oz **mixed dried mushrooms**
2 pints boiling **vegetable stock**
¼ cup **Oloroso sherry** or **fresh orange juice**
1 **onion**, finely chopped
1 teaspoon **ground cumin**
2 **garlic cloves**, minced
¼ cup **golden raisins**
½ cup **pearl barley**
4 **lamb loin chops**,
    about 5 oz each
1¾ cups diced **ready-prepared pumpkin** or **butternut squash**,
    cut into ¾ inch pieces
salt and **pepper**
chopped **mint** and **parsley**, to garnish

Preheat the slow cooker if necessary. Add the dried mushrooms to the slow-cooker pot and pour in the boiling stock, then stir in the sherry or orange juice, onion, cumin, garlic, and golden raisins. Spoon in the barley and season with salt and pepper.

Arrange the chops on top in a single layer, season, then tuck the pumpkin or squash into the gaps between the chops. Press the chops and squash down lightly into the stock, then cover with the lid and cook on low for 7 to 8 hours until the lamb and vegetables are tender.

Lift the chops out of the slow cooker, stir the barley, then spoon onto plates, top with the chops, broken into pieces. Scatter with the herbs and serve with spoonfuls of harissa, if liked.

FOR PUMPKIN & BARLEY RISOTTO, omit the lamb and use 1¾ cups ready-prepared diced pumpkin. Cook as above, then add ¼ lb spinach, rinsed and drained, to the risotto for the last 15 minutes of cooking. Serve topped with spoonfuls of Greek yogurt, chopped mint and parsley, and buttery fried sliced almonds.

POT-ROAST LAMB WITH ZA'ATAR RUB

Serves **4**
Preparation time **20 minutes**
Cooking temperature **high**
Cooking time **5 to 6 hours**

1 tablespoon **extra virgin olive oil**
2 **onions**, thinly sliced
2 **garlic cloves**, minced
1 cup **lamb stock**
1 tablespoon **tomato paste**
2 teaspoons **za'atar spice mix**
1 cup **dry white wine** or **extra lamb stock**
1 tablespoon **cornstarch**
¾ lb **new potatoes**, scrubbed and thickly sliced
½ **boneless lamb shoulder**, about 1½ lb
salt and **pepper**
chopped **parsley** and **mint**, to garnish

TO SERVE
2 **zucchini**, thinly sliced
1 tablespoon **olive oil**
½ teaspoon **za'atar spice mix**
1½ cups **hummus**

Preheat the slow cooker if necessary. Heat the oil in a large skillet, add the onions, and fry for 5 minutes until softened and just beginning to brown. Stir in the garlic, stock, tomato paste, and half the za'atar. Pour in the wine or extra stock, reserving about 2 tablespoons.

Stir the cornstarch into the reserved wine or stock until smooth, then add to the skillet. Bring to a boil, stirring.

Add the potatoes to the bottom of the slow-cooker pot, then pour in the hot stock mixture. Remove the strings from the lamb, open it out flat, and rub with the reserved za'atar, then season with salt and pepper. Add to the slow-cooker pot and press the meat beneath the liquid. Cover with the lid and cook on high for 5 to 6 hours or until the lamb is almost falling apart.

When almost ready to serve, toss the sliced zucchini with the oil, za'atar, and a little salt and pepper. Cook in a preheated ridged grill pan until lightly browned and tender. Divide the hummus between 4 serving plates, spread into an even layer, and make a thin ridge around the sides to contain the lamb sauce. Break the lamb into pieces, then spoon it onto the hummus with the sauce. Add the zucchini and scatter with chopped parsley and mint.

FOR POT ROAST LAMB WITH ROSEMARY, add 1 cup red wine in place of the white wine, if using, in the sauce, plus 2 tablespoons redcurrant jelly and 3 rosemary sprigs. Mix the cornstarch with the reserved wine or stock as above. Add the potatoes and plain bone-in lamb leg to the slow cooker, then pour over the hot stock mixture. Cook as above and serve with mixed steamed vegetables.

LAMB RAGÙ

Serves **4**
Preparation time **15 minutes**
Cooking temperature **low**
Cooking time **8 to 9 hours**

1¼ lb jar **tomato and bell pepper ragù sauce**
½ cup **red wine** or **lamb stock**
10 oz **baby new potatoes**, scrubbed and
    thickly sliced
1¼ lb diced **lamb**
1 **red bell pepper**, cored, seeded, and cut into chunks
1 **yellow bell pepper**, cored, seeded, and cut into chunks
basil leaves, to garnish

Preheat the slow cooker if necessary. Pour the ragù sauce and wine or stock into a saucepan and bring to a boil. Alternatively, heat the mixture in a microwave.

Place the potato slices on the bottom of the slow-cooker pot, arrange the lamb on top, then add the red and yellow bell peppers. Add the hot sauce, then cover with the lid and cook on low for 8 to 9 hours until the potatoes and lamb are tender.

Stir the ragù. Serve garnished with basil leaves and accompanied by warm garlic bread, if liked.

FOR BEEF & MUSHROOM RAGÙ, make the recipe as above adding 1¼ lb diced beef instead of the lamb and 2 cups sliced white mushrooms in place of the yellow bell pepper.

LAMB SHANKS WITH JUNIPER

Serves **4**
Preparation time **15 minutes**
Cooking temperature **high**
Cooking time **5 to 7 hours**

2 tablespoons **butter**
4 **lamb shanks**, about 3 lb in total
2 small **red onions**, cut into wedges
2 tablespoons **all-purpose flour**
1 cup **red wine**
2 cups **lamb stock**
2 tablespoons **cranberry sauce** (optional)
1 tablespoon **tomato paste**
2 **bay leaves**
1 teaspoon **juniper berries**, coarsely crushed
1 small **cinnamon stick**, halved
pared zest of 1 small **orange**
salt and **pepper**

Preheat the slow cooker if necessary. Heat the butter in a skillet, add the lamb shanks, and fry over medium heat, turning, until browned all over. Drain and put into the slow-cooker pot.

Add the onions to the pan and fry for 4 to 5 minutes or until just beginning to turn golden. Stir in the flour. Slowly stir in the wine and stock, then add the cranberry sauce, if using, and the remaining ingredients. Bring to a boil, stirring.

Transfer to the slow-cooker pot, cover with the lid, and cook on high for 5 to 7 hours or until the lamb is beginning to fall off the bone. If you prefer a thick sauce, pour it into a saucepan and boil rapidly for 5 minutes or until reduced by one-third.

FOR LAMB SHANKS WITH LEMON, fry the lamb shanks as above, then fry 2 sliced white onions. Mix with the flour and add 1 cup dry white wine, the lamb stock, 4 teaspoons coarsely crushed coriander seeds, the bay leaves, the pared zest of 1 lemon, and 2 teaspoons liquid honey. Season and bring to a boil, pour over the lamb, and cook as above.

MINTED LAMB WITH COUSCOUS

Serves **4**
Preparation time **25 minutes**
Cooking temperature **high**
Cooking time **7 to 8 hours**

1 tablespoon **olive oil**
½ **shoulder of lamb**, about
    1¾ to 2 lb
1 **onion**, sliced
2 **garlic cloves**, minced
2 tablespoons **all-purpose flour**
3 tablespoons **mint jelly**
¾ cup **red wine**
1¼ cups **lamb stock**
salt and **pepper**

COUSCOUS WITH HERBS
1 cup **couscous**
1 cup peeled and diced **cooked beets**
1¾ cups boiling **water**
grated zest and juice of 1 **lemon**
2 tablespoons **olive oil**
small bunch of **parsley**,
    finely chopped
small bunch of **mint**, finely chopped

Preheat the slow cooker if necessary. Heat the oil in a skillet, add the lamb, and fry on both sides until browned. Lift out with 2 slotted spoons and transfer to the slow-cooker pot. Fry the onion, stirring, for 5 minutes or until softened and just turning golden.

Stir in the garlic, then the flour. Add the mint jelly and wine and mix until smooth. Pour in the stock, season, and bring to a boil, stirring. Pour the sauce over the lamb, cover with the lid, and cook on high for 7 to 8 hours or until the lamb is almost falling off of the bone.

When almost ready to serve, put the couscous and beets into a bowl, pour over the boiling water, then add the lemon zest and juice, oil, and some seasoning. Cover with a plate and let soak for 5 minutes.

Add the herbs to the couscous and fluff up with a fork, then spoon onto plates. Lift the lamb onto a serving plate and carve into rough pieces, discarding the bone. Divide between the plates and serve the sauce separately in a pitcher to pour over as needed.

FOR CORIANDER & HONEY-BRAISED LAMB, fry the onion and garlic as above. Add 1 tablespoon coarsely crushed coriander seeds with the flour. Stir in 1 tablespoon honey instead of the mint jelly and ¾ cup dry white wine instead of red. Add the lamb stock, 1 bay leaf, and seasoning. Bring to a boil, then add to the browned lamb in the slow-cooker pot. Cover and cook as above. Serve with rice and green beans.

PORK

PRUNE-STUFFED PORK TENDERLOIN

Serves **4**
Preparation time **40 minutes**
Cooking temperature **high**
Cooking time **3½ to 4 hours**

2 **pork tenderloins**, just under
  ¾ lb each
1 slice of **bread**, crusts removed
1 small **onion**, quartered
2 **garlic cloves**, halved
1½-inch piece of **fresh ginger root**,
  peeled and sliced
¼ teaspoon **ground allspice**
10 **ready-to-eat pitted prunes**
4 **slices smoked bacon**
1 tablespoon **olive oil**
12 **shallots**, halved if large
2 tablespoons **cornstarch**
1 cup **red wine**
1¼ cups **chicken stock**
1 tablespoon **tomato paste**
salt and **pepper**

Preheat the slow cooker if necessary. Trim the thinnest end off of each pork tenderloin so that each is 9 inches long, reserving the trimmings. Make a slit along the length of each and open out flat.

Put the pork trimmings into a food processor with the bread, onion, garlic, ginger, allspice, and salt and pepper and mix until finely chopped. Spoon half the mixture along the length of 1 piece of pork, press the prunes on top, then cover with the rest of the stuffing and the remaining tenderloin. Season, then wrap the bacon around the pork and tie in place with string.

Heat the oil in a large skillet, add the pork and shallots, and fry, turning the pork over, until golden on all sides. Transfer to the slow-cooker pot. Make a smooth paste with the cornstarch and a little cold water, then add to the pan with the remaining ingredients. Bring to a boil, stirring until thickened, then pour over the pork.

Cover with the lid and cook on high for 3½ to 4 hours or until the pork is cooked through and tender. Transfer the pork to a serving plate. Serve cut into thick slices, with the shallots and sauce, accompanied with steamed asparagus and creamy potato dauphinoise, if liked.

FOR APRICOT & PISTACHIO STUFFED PORK TENDERLOIN, slit the tenderloins as above. Replace the prunes with 3 tablespoons coarsely chopped pistachio nuts, the grated zest of ½ orange and ½ cup chopped ready-to-eat dried apricots, and add to the pork trimmings mixture, then continue as above. To make the sauce, replace the red wine with 1 cup hard dry cider.

ORIENTAL PORK WITH BOK CHOY

Serves **4**
Preparation time **20 minutes**
Cooking temperature **low** and **high**
Cooking time **6¼ to 7¼ hours**

4 **pork medallions**, ¾ lb in total
1 **red onion**, thinly sliced
1-inch piece of **fresh ginger root**,
    peeled and thinly sliced
1 **garlic clove**, thinly sliced
small handful of **cilantro**
    leaves, divided
¼ teaspoon **crushed dried**
    red chiles
2 small **star anise**
1 teaspoon **Thai fish sauce**
2 teaspoons **tomato paste**
4 teaspoons **dark soy sauce**
1½ cups hot **chicken stock**
7 oz **bok choy**, thickly sliced
1 cup **asparagus tips**
8 oz **dried egg noodles**

Preheat the slow cooker if necessary. Place the pork medallions in the slow-cooker pot in a single layer and scatter with the onion, ginger, and garlic. Scatter half the cilantro leaves on top.

Stir the chiles, star anise, fish sauce, tomato paste, and soy sauce into the hot chicken stock, then pour over the pork. Cover and cook on low for 6 to 7 hours until the pork is tender.

Add the bok choy and asparagus to the pot, cover, and cook on high for 15 minutes until the vegetables are just tender and still bright green.

Meanwhile, cook the egg noodles following the package instructions.

Drain and divide between 4 bowls, top with the pork and vegetables, then spoon over the broth and serve garnished with the remaining cilantro.

FOR ORIENTAL PORK WITH MIXED VEGETABLES, follow the recipe above, adding 10 oz ready-prepared mixed stir-fry vegetables instead of the bok choy and asparagus.

SHAKSHUKA

Serves **4**
Preparation time **20 minutes**
Cooking temperature **high**
Cooking time **3¼ to 4¼ hours**

low-calorie cooking oil spray
2 **red onions**, coarsely chopped
3 oz **chorizo sausage**, casing
    removed, diced
3½ cups chopped **tomatoes**
½ teaspoon crushed **dried red chiles**
1 tablespoon **tomato paste**
2 teaspoons **granulated sweetener**
2 teaspoons **paprika**
1 teaspoon **dried oregano**
4 **eggs**
salt and **pepper**

TO SERVE
chopped **parsley**
4 small slices of **wholewheat
    bread**, toasted

Preheat the slow cooker if necessary. Spray a large skillet with a little low-calorie cooking oil spray and place over medium heat until hot. Add the onions and chorizo and cook for 5 minutes, stirring, until the onions have softened.

Add the chopped tomatoes, chiles, tomato paste, sweetener, paprika, and oregano. Season to taste and transfer the mixture to the slow-cooker pot, cover, and cook on high for 3 to 4 hours until the tomatoes have softened and the sauce is thick.

Make 4 indents in the tomato mixture with the back of a tablespoon, then break an egg into each one. Cover again and cook, still on high, for 15 minutes or until the eggs are set to your liking. Scatter with a little chopped parsley, then spoon onto plates and serve with toast.

FOR MIXED VEGETABLE SHAKSHUKA, follow the recipe above, omitting the chorizo and using just 1 chopped red onion. Add 1 cored, seeded, and diced red bell pepper, 1 large diced zucchini, and 2 minced garlic cloves to the skillet with the onion and continue as above.

PULLED PORK

Serves **4**
Preparation time **15 minutes**
Cooking temperature **high**
Cooking time **5 to 6 hours**

1 lb 6 oz **boneless pork shoulder**,
   trimmed of fat
1 tablespoon **molasses**
½ teaspoon **ground allspice**
½ teaspoon **ground ginger**
½ teaspoon **ground cumin**
½ teaspoon **crushed dried red chiles**
¼ teaspoon **salt**
leaves from 2 to 3 **thyme sprigs**
1 **onion**, sliced
1 cup hot **chicken stock**
pepper

TO SERVE
4 **hamburger buns**, split
4 **lettuce leaves,** shredded
3 **tomatoes**, thinly sliced
1 **dill pickle**, drained and sliced

Preheat the slow cooker if necessary. Remove the strings, unroll the pork shoulder, and make a cut through the middle to reduce the thickness by half. Place in the slow-cooker pot and spread with the molasses.

Mix the ground spices, chiles, salt, and thyme leaves together and season with pepper. Rub all over the pork, then tuck the onion slices around it. Pour the hot stock over the onions, then cover and cook on high for 5 to 6 hours or until the pork is very tender.

Place the pork on a cutting board and pull into shreds using 2 forks. Top the bottom halves of the buns with the lettuce, tomato, and dill pickle, then pile the hot pork on top. Add a few of the onion slices to each bun and drizzle with the cooking juices. Replace the tops of the buns and serve immediately.

FOR PULLED PORK WITH HERBS, follow the recipe above to prepare the pork and spread it with the molasses. Mix the crushed dried red chiles, salt, and thyme leaves with 2 finely chopped sage sprigs and rub over the molasses-covered pork. Add the onion and stock and continue as above.

PORK & HARD CIDER WITH SAGE DUMPLINGS

Serves **4**
Preparation time **25 minutes**
Cooking temperature **low**
Cooking time **9 to 11 hours**

1 tablespoon **sunflower oil**
1½ lb **pork shoulder steaks**, trimmed
   of fat and cubed
1 **leek**, thinly sliced, the white and
   green parts kept separate
2 tablespoons **all-purpose flour**
1¼ cups **dry hard cider**
1¼ cups **chicken stock**
1½ cups diced **carrots**
1 **apple**, cored and diced
2 to 3 **sage sprigs**
salt and **pepper**

DUMPLINGS
1¼ cups **all-purpose flour**, sifted with
   1¼ teaspoons **baking powder**,
   plus extra flour for dusting
¼ cup **vegetable shortening**, shredded
1 tablespoon chopped **sage**
2 tablespoons chopped **parsley**
5 to 7 tablespoons **water**

Preheat the slow cooker if necessary. Heat the oil in a skillet, add the pork a few pieces at a time until all the meat is in the pan, then fry over high heat until lightly browned. Lift out of the pan with a slotted spoon and transfer to the slow-cooker pot.

Add the white leek slices to the pan and fry for 2 to 3 minutes or until softened. Stir in the flour, then gradually mix in the hard cider and stock. Add the carrot, apple, sage, and some salt and pepper. Bring to a boil, stirring. Pour the mixture into the slow-cooker pot, cover with the lid, and cook on low for 8 to 10 hours or until the pork is tender.

Make the dumplings. Put the flour and baking powder mixture, shortening, herbs, and a little salt and pepper into a bowl and mix together, then gradually stir in enough of the measurement water to make a soft but not sticky dough. Cut into 12 pieces and roll into balls with floured hands. Stir the green leek slices into the pork casserole and arrange the dumplings on the top. Cover and cook, still on low, for 1 hour until they are well risen. Spoon into shallow bowls to serve.

FOR PORK WITH BEER & ROSEMARY DUMPLINGS, make the recipe as above, adding 1¼ cups blonde beer or lager instead of the hard cider and 2¼ cups mixed diced parsnip, carrot, and turnip instead of the carrot and apple. Flavor with 2 rosemary sprigs instead of the sage and add 1 tablespoon chopped rosemary instead of sage to the dumplings.

BAKED HAM IN COLA

Serves **4**
Preparation time **20 minutes, plus
  overnight soaking**
Cooking temperature **high**
Cooking time **6 to 7 hours**

2½ lb **boneless smoked ham**, soaked
  overnight in cold water
5 **cloves**
1 **onion**, cut into 8 wedges
2 **carrots**, thickly sliced
14 oz can **black beans** or **red kidney
  beans**, drained
2 **bay leaves**
2 pints **cola**
1 tablespoon **dark brown sugar**
1 tablespoon **tomato paste**
2 teaspoons **English mustard**

Preheat the slow cooker if necessary. Drain the ham and put it into the slow-cooker pot. Press the cloves into 5 of the onion wedges and add to the ham along with the remaining onion wedges and carrot slices. Tip in the drained beans and add the bay leaves.

Pour the cola into a saucepan, add the sugar, tomato paste, and mustard and bring to a boil, stirring. Pour evenly over the ham, cover with the lid, and cook on high for 6 to 7 hours or until the ham is tender.

Strain the cooking liquid into a saucepan and boil rapidly for 10 minutes to reduce by half. Keep the ham and vegetables hot in the turned-off slow cooker with the lid on.

Slice the ham thinly and arrange on plates with the vegetables, beans, and a drizzle of sauce. Serve with baked potatoes and broccoli, if liked.

FOR BAKED HAM WITH PARSLEY SAUCE, soak the ham as above and cook in the slow-cooker pot with the cloves, onion, carrots, bay leaves, and 2 pints boiling water instead of the cola. Omit the beans and remaining ingredients. Melt 2 tablespoons butter in a saucepan for the parsley sauce. Stir in 3½ tablespoons all-purpose flour, cook for 1 minute, then mix in 1¼ cups milk. Bring to a boil, stirring, until thickened and smooth. Stir in 1 teaspoon English mustard, 3 tablespoons chopped parsley, and salt and pepper. Serve with the sliced ham and drained onion and carrots.

SAUSAGES WITH ONION GRAVY

Serves **4**
Preparation time **15 minutes**
Cooking temperature **low**
Cooking time **6 to 8 hours**

1 tablespoon **sunflower oil**
8 **garlicky sausages**, such as Sicilian
   or Toulouse
2 **red onions**, halved and thinly sliced
2 teaspoons **light brown sugar**
2 tablespoons **all-purpose flour**
2 cups **beef stock**
1 tablespoon **sun-dried tomato paste**
   or **regular tomato paste**
1 **bay leaf**
salt and **pepper**

TO SERVE
4 large **ready-made**
   Yorkshire puddings
steamed **carrots**
steamed **broccoli**

Preheat the slow cooker if necessary. Heat the oil in a skillet, add the sausages, and fry over high heat for 5 minutes, turning, until browned on all sides but not cooked through. Drain and transfer to the slow-cooker pot.

Add the onions to the skillet and fry over medium heat for 5 minutes or until softened. Add the sugar and fry, stirring, for 5 more minutes or until the onion slices are caramelized around the edges.

Stir in the flour, then gradually mix in the stock. Add the tomato paste, the bay leaf, and some salt and pepper and bring to a boil, stirring. Pour over the sausages. Cover with the lid and cook on low for 6 to 8 hours or until the sausages are tender.

Serve spooned into the Yorkshire puddings, reheated following the package instructions, accompanied by steamed carrots and broccoli.

FOR SAUSAGES WITH BEER & ONION GRAVY, fry 8 large traditional herb-flavored sausages instead of the garlicky ones until browned. Drain, then fry 2 sliced white onions until softened, and omit the sugar. Stir in the all-purpose flour, then mix in ¾ cup stout or brown ale and reduce the beef stock to 1¼ cups. Replace the tomato paste with 1 tablespoon wholegrain mustard and 2 tablespoons Worcestershire sauce. Season and bring to a boil. Cook in the slow cooker for 6 to 8 hours.

MAPLE-GLAZED RIBS

Serves **4**
Preparation time **25 minutes**
Cooking temperature **high**
Cooking time **5 to 7 hours**

2½ lb **pork ribs**, rinsed and drained
1 **onion**, quartered
1 **carrot**, thickly sliced
2 **bay leaves**
2 tablespoons **malt vinegar**
1 teaspoon **black peppercorns**
½ teaspoon **salt**
2 pints boiling **water**

GLAZE
2 teaspoons **English mustard**
1 teaspoon **ground allspice**
2 tablespoons **tomato paste**
2 tablespoons **brown sugar**
½ cup **maple syrup**

COLESLAW
2 **carrots**, grated
¼ **red cabbage**, shredded
3 **scallions**, sliced
¾ cup **kernel corn**, defrosted
  if frozen
2 tablespoons **mayonnaise**
2 tablespoons **plain yogurt**

Preheat the slow cooker if necessary. Put the pork ribs, onion, carrot, bay leaves, vinegar, peppercorns, salt, and measurement boiling water into the slow-cooker pot, cover with the lid, and cook on high for 5 to 7 hours or until the ribs are tender.

Lift the ribs out of the slow cooker using a slotted spoon and transfer to a foil-lined broiler pan. Mix together the ingredients for the glaze with ¾ cup hot stock from the slow-cooker pot. Spoon over the ribs, then cook under a preheated hot broiler for 10 to 15 minutes, turning once or twice, until browned and sticky.

Meanwhile, mix the ingredients for the coleslaw together and spoon into 4 small bowls. Place these on serving plates, then pile the ribs onto the plates to serve.

FOR CHINESE RIBS, cook the pork ribs in the slow cooker as above. Drain and transfer to a foil-lined broiler pan, then glaze with a mixture of 2 tablespoons each tomato paste and soy sauce, ¼ cup hoisin sauce, 2 tablespoons light brown sugar, the juice of 1 orange and ¾ cup stock from the slow-cooker pot. Broil for 10 to 15 minutes as above.

HONEY-GLAZED HAM

Serves **4**

Preparation time **20 minutes, plus overnight soaking**

Cooking temperature **high**

Cooking time **5 to 7 hours**

2¼ lb **boneless smoked ham**, soaked overnight in cold water

1 **onion**, cut into wedges

10 oz **carrots**, halved lengthwise and cut into 1-inch chunks

1 lb **baking potatoes**, scrubbed and quartered

2 **bay leaves**

6 **cloves**

½ teaspoon **black peppercorns**

2 pints boiling **water**

GLAZE

2 tablespoons **liquid honey**

2 teaspoons **English mustard**

Preheat the slow cooker if necessary. Put the ham into the slow-cooker pot. Tuck the vegetables around the sides, then add the bay leaves, cloves, and peppercorns. Pour in enough of the measurement boiling water to just cover the ham.

Cover with the lid and cook on high for 5 to 7 hours or until the ham and vegetables are cooked through and tender. Lift the ham out of the slow-cooker pot and transfer to a broiler pan. Cut away the skin and discard.

Mix the honey and mustard together for the glaze, spoon over the top and sides of the ham, then add 3 ladlefuls of stock from the slow-cooker pot to the bottom of the broiler pan. Cook under a preheated medium broiler until the ham is golden brown. Carve into slices and serve with the sauce from the broiler pan and drained vegetables from the slow-cooker pot. Accompany with steamed green beans, if liked.

FOR GLAZED HAM WITH PEASE PUDDING, soak 1 cup dried yellow split peas in cold water overnight while soaking the ham in a separate bowl of cold water. Next day, drain the peas, add to a saucepan with 2 pints water, bring to a boil, and boil rapidly for 10 minutes. Add the ham, onion, carrots, bay leaves, cloves, and peppercorns to the slow-cooker pot, omitting the potatoes. Pour in the hot peas and their water, then continue as above. When the glazed ham is broiled, drain off most of the stock from the peas and carrots, then mash and stir in 2 tablespoons butter and a little salt, if needed. Serve the pease pudding with the sliced ham.

BACON & LEEK SUET PUDDING

Serves **4**
Preparation time **30 minutes**
Cooking temperature **high**
Cooking time **4 to 5 hours**

2 tablespoons **butter**
2 **smoked ham steaks**, about 14½ oz in total, trimmed of fat and rind, diced
2¾ cups **leeks**, sliced
2½ cups **all-purpose flour**, sifted with 2½ teaspoons **baking powder**, plus extra flour for dusting
¼ cup **suet**, shredded
3 teaspoons **mustard powder**
1 cup **water**
salt and **pepper**

PARSLEY SAUCE
2 tablespoons **butter**
3½ tablespoons **all-purpose flour**
1¼ cups **milk**
¼ cup **parsley**, finely chopped

Preheat the slow cooker if necessary. Heat the butter in a skillet, add the ham and leeks, and fry, stirring, for 4 to 5 minutes or until the leeks have just softened. Season with pepper only. Let cool slightly.

Put the flour, ½ teaspoon salt, a large pinch of pepper, the suet, and mustard powder in a bowl and mix well. Gradually stir in enough of the measurement water to make a soft but not sticky dough. Knead lightly, then roll out on a large piece of floured nonstick parchment paper to a rectangle 9 x 12 inches. Turn the paper so that the shorter edges are facing you.

Spoon the ham mixture over the pastry, leaving ¾ inch around the edges. Roll up, starting at the shorter edge, using the paper to help. Wrap in the paper, then in a sheet of foil. Twist the ends together tightly, leaving some space for the pudding to rise.

Transfer the pudding to the slow-cooker pot and raise off the bottom slightly by standing it on 2 ramekins. Pour boiling water into the pot to come a little up the sides of the pudding, being careful that the water cannot seep through any joins. Cover with the lid and cook on high for 4 to 5 hours or until the pudding is well risen.

When almost ready to serve, melt the butter for the sauce in a saucepan. Stir in the flour, then gradually mix in the milk and bring to a boil, stirring until smooth. Cook for 1 to 2 minutes, then stir in the parsley and season. Lift the pudding out of the slow-cooker pot using a dish towel, unwrap, and cut into slices. Arrange on serving plates and spoon over a little sauce. Serve with snow peas, if liked.

BALSAMIC-BRAISED PORK CHOPS

Serves **4**
Preparation time **15 minutes**
Cooking temperature **high** and **low**
Cooking time **7 to 8 hours**

4 **spare rib pork chops**, about 1½ lb
   in total
3 tablespoons **apple balsamic** or
   plain balsamic vinegar
2 tablespoons **light brown sugar**
2 **onions**, thinly sliced
2 **apples**, peeled, cored, and quartered
2 tablespoons **cornstarch**
3 teaspoons **English mustard**
1 cup boiling **chicken stock**
snipped **chives**, to garnish (optional)

Preheat the slow cooker if necessary. Put the pork chops into the bottom of the slow-cooker pot and spoon over the vinegar and sugar. Scatter the onion slices on top, then add the apples.

Put the cornstarch and mustard in a small bowl and mix with a little cold water to make a smooth paste, then gradually stir in the boiling stock until smooth. Pour over the pork. Cover with the lid and cook on high for 30 minutes. Reduce the heat and cook on low for 6½ to 7½ hours, or set to auto for 7 to 8 hours, until the pork is cooked through and tender.

Transfer the pork to serving plates, stir the sauce, and spoon over the chops. Sprinkle with snipped chives and serve with mashed potatoes and Brussels sprouts, if liked.

FOR HARD CIDER-BRAISED PORK, prepare the pork chops as above, omitting the vinegar. Bring 1 cup hard dry cider to a boil in a saucepan. Make the cornstarch paste as above, then gradually stir in the boiling hard cider instead of the stock. Pour over the chops and continue as above.

PORK WITH BLACK BEAN SAUCE

Serves **4**

Preparation time **20 minutes, plus overnight marinating**

Cooking temperature **high** and **low**

Cooking time **8 to 10 hours**

4 **spare rib pork steaks**, about 6 oz each

2 tablespoons **cornstarch**

¼ cup **soy sauce**

1½-inch piece of **fresh ginger root**, peeled and finely chopped

2 **garlic cloves**, minced

¼ cup **black bean sauce**

1¼ cups boiling **chicken stock**

pepper

TO SERVE

1 tablespoon **sunflower oil**

10 oz **ready-prepared mixed stir-fry vegetables**

cooked **rice**

Put the pork steaks into a shallow nonmetallic dish. Put the cornstarch and soy sauce in a small bowl and mix to a smooth paste, then add the ginger, garlic, black bean sauce, and a little pepper. Pour over the pork, cover with plastic wrap, and marinate in the refrigerator overnight.

Preheat the slow cooker if necessary. Put the pork and marinade into the slow-cooker pot. Pour over the boiling stock, cover, and cook on high for 30 minutes. Reduce the heat and cook on low for 7½ to 9½ hours, or set to auto for 8 to 10 hours, until the pork is cooked through and tender.

When almost ready to serve, heat the oil in a large skillet, add the mixed vegetables, and stir-fry for 2 to 3 minutes or until just tender. Spoon the pork onto plates lined with rice and top with the vegetables.

FOR SWEET & SOUR PORK, omit the black bean sauce from the marinade and add the marinated pork to the slow-cooker pot with a bunch of sliced scallions, 1 cored, seeded, and sliced red bell pepper and 1½ cups sliced mushrooms. Replace the chicken stock with a 14 oz jar sweet and sour sauce. Bring the sauce to a boil in a saucepan or the microwave, then pour into the slow-cooker pot. Continue as above.

ASIAN GLAZED RIBS

Serves **4**
Preparation time **25 minutes, plus overnight marinating**
Cooking temperature **high** and **low**
Cooking time **8 to 10 hours**

1 **onion**, quartered
2-inch piece of **fresh ginger root**, peeled and sliced
2 tablespoons **rice** or **white wine vinegar**
4 **star anise**
1 **cinnamon stick**, halved
2½ lb **pork ribs**
2 pints boiling **water**
2 **English Breakfast teabags**

GLAZE
¼ cup **liquid honey**
¼ cup **soy sauce**

Put the onion, ginger, vinegar, star anise, and cinnamon into a bowl and cover with plastic wrap. Let chill in the refrigerator overnight.

Preheat the slow cooker if necessary. Pour the measurement boiling water over the teabags and let brew for 2 to 3 minutes, then squeeze out the bags and discard. Rinse the ribs, drain, and put into the slow-cooker pot with the spiced onion mixture and the hot tea.

Cover with the lid and cook on high for 30 minutes. Reduce the heat and cook on low for 7½ to 9½ hours, or set to auto for 8 to 10 hours, until the meat is almost falling off of the bones.

Lift the ribs out of the slow-cooker pot and transfer to a foil-lined broiler pan. Put ¼ cup of stock from the pot into a bowl and mix in the honey and soy sauce. Spoon over the ribs, then cook under a preheated hot broiler for 10 to 15 minutes, turning several times and spooning soy mixture over, until browned and glazed. Serve with Pickled Cucumber (*see* below) and rice, if liked.

FOR PICKLED CUCUMBER TO ACCOMPANY THE RIBS, mix together ¼ to ½ mild red chile, seeded and finely chopped, 3 tablespoons chopped cilantro, 1 tablespoon rice or white wine vinegar, 1 teaspoon fish sauce, and ½ teaspoon superfine sugar in a salad bowl. Very thinly slice ½ cucumber, add to the dressing, and toss together gently. This dish can be made, covered with plastic wrap, and kept in the refrigerator overnight.

STICKY
JERK RIBS ♥

Serves **4**
Preparation time **20 minutes**
Cooking temperature **high**
Cooking time **5 to 6 hours**

2½ lb **lean pork ribs**
1 **onion**, cut into wedges
1 large **carrot**, sliced
3 **bay leaves**
2 tablespoons **malt vinegar**
low-calorie cooking oil spray
salt and **pepper**

JERK GLAZE
½ cup **tomato purée**
3 tablespoons **soy sauce**
½ teaspoon **ground cinnamon**
½ teaspoon **ground allspice**
¼ teaspoon **chili powder**
1 tablespoon **dark brown sugar**
grated zest and juice of ½ **orange**
4 **scallions**, finely chopped

Preheat the slow cooker if necessary. Place the pork ribs, onion, and carrot in the slow-cooker pot and add the bay leaves and vinegar. Season generously, then pour over enough boiling water to cover the ribs, making sure the level is at least 1 inch from the top of the pot. Cover and cook on high for 5 to 6 hours until the meat is starting to fall away from the bones. Transfer the ribs to a foil-lined broiler pan or baking pan.

Mix together the glaze ingredients, then brush all over the ribs. Spray with a little low-calorie cooking oil spray and cook under a preheated hot broiler, with the ribs about 2 inches away from the heat, for about 10 minutes, turning from time to time and brushing with the pan juices, until a deep brown. Serve with a salad, if liked.

FOR STICKY HOISIN RIBS, follow the recipe above to cook the ribs in the slow cooker. Make a glaze by mixing together 3 tablespoons hoisin sauce, ½ cup tomato purée, ¼ teaspoon chili powder, the grated zest and juice of ½ orange, and 4 finely chopped scallions. Brush over the ribs and broil as above.

PORK, ORANGE
& STAR ANISE

Serves **4**
Preparation time **20 minutes**
Cooking temperature **low**
Cooking time **8 to 10 hours**

1 tablespoon **sunflower oil**
4 **pork shoulder steaks** or **boneless spare rib chops**,
    about 1 lb 6 oz in total, each cut into 3
1 **onion**, chopped
2 tablespoons **all-purpose flour**
2 cups **chicken stock**
grated zest and juice of 1 **orange**
3 tablespoons **plum sauce**
2 tablespoons **soy sauce**
3 to 4 **star anise**
1 fresh or dried **red chile**, halved (optional)
salt and **pepper**
grated zest of 1 **orange**
mashed potatoes mixed with **steamed green
    vegetables**, to serve

Preheat the slow cooker if necessary. Heat the oil in a large skillet, add the pieces of pork, and fry over high heat until browned on both sides. Lift the pork out of the pan with a slotted spoon and transfer to a plate.

Add the onion to the pan and fry, stirring, for 5 minutes or until lightly browned. Stir in the flour, then mix in the stock, orange zest and juice, plum sauce, soy sauce, star anise, and chile, if using. Season with salt and pepper and bring to a boil, stirring.

Transfer the pork to the slow-cooker pot and pour the sauce over it. Cover and cook on low for 8 to 10 hours. Scatter with grated orange zest and serve with mashed potatoes mixed with steamed green vegetables.

FOR PORK, ORANGE & BAY LEAVES, prepare the dish as above, but replace the plum sauce, soy sauce, star anise, and red chile with 2 bay leaves, 2 teaspoons light brown sugar, and 1 tablespoon balsamic vinegar.

TIPSY MUSTARD PORK

Serves **4**
Preparation time **20 minutes**
Cooking temperature **high**
Cooking time **4 to 5 hours**

low-calorie cooking oil spray
4 **pork loin chops on the bone**,
   8 oz each, trimmed of fat
1 **onion**, chopped
1 tablespoon **all-purpose flour**
2 teaspoons **wholegrain mustard**
1 teaspoon **ground turmeric**
¾ cup **hard dry cider**
1¼ cups **chicken stock**
4 cups cubed **turnip**, cut into
   1-inch pieces
1½ cups cubed **potatoes**, cut into
   1-inch pieces
1 **apple**, cored and thickly sliced
salt and **pepper**
7 oz **snow peas**, steamed, to serve

Preheat the slow cooker if necessary. Spray a large skillet with a little low-calorie cooking oil spray and place over high heat until hot. Add the chops in a single layer and cook for 5 minutes, turning once, until browned on both sides, then transfer to a plate.

Add a little extra low-calorie cooking oil spray to the pan if necessary, then add the onion and cook over medium heat for 4 to 5 minutes until softened. Stir in the flour, then add the mustard, turmeric, cider, and stock. Season to taste and bring to a boil, stirring.

Place the turnip and potatoes in the slow-cooker pot. Arrange the chops in a single layer on top, then add the apple slices. Pour over the hot stock mixture, cover with the lid, and cook on high for 4 to 5 hours until the pork is very tender.

Transfer the pork to a plate. Divide the vegetables between 4 shallow dishes, top with the chops, and drizzle with the sauce. Serve with the steamed snow peas.

FOR MUSTARD CHICKEN WITH CELERIAC, follow the recipe above, browning 4 skinless chicken leg pieces in the skillet instead of the pork chops. Continue, replacing the turnip with 3¼ cups diced celeriac. Cook on low for 8 to 10 hours until the chicken is cooked through with no hint of pink juices and the celeriac is tender.

VEGETARIAN

HOPPIN' JOHN RICE

Serves **4**
Preparation time **15 minutes,**
   plus soaking
Cooking temperature **high**
Cooking time **1½ to 2 hours**

1 cup **white basmati rice**, soaked in cold
   water for 10 minutes
4 **scallions**, chopped
1 **red bell pepper**, cored, seeded,
   and diced
1 cup peeled, seeded diced **pumpkin**
   or **butternut squash**, cut into
   ½-inch pieces
2 **tomatoes**, diced
14 oz can **black-eye beans**, drained
leaves from 2 **thyme sprigs**
½ to 1 **red chile**, seeded
½ teaspoon **ground allspice**
½ teaspoon **salt**
3¼ cups boiling **water**
¼ cup **cilantro**, finely chopped
pepper

Preheat the slow cooker if necessary. Drain the soaked rice in a sieve and rinse under cold running water. Drain again and place in the slow-cooker pot with the scallions, red bell pepper, pumpkin or butternut squash, tomatoes, beans, thyme, and chile, to taste.

Stir the allspice and salt into the measurement boiling water and pour over the rice. Season generously with pepper. Cover and cook on high for 1½ to 2 hours until the rice is tender and has absorbed the water, stirring once during cooking and adding a little more hot water if the rice is too dry. Add the cilantro and fluff up the rice with a fork before serving.

FOR PUMPKIN RICE, place the soaked and rinsed rice in the slow cooker pot with the scallions, 2½ cups peeled, seeded, and diced pumpkin, 2 chopped garlic cloves, leaves from 2 thyme sprigs, a 1-inch piece of fresh ginger root, peeled and grated, and ½ to 1 red chile. Pour over 3¼ cups boiling water, season generously, and cook as above. Stir in the chopped cilantro just before serving.

BARLEY RISOTTO WITH BLUE CHEESE

Serves **4**
Preparation time **20 minutes**
Cooking temperature **low**
Cooking time **6¼ to 8¼ hours**

¾ cup **pearl barley**
1 **onion**, finely chopped
2 **garlic cloves**, minced
3¼ cups peeled, seeded, and
    cubed **butternut squash**, cut
    into ¾-inch pieces
2 pints boiling **vegetable stock**
¼ lb **baby spinach**, rinsed and
    well drained

BLUE CHEESE BUTTER
1 stick **butter**, at room temperature
3½ oz **blue cheese** (rind removed)
1 **garlic clove**, minced
¼ teaspoon **crushed dried
    red chiles**
salt and **pepper**

Preheat the slow cooker if necessary. Put the pearl barley, onion, garlic, and butternut squash into the slow-cooker pot. Add the boiling stock and a little salt and pepper. Cover with the lid and cook on low for 6 to 8 hours or until the barley and squash are tender.

Meanwhile, make the blue cheese butter. Put the butter on a plate, crumble the cheese on top, add the garlic and chiles, and mash together with a fork. Spoon the butter into a line on a piece of nonstick parchment paper, then wrap it up in the paper and roll it back and forth to make a neat sausage shape. Twist the ends to seal, the let chill in the refrigerator until required.

When almost ready to serve, stir the risotto, slice half the blue cheese butter, and add to the slow-cooker pot. Mix together until just beginning to melt, then add the spinach. Replace the lid and cook, still on low, for 15 minutes or until the spinach has just wilted. Ladle into shallow bowls and top with slices of the remaining butter.

FOR BARLEY RISOTTO WITH GARLIC & CILANTRO CREAM, make the risotto as above, replacing the squash with 4 cups peeled and diced sweet potato, cut into ¾-inch pieces, and adding 2 cups sliced white mushrooms with the stock. Cook as above, omitting the spinach and blue cheese butter. Mix together 1 cup crème fraîche, 1 minced garlic clove, 3 tablespoons finely chopped cilantro, and 3 chopped scallions. Ladle the risotto into bowls and top with spoonfuls of the cream.

GREEN BEAN RISOTTO WITH PESTO

Serves **4**
Preparation time **20 minutes**
Cooking temperature **low**
Cooking time **2 hours 5 minutes to**
  2½ hours

2 tablespoons **butter**
1 tablespoon **olive oil**
1 **onion**, chopped
2 **garlic cloves**, chopped
1 cup **risotto rice**
2½ pints hot **vegetable stock**, divided
2 teaspoons **pesto**
4 oz **extra-fine frozen**
  green snap beans
¾ cup **frozen peas**
salt and **pepper**

TO GARNISH
vegetarian hard cheese shavings
basil leaves

Preheat the slow cooker if necessary. Heat the butter and oil in a saucepan, add the onion, and fry, stirring, for 5 minutes or until softened and just beginning to brown.

Stir in the garlic and rice and cook for 1 minute. Add all but ¾ cup of the stock, season with salt and pepper, then bring to a boil. Transfer to the slow-cooker pot, cover with the lid, and cook on low for 1¾ to 2 hours.

Stir in the pesto and the remaining stock if more liquid is needed. Place the frozen vegetables on top of the rice, replace the lid, and cook for another 20 to 30 minutes or until the vegetables are hot. Serve, garnished with vegetarian hard cheese shavings and basil leaves.

FOR GREEN BEAN RISOTTO WITH SAGE, make the risotto as above, replacing the pesto with 2 sage sprigs. Replace the basil leaves with some tiny sage leaves.

DUM ALOO

Serves **4**
Preparation time **15 minutes**
Cooking temperature **high**
Cooking time **6¼ to 7¼ hours**

2 tablespoons **sunflower oil**
1 large **onion**, sliced
1 teaspoon **cumin seeds**, crushed
4 **cardamom pods**, crushed
1 teaspoon **black onion
    seeds** (optional)
1 teaspoon **ground turmeric**
½ teaspoon **ground cinnamon**
1-inch piece of **fresh ginger root**,
    peeled and finely chopped
14 oz can **diced tomatoes**
1¼ cups **vegetable stock**
1 teaspoon **superfine sugar**
1½ lb **baby new potatoes**, scrubbed
¼ lb **baby leaf spinach**, rinsed
    and drained
salt and **pepper**
torn **cilantro leaves**, to garnish

Preheat the slow cooker if necessary. Heat the oil in a large skillet, add the onion, and fry, stirring, for 5 minutes or until lightly browned.

Mix in the crushed cumin seeds and cardamom pods with their black seeds, onion seeds, if using, ground spices, and ginger. Cook for 1 minute, then mix in the tomatoes, stock, and sugar and season with salt and pepper. Bring to a boil, stirring.

Cut the potatoes into thick slices or halves (if they are small) so that all the pieces are of a similar size. Transfer to the slow-cooker pot and pour the sauce over the top. Cover and cook on high for 6 to 7 hours or until the potatoes are tender.

Add the spinach and cook on high for 15 minutes until it is just wilted. Stir the curry and serve scattered with torn cilantro leaves and accompanied by warmed naan bread, a lentil dahl, and boiled rice, if liked.

FOR DUM ALOO WITH SAFFRON & CHICKPEAS, add 2 large pinches of saffron threads instead of the turmeric and mix into the pan when you add the tomatoes. Reduce the amount of potatoes to 1 lb. Drain a 14 oz can chickpeas and stir into the mixture. Pour over the hot sauce and cook as above.

MOROCCAN SEVEN-VEGETABLE STEW

Serves **4**

Preparation time **25 minutes**

Cooking temperature **low** and **high**

Cooking time **6¼ hours to 8 hours
20 minutes**

2 tablespoons **olive oil**

1 large **onion**, chopped

2 **carrots**, diced

2¼ cups diced **turnip**

1 **red bell pepper**, cored, seeded,
and chopped

3 **garlic cloves**, minced

7 oz **frozen fava beans**

14 oz can **diced tomatoes**

3 teaspoons **harissa**

1 teaspoon **ground turmeric**

¾-inch piece of **fresh ginger root**,
peeled and finely chopped

1 cup **vegetable stock**

1 cup thickly sliced **okra**

salt and **pepper**

torn **mint leaves**, to garnish

prepared **couscous**, flavored with
olive oil, **lemon juice**, and **golden
raisins**, to serve

Preheat the slow cooker if necessary. Heat the oil in a large skillet, add the onion, and fry, stirring, for 5 minutes or until lightly browned.

Add the carrots and turnip to the pan with the red bell pepper, garlic, beans, and tomatoes. Mix in the harissa, turmeric, and ginger, then pour on the stock and season with salt and pepper. Bring to a boil, stirring.

Spoon the mixture into the slow-cooker pot and press the vegetables beneath the surface of the stock. Cover and cook on low for 6 to 8 hours or until the root vegetables are tender.

Stir in the sliced okra, cover, and cook on high for 15 to 20 minutes or until the okra is tender but still bright green. Garnish with torn mint leaves and serve with couscous flavored with olive oil, lemon juice, and golden raisins.

RATATOUILLE WITH RICOTTA DUMPLINGS

Serves **4**
Preparation time **25 minutes**
Cooking temperature **high**
Cooking time **3¼ to 4 hours**
    20 minutes

3 tablespoons **olive oil**
1 **onion**, chopped
1 **eggplant**, sliced
2 **zucchini**, about ¾ lb in total, sliced
1 **red bell pepper**, cored, seeded,
    and cubed
1 **yellow bell pepper**, cored, seeded,
    and cubed
2 **garlic cloves**, minced
1 tablespoon **all-purpose flour**
14 oz can **diced tomatoes**
1¼ cups **vegetable stock**
2 to 3 **rosemary sprigs**
salt and **pepper**

DUMPLINGS
¾ cup **all-purpose flour**, plus extra
    for dusting
¼ cup **ricotta cheese**
grated zest of ½ **lemon**
1 **egg**, beaten

Preheat the slow cooker if necessary. Heat the oil in a skillet, add the onion and eggplant, and fry, stirring, for 5 minutes or until softened and just beginning to turn golden.

Stir in the zucchini, bell peppers, and garlic and fry for 3 to 4 minutes. Mix in the flour, then the tomatoes, stock, rosemary, and a little salt and pepper. Bring to a boil, then spoon into the slow-cooker pot. Cover and cook on high for 3 to 4 hours until the vegetables are tender.

When almost ready to serve, make the dumplings. Put the flour, ricotta, lemon zest, and a little salt and pepper into a bowl. Add the egg and mix to a soft but not sticky dough. Cut into 12 pieces and roll each piece into a ball with floured hands.

Stir the ratatouille and arrange the dumplings on the top. Replace the lid and cook for 15 to 20 minutes or until light and firm to the touch. Spoon into bowls and eat with a spoon and fork.

PUMPKIN & CHEESE GNOCCHI

SPANISH POTATOES

Serves **4**
Preparation time **20 minutes**
Cooking temperature **low**
Cooking time **6 to 8 hours**

1 tablespoon **olive oil**
2 tablespoons **butter**
1 **onion**, thinly sliced
2 **garlic cloves**, minced
2 tablespoons **all-purpose flour**
¾ cup **dry white wine**
1¼ cups **vegetable stock**
2 to 3 **sage sprigs**, plus extra leaves to garnish (optional)
2½ cups peeled and seeded diced **pumpkin**
    or **butternut squash**
1 lb **gnocchi**, chilled
½ cup **heavy cream**
freshly grated **vegetarian hard cheese**
salt and **pepper**

Preheat the slow cooker if necessary. Heat the oil and butter in a skillet, add the onion, and fry, stirring, for 5 minutes or until just beginning to turn golden.

Stir in the garlic and cook for 2 minutes, then stir in the flour. Gradually mix in the wine and stock and heat, stirring, until smooth. Add the sage and season well.

Add the pumpkin or squash to the slow-cooker pot, pour over the hot sauce, then press the pumpkin or squash beneath the surface of the liquid. Cover with the lid and cook on low for 6 to 8 hours or until the pumpkin (or squash) is tender.

When almost ready to serve, bring a large saucepan of water to a boil, add the gnocchi, bring the water back to a boil, and cook for 2 to 3 minutes or until the gnocchi float to the surface and are piping hot. Pour into a colander to drain.

Stir the cream, then the gnocchi into the slow-cooker pot and mix together lightly. Spoon into shallow bowls and serve topped with freshly grated vegetarian hard cheese and a few extra sage leaves, if liked.

Serves **4**
Preparation time **15 minutes**
Cooking temperature **high**
Cooking time **4 to 5 hours**

2 tablespoons **olive oil**
1 large **red onion**, thinly sliced
2 **garlic cloves**, minced
1 teaspoon **smoked paprika**
¼ to ½ teaspoon **crushed dried red chiles**, to taste
1 **red bell pepper**, cored, seeded, and diced
1 **yellow bell pepper**, cored, seeded, and diced
14 oz can **diced tomatoes**
1¼ cups **vegetable stock**
2 to 3 **thyme sprigs**
¼ cup **pitted dry olives**
1¼ lb **baking potatoes**, cut into 1-inch chunks
salt and **pepper**

Preheat the slow cooker if necessary. Heat the oil in a skillet, add the onion, and fry, stirring, for 5 minutes or until just beginning to turn golden.

Stir in the garlic, paprika, chiles, and peppers and cook for 2 minutes. Mix in the tomatoes, stock, thyme, olives, and some salt and pepper, then bring to a boil.

Add the potatoes to the slow-cooker pot, pour over the hot tomato mixture, cover with the lid, and cook on high for 4 to 5 hours or until the potatoes are tender. Serve with warm crusty bread and a dressed green salad, if liked.

FOR SPANISH SWEET POTATOES, make the recipe as above, using sweet potatoes instead of baking potatoes and omitting the olives. Cook on high for 3 to 4 hours and serve in bowls topped with spoonfuls of Greek yogurt and torn cilantro leaves.

SWEET POTATO & EGG CURRY

Serves **4**
Preparation time **15 minutes**
Cooking temperature **low**
Cooking time **6¼ to 8¼ hours**

1 tablespoon **sunflower oil**
1 **onion**, chopped
1 teaspoon **cumin seeds**,
   coarsely crushed
1 teaspoon **ground coriander**
1 teaspoon **ground turmeric**
1 teaspoon **garam masala**
½ teaspoon **crushed dried red chiles**
3¼ cups peeled diced **sweet potatoes**
2 **garlic cloves**, minced
14 oz can **diced tomatoes**
14 oz can **lentils**, drained
1¼ cups **vegetable stock**
1 teaspoon **superfine sugar**
6 **eggs**
1 cup **frozen peas**
¾ cup **heavy cream**
small bunch of **cilantro**, torn into pieces
salt and **pepper**

Preheat the slow cooker if necessary. Heat the oil in a skillet, add the onion, and fry, stirring, for 5 minutes or until softened and just beginning to turn golden.

Stir in the spices, sweet potatoes, and garlic and fry for 2 minutes. Add the tomatoes, lentils, stock, and sugar and season with a little salt and pepper. Bring to a boil, stirring. Spoon into the slow-cooker pot, cover with the lid, and cook on low for 6 to 8 hours.

When almost ready to serve, put the eggs in a small saucepan, cover with cold water, and bring to a boil, then simmer for 8 minutes. Drain, crack the shells, and cool under cold running water. Peel and halve, then add to the slow-cooker pot with the peas, cream, and half the cilantro. Cover and cook on low for 15 minutes.

Spoon into bowls, garnish with the remaining cilantro and serve with rice or warmed naan bread, if liked.

FOR SWEET POTATO & PANEER CURRY, make up the curry as above, adding 13 oz diced paneer (Indian cheese) instead of the boiled eggs, reducing the peas to ¾ cup and adding 3½ oz baby corn, halved if large.

MIXED MUSHROOM & LENTIL BRAISE

Serves **4**
Preparation time **25 minutes**
Cooking temperature **low**
Cooking time **6 to 8 hours**

2 tablespoons **olive oil**, plus extra
  to serve
1 large **onion**, chopped
3 **garlic cloves**, chopped
14 oz can **diced tomatoes**
1¼ cups **vegetable stock**
¾ cups **red wine** or extra **stock**
1 tablespoon **tomato paste**
2 teaspoons **superfine sugar**
½ cup **dried Puy lentils**
4 cups halved or quartered
  white mushrooms
4 oz **shiitake mushrooms**, halved
  if large
4 large **field mushrooms**, about
  ½ lb in total
salt and **pepper**

TO SERVE
arugula
vegetarian hard cheese shavings
fried slices of **polenta**

Preheat the slow cooker if necessary. Heat the oil in a large skillet, add the onion, and fry, stirring, for 5 minutes or until lightly browned. Mix in the garlic, tomatoes, stock, wine or extra stock, tomato paste, and sugar. Season with salt and pepper, add the Puy lentils, and bring to a boil.

Put the mushrooms in the slow-cooker pot and pour over the lentil mixture, then cover with the lid and cook on low for 6 to 8 hours, stirring once if possible.

Serve with arugula tossed with vegetarian hard cheese shavings and a drizzle of olive oil and fried slices of polenta.

FOR MIXED MUSHROOMS & LENTILS BAKED WITH CHEESE, make and cook the mushroom and lentil mixture as above. Mix together 3 eggs, 1 cup plain yogurt, ½ cup crumbled feta cheese, and a pinch of grated nutmeg. Press the cooked mushroom mixture into an even layer, then spoon the yogurt mixture on top. Arrange 2 sliced tomatoes on top and cook on high for 45 minutes to 1¼ hours until the topping is set. Lift the pot out of the housing using oven mitts and brown under a preheated hot broiler, if liked.

BEET & MASCARPONE RISOTTO

Serves **4**
Preparation time **20 minutes**
Cooking temperature **low**
Cooking time **1¾ to 2 hours**

2 tablespoons **butter**
1 tablespoon **olive oil**
1 **red onion**, chopped
1 **garlic clove**, minced
8 oz package **cooked beets in natural juice**, drained and diced
1 cup **risotto rice**
¾ cup **red wine**
2 pints **vegetable stock**
2 **thyme sprigs**
salt and **pepper**

TO SERVE
¾ cup **mascarpone cheese**
¼ cup chopped **thyme leaves**
vegetarian hard cheese shavings

Preheat the slow cooker if necessary. Heat the butter and oil in a large skillet, add the onion, and fry, stirring, for 5 minutes or until softened.

Stir in the garlic, beets, and rice and cook for 1 minute, then mix in the wine and stock. Add the thyme and a little salt and pepper and bring to a boil, stirring.

Pour the mixture into the slow-cooker pot. Cover with the lid and cook on low for 1¾ to 2 hours or until the rice is tender and almost all the stock has been absorbed.

Spoon into bowls and top with spoonfuls of the mascarpone mixed with the chopped thyme leaves, a little pepper and a generous sprinkling of vegetarian hard cheese shavings.

FOR MUSHROOM & THYME RISOTTO, soak ½ oz dried porcini mushrooms in ¾ cup boiling water for 15 minutes. Fry the onion in butter and oil as above, then add the garlic, 3½ cups mixed sliced mushrooms, and an extra 2 tablespoons butter and fry briefly. Omit the beets. Add the rice and cook for 1 minute, then add the soaked mushrooms and their soaking liquid, the red wine, stock, and thyme. Season with salt and pepper and bring to a boil. Continue as above.

EGGPLANT WITH BAKED EGGS

Serves **4**
Preparation time **20 minutes**
Cooking temperature **high**
Cooking time **2¾ to 3 hours
20 minutes**

¼ cup **olive oil**
1 **onion**, chopped
2 **eggplant**, cubed
2 **garlic cloves**, minced
2¾ cups chopped **tomatoes**, cut into
    large chunks
½ teaspoon **smoked paprika**
½ teaspoon **ground cumin**
½ teaspoon **ground coriander**
½ cup **quinoa**
1¼ cups **vegetable stock**
¾ cup **frozen peas** (optional)
4 **eggs**
salt and **pepper**
chopped **mint**, to garnish

Preheat the slow cooker if necessary. Heat the oil in a large skillet, add the onion and eggplant, and fry, stirring, until the eggplant cubes are golden.

Stir in the garlic, tomatoes, and spices and cook for 1 minute. Mix in the quinoa and stock, add a little salt and pepper, and bring to a boil. Transfer the mixture to the slow-cooker pot. Cover with the lid and cook on high for 2½ to 3 hours.

Stir in the frozen peas, if using, and add a little boiling water if the quinoa has begun to stick around the edges of the pot. Make 4 indents with the back of a tablespoon, then break and drop an egg into each one. Cover with the lid and cook for 15 to 20 minutes or until the egg whites are set and the yolks still soft.

Spoon onto plates, season the eggs with a little extra salt and pepper, and garnish with chopped mint. Serve with toasted pitta bread, cut into strips, if liked.

FOR EGGPLANT RATATOUILLE WITH BAKED EGGS, omit the ground spices and quinoa and make the recipe as above, adding 1 diced zucchini and 1 cored, seeded, and diced orange bell pepper with the garlic, tomatoes, and smoked paprika. Add 1 cup vegetable stock, season with salt and pepper, and continue as above, omitting the peas. Serve sprinkled with torn basil leaves, and spooned over toasted rustic-style bread.

SOY SAUSAGES WITH ONION GRAVY

Serves **4**
Preparation time **20 minutes**
Cooking temperature **high**
Cooking time **4 to 5 hours**

low-calorie cooking oil spray
2 x 7½ oz packages **soy sausages**
2 cups thinly sliced **onions**
2 teaspoons **dark brown sugar**
1½ cups **vegetable stock**
1 tablespoon **tomato paste**
2 teaspoons **wholegrain mustard**
2 teaspoons **cornstarch**
1 lb 6 oz **celeriac**, peeled and cubed
  just before cooking
salt and **pepper**
chopped **parsley**, to garnish (optional)

TO SERVE
¾ lb **fine green snap beans**, steamed

Preheat the slow cooker if necessary. Spray a large skillet with a little low-calorie cooking oil spray and place over high heat until hot. Add the sausages and cook for 2 to 3 minutes until browned all over. Transfer to the slow-cooker pot in a single layer.

Add a little extra low-calorie cooking oil spray to the skillet, add the onions, and cook over medium heat for 5 minutes until just beginning to soften. Add the sugar and continue to cook for 5 minutes until deep brown, being careful not to burn the onions.

Stir in the stock, tomato paste, and mustard. Mix the cornstarch to a smooth paste with a little cold water and stir into the pan. Season to taste and bring to a boil, stirring. Pour over the sausages, cover, and cook on high for 4 to 5 hours until the sausages are cooked through.

When almost ready to serve, cook the celeriac in a saucepan of lightly salted boiling water for 15 to 20 minutes until tender. Drain and mash with 3 to 4 tablespoons of the cooking water and season to taste. Divide the mashed celeriac between 4 serving plates and top with the sausages and onion gravy. Scatter with a little chopped parsley, if liked, and serve with the steamed green snap beans.

CHILE, MUSHROOM & TOMATO RAGÙ

Serves **4**
Preparation time **20 minutes**
Cooking temperature **low**
Cooking time **7 to 8 hours**

1 tablespoon **olive oil**
1 **red onion**, coarsely chopped
2 **garlic cloves**, minced
1 teaspoon **paprika**
½ teaspoon **crushed dried red chiles**
1 teaspoon **dried
   Mediterranean herbs**
1 cup **tomato purée**
2 teaspoons **granulated sweetener**
10 oz **baby mushrooms**
2 cups **cherry tomatoes**
salt and **pepper**

TO SERVE
7 oz **dried penne pasta**
large pinch of **crushed dried red
   chiles** (optional)
handful of **arugula**

Preheat the slow cooker if necessary. Heat the oil in a large skillet over medium heat until hot, add the onion, and cook for 4 to 5 minutes, stirring until just beginning to soften. Add the garlic, paprika, and chiles, then the dried herbs, tomato purée, and sweetener. Season to taste and bring to a boil.

Place the mushrooms and cherry tomatoes in the slow-cooker pot, pour over the hot tomato mixture, and stir well. Cover and cook on low for 7 to 8 hours.

When almost ready to serve, cook the pasta in a saucepan of lightly salted boiling water following the package instructions until just tender. Drain and stir into the ragù, then spoon into shallow bowls, sprinkle with the chiles, if liked, and top with the arugula. Serve immediately.

FOR ZUCCHINI & TOMATO ARRABIATA, follow the recipe above, using 1¾ cups diced zucchini and 1 cored, seeded, and diced red bell pepper instead of the mushrooms.

LENTIL TAGINE WITH POMEGRANATE

Serves **4**
Preparation time **15 minutes**
Cooking temperature **high**
Cooking time **4 to 5 hours**

1 tablespoon **olive oil**
1 **onion**, chopped
2-inch piece of **fresh ginger**
    root, peeled and finely chopped
3 **garlic cloves**, minced
2 teaspoons **cumin seed**s, crushed
1 teaspoon **coriander seeds**, crushed
1 cup **dried Puy lentils**
2 **celery stalks**, sliced
1¾ cups halved **cherry tomatoes**
1¾ cups hot **vegetable stock**
juice of **1 lemon**
¼ cup **flat-leaf parsley**,
    coarsely chopped
3 tablespoons **mint**, coarsely chopped
salt and **pepper**

TO SERVE
½ cup **0% fat Greek yogurt**
1 tablespoon **harissa**
seeds from ½ **pomegranate**

Preheat the slow cooker if necessary. Heat the oil in a large skillet over medium heat, add the onion, and cook for 4 to 5 minutes until just beginning to soften. Stir in the ginger, garlic, and crushed cumin and coriander seeds.

Place the lentils in a sieve and rinse under cold running water. Drain and transfer to the slow-cooker pot. Spoon the onion mixture on top, then add the celery and tomatoes. Pour over the hot stock, season to taste, cover, and cook on high for 4 to 5 hours until the lentils are tender.

Stir in the lemon juice and herbs and spoon into bowls. Top with the yogurt and harissa, then scatter with the pomegranate seeds and serve.

FOR CHICKPEA & LENTIL TAGINE, follow the recipe above, adding ½ teaspoon chili powder with the other spices and using ½ cup dried Puy lentils and a 14 oz can chickpeas, drained, instead of 1 cup lentils. Omit the mint and pomegranate, but stir in ½ cup coarsely chopped parsley and serve topped with the yogurt and harissa.

MUSHROOM & WALNUT COBBLER

Serves **4**
Preparation time **30 minutes**
Cooking temperature **low** and **high**
Cooking time **6¾ to 8¾ hours**

2 tablespoons **olive oil**
1 **onion**, chopped
2 **garlic cloves**, chopped
½ lb **flat mushrooms**, peeled
    and quartered
½ lb **cremino mushrooms**, quartered
1 tablespoon **all-purpose flour**
1 cup **red wine**
14 oz can **diced tomatoes**
¾ cup **vegetable stock**
1 tablespoon **redcurrant jelly**
2 to 3 **thyme sprigs**
salt and **pepper**

WALNUT TOPPING
1½ cups **all-purpose flour**, sifted with
    1½ teaspoons **baking powder**, plus
    extra flour for dusting
½ stick **butter**, diced
½ cup chopped **walnuts**
¾ cup shredded **Cheddar cheese**
1 **egg**, beaten
4 to 5 tablespoons **milk**

Preheat the slow cooker if necessary. Heat the oil in a skillet, add the onion, garlic, and mushrooms and fry, stirring, for 5 minutes or until just turning golden.

Stir in the flour, then mix in the wine, tomatoes, and stock. Add the redcurrant jelly, thyme, and salt and pepper and bring to a boil. Pour into the slow-cooker pot, cover with the lid, and cook on low for 6 to 8 hours.

When almost ready to serve, make the topping. Put the flour and butter in a bowl, then rub in the butter with your fingertips until fine bread crumbs form. Stir in the walnuts, cheese, and salt and pepper. Add half the egg, then mix in enough milk to make a soft dough.

Knead lightly, then roll out the dough on a lightly floured surface until ¾ inch thick. Stamp out 8 circles with a 2½-inch plain cookie cutter, rerolling the trimmings as needed. Stir the mushroom mixture, then arrange the dough circles, slightly overlapping, around the edge of the dish. Cover and cook on high for 45 minutes or until well risen. Lift the pot out of the housing using oven mitts, brush the tops of the dough with the remaining egg, and brown under a preheated medium broiler, if liked.

FOR CHEAT'S MUSHROOM PIE, make the mushroom mixture as above, but omit the stock and dough topping. Unroll 1 pastry sheet from a 14-oz package of 2 and trim the edges to make an oval shape. Transfer to an oiled cookie sheet, brush with beaten egg, and bake in a preheated oven, 400°F, for 15 to 20 minutes or until golden. Cut into wedge shapes and serve on top of the mushroom mixture.

TARKA DAHL

Serves **4**
Preparation time **15 minutes**
Cooking temperature **high**
Cooking time **3 to 4 hours**

1¼ cups **dried red lentils**
1 **onion**, finely chopped
½ teaspoon **ground turmeric**
½ teaspoon **cumin seeds**, coarsely crushed
¾-inch piece of **fresh ginger root**, peeled and
    finely chopped
7 oz **can diced tomatoes**
2½ cups boiling **vegetable stock**
¾ cup **plain yogurt**
salt and **pepper**
torn **cilantro leaves**, to garnish

TARKA
1 tablespoon **sunflower oil**
2 teaspoons **black mustard seeds**
½ teaspoon **cumin seeds**, coarsely crushed
pinch of **ground turmeric**
2 **garlic cloves**, minced

Preheat the slow cooker if necessary. Rinse the lentils
well with cold running water, drain, and put into
the slow-cooker pot with the onion, spices, ginger,
tomatoes, and boiling stock.

Stir in a little salt and pepper, cover with the lid, and
cook on high for 3 to 4 hours or until the lentils are soft
and tender.

When almost ready to serve, make the tarka. Heat
the oil in a small skillet, add the remaining tarka
ingredients, and fry, stirring, for 2 minutes. Coarsely
mash the lentil mixture, then spoon into bowls, add
spoonfuls of yogurt, and drizzle with the tarka. Scatter
with cilantro leaves and serve with warmed naan bread,
if liked.

FOR TARKA DAHL WITH SPINACH, cook the lentils in the
same way as above, adding ¼ lb rinsed, drained, and
coarsely shredded spinach for the last 15 minutes. Fry
the tarka spices as above, adding ¼ teaspoon crushed
dried red chiles, if liked.

NUT & APRICOT PILAF

Serves **4**
Preparation time **25 minutes**
Cooking temperature **low**
Cooking time **3 to 3½ hours**

1 tablespoon **olive oil**
1 large **onion**, chopped
3 oz mixed **pistachios, walnuts,** and **hazelnuts,**
    plus extra, lightly toasted, to garnish
3 tablespoons **sunflower seeds**
1 cup **converted long-grain brown rice**
2 pints **vegetable stock**
½ cup **ready-to-eat dried apricots**, chopped
¼ cup **currants**
1 **cinnamon stick**, halved
6 **cloves**
3 **bay leaves**
1 tablespoon **tomato paste**
salt and **pepper**

Preheat the slow cooker if necessary. Heat the oil in a
skillet, add the onion, and fry, stirring, for 5 minutes or
until lightly browned.

Add the nuts and seeds and fry until lightly browned.
Stir in the rice and stock, followed by the dried fruit,
spices, bay leaves, and tomato paste, then season with
salt and pepper to taste. Bring to a boil, stirring.

Transfer the mixture to the slow-cooker pot. Cover
with the lid and cook on low for 3 to 3½ hours or until
the rice is tender and the stock has been absorbed.
Discard the cinnamon, cloves, and bay leaves. Garnish
with extra, toasted nuts to serve.

FOR EGGPLANT & APRICOT PILAF, heat 3 tablespoons
olive oil, add the onion, and 1 sliced eggplant. Fry
until lightly browned. Continue as above, replacing
the hazelnuts with almonds and adding the sunflower
seeds, the rice, stock, and just ¼ cup of the apricots
plus ¼ cup chopped pitted dates. Add the remaining
ingredients and continue as above.

VEGETABLE GOULASH

Serves **4**
Preparation time **20 minutes**
Cooking temperature **high**
Cooking time **4 to 5 hours**

1 tablespoon **sunflower oil**
1 **onion**, chopped
2 cups diced **turnips**
2 cups diced **carrots**
1½ cups diced **potatoes**
1 **red bell pepper**, cored, seeded, and diced
2 **celery stalks**, sliced
2 cups halved **white mushrooms**
1 teaspoon **smoked paprika**, plus extra
   to garnish (optional)
¼ teaspoon **crushed dried red chiles**
1 teaspoon **caraway seeds**
1 tablespoon **all-purpose flour**
14 oz can **diced tomatoes**
1¼ cups **vegetable stock**
2 **bay leaves**
salt and **pepper**

TO SERVE
¾ cup **sour cream**
boiled **rice**

Preheat the slow cooker if necessary. Heat the oil in
a large skillet, add the onion, and fry, stirring, until
softened. Add the vegetables and fry for 1 to 2 minutes,
then stir in the paprika, chiles, and caraway seeds. Cook
for 1 minute.

Stir in the flour, then mix in the canned tomatoes and
stock, add the bay leaves, and a little salt and pepper.
Bring to a boil. Transfer to the slow-cooker pot and
press the vegetables below the surface of the liquid.
Cover with the lid and cook on high for 4 to 5 hours or
until the root vegetables are tender.

Stir the goulash and discard the bay leaves. Spoon
onto plates and top with spoonfuls of the sour cream
and a sprinkling of extra paprika, if liked. Serve with
boiled rice.

MUSHROOM & TOMATO RIGATONI ♥

Serves **4**
Preparation time **20 minutes**
Cooking temperature **low**
Cooking time **2½ to 3 hours**

8 oz **dried rigatoni** or **pasta quills**
3 tablespoons **olive oil**
1 **onion**, sliced
2 to 3 **garlic cloves**, minced
3½ cups sliced **white mushrooms**
½ lb **portabello mushrooms**, sliced
1½ cups chopped **tomatoes**, cut into chunks
14 oz can **diced tomatoes**
1 cup **vegetable stock**
1 tablespoon **tomato paste**
3 **rosemary sprigs**
salt and **pepper**

Preheat the slow cooker if necessary. Place the pasta in
a large bowl, cover with boiling water, and let soak for
10 minutes.

Meanwhile, heat 1 tablespoon of the oil in a large
skillet over medium heat, add the onion, and cook
for 5 minutes until softened. Stir in the remaining oil,
the garlic, and mushrooms. Cook, stirring, until the
mushrooms are just beginning to brown.

Stir in the fresh and canned tomatoes, stock, and
tomato paste. Add the rosemary, season to taste, and
bring to a boil.

Drain the pasta and put it in the slow-cooker pot. Pour
over the hot mushroom mixture and spread into an even
layer. Cover and cook on low for 2½ to 3 hours or until
the pasta is just tender. Spoon into bowls and scatter
with freshly shredded vegetarian hard cheese, if liked.

FOR MUSHROOM PASTICHIO, follow the recipe above,
using 8 oz dried macaroni instead of the rigatoni.
Mix 3 eggs with 1 cup plain yogurt, ½ cup crumbled
feta cheese, and a pinch of grated nutmeg. Spoon
the mixture over the top of the mushroom and pasta
mixture for the last hour of cooking until set. Place under
a preheated hot broiler to brown the top before serving.

SPICY FLAVORS

EASY CAULIFLOWER DAHL

Serves **4**
Preparation time **15 minutes**
Cooking temperature **high**
Cooking time **3 to 4 hours**

1 cup **dried red lentils**, rinsed
    and drained
3¼ cups hot **water**
2 teaspoons **medium curry powder**
½ teaspoon **salt**
pepper

SPICED CAULIFLOWER
¾ lb **cauliflower**, trimmed and cut
    into small florets
¼ cup **water**
1 **onion**, thinly sliced
low-calorie cooking oil spray
1 teaspoon **cumin seeds**,
    coarsely crushed
1 teaspoon **ground turmeric**
1 teaspoon **garam masala**

Preheat the slow cooker if necessary. Place the lentils, measurement hot water, curry powder, and salt in the slow-cooker pot, then season with pepper. Cover and cook on high for 3 to 4 hours or until the lentils are soft.

Meanwhile, place the cauliflower in a large skillet with the measurement water, cover, and cook over medium heat for 5 minutes until the cauliflower is almost tender. Drain off any excess water, then add the onion and a little low-calorie cooking oil spray, increase the heat, and cook for 2 to 3 minutes, stirring.

Sprinkle the cumin, turmeric, and garam masala over the cauliflower and cook, stirring, for 4 to 5 minutes until the cauliflower is golden brown. Season to taste. Stir the lentil dahl, spoon into shallow bowls, and top with the spiced cauliflower.

FOR EASY EGGPLANT & MUSHROOM DAHL, follow the recipe above to cook the lentil dahl. Spray a large skillet with a little low-calorie cooking oil spray, add 1 large diced eggplant and 1½ cups sliced button mushrooms, and cook over medium heat for 2 to 3 minutes until beginning to soften. Add a little more low-calorie cooking oil spray, then the cumin, turmeric, and garam masala, as above, and continue to cook until the eggplant is soft. Spoon the spiced vegetables over the dahl and scatter with chopped cilantro.

INDIAN BLACK PEPPER CHICKEN

Serves **4**
Preparation time **20 minutes**
Cooking temperature **low** and **high**
Cooking time **7¼ to 8½ hours**

1 large **onion**, quartered
3 **garlic cloves**, halved
1½-inch piece of **fresh ginger root**,
    peeled and sliced
1 cup fresh **cilantro**
8 small **skinless chicken
    drumsticks**, 1¾ lb in total
low-calorie cooking oil spray
2-inch **cinnamon stick**
1 teaspoon **ground cumin**
1 teaspoon **ground turmeric**
2 teaspoons **black peppercorns**,
    coarsely crushed
juice of ½ **lemon**
1½ cups **chicken stock**
5 oz **baby spinach**, rinsed
    and drained
salt

Preheat the slow cooker if necessary. Place the onion, garlic, ginger, and cilantro in a food processor and blend until very finely chopped.

Slash each chicken drumstick 2 or 3 times with a sharp knife. Spray a large skillet with a little low-calorie cooking oil spray and place over high heat until hot. Add the chicken and cook for 4 to 5 minutes, turning, until browned all over. Transfer the drumsticks to the slow-cooker pot, packing them in tightly together.

Add the chopped onion mixture to the skillet and cook for 2 minutes until just softened. Stir in the cinnamon, cumin, turmeric, and crushed peppercorns, then add the lemon juice and stock. Season to taste and bring to a boil, stirring.

Pour the hot stock over the chicken, cover, and cook on low for 7 to 8 hours until the chicken is cooked through and beginning to shrink on the bones. Stir the sauce, add the spinach, cover again, and cook on high for 15 to 30 minutes until the spinach has wilted. Spoon into shallow bowls and serve.

FOR INDIAN CHICKEN & CHICKPEA CURRY, follow the recipe above, using just 4 chicken drumsticks and adding ¼ teaspoon chili powder instead of the crushed black peppercorns. Place the browned drumsticks in the slow-cooker pot with a 14 oz can chickpeas, drained, then pour over the hot stock and cook as above.

SMOKY SWEET POTATO & QUORN CHILI

Serves **4**
Preparation time **20 minutes**
Cooking temperature **low**
Cooking time **7 to 8 hours**

1 to 2 small **dried smoked
    chipotle chiles**
¼ cup boiling **water**
low-calorie cooking oil spray
1 **onion**, chopped
2 **garlic cloves**, minced
1 teaspoon **ground cumin**
1 teaspoon **paprika**
2 x 14 oz cans **diced tomatoes**
14 oz can **red kidney beans**, rinsed
    and drained
1 tablespoon **Worcestershire
    sauce** (optional)
11½ oz **Quorn grounds**
2¼ cups cubed **sweet potato**, cut
    into 1-inch pieces
salt and **pepper**

SALSA
½ **red onion**, finely chopped
3 tablespoons chopped **cilantro**
2 **tomatoes**, halved, seeded, and diced

Preheat the slow cooker if necessary. Place the dried chiles in a small bowl, pour over the boiling water, and let stand for 10 minutes.

Meanwhile, spray a large skillet with a little low-calorie cooking oil spray and place over medium heat until hot. Add the onion and fry for 4 to 5 minutes until softened, then add the garlic, cumin, and paprika. Stir in the tomatoes, kidney beans, and Worcestershire sauce, if using, then the Quorn grounds and sweet potato. Season to taste.

Drain the chiles, reserving the soaking water, then finely chop. Stir into the Quorn grounds mixture with the soaking water. Bring to a boil, stirring, then transfer to the slow-cooker pot. Cover and cook on low for 7 to 8 hours until the sweet potato is tender. Mix the salsa ingredients together, then sprinkle over the chili to serve.

FOR SWEET POTATO & QUORN GROUNDS CURRY, follow the recipe above, omitting the chipotle chiles. Add 1 teaspoon ground turmeric, 1 teaspoon garam masala, and ½ teaspoon crushed dried red chiles with the cumin and paprika, and a 14 oz can lentils, drained, when adding the Quorn grounds. Cook as above, then stir in ¾ cup frozen peas and ¼ cup chopped cilantro, cover the pot again, and cook on high for 15 minutes.

COCONUT, PUMPKIN & CHICKPEA CURRY

Serves **4**
Preparation time **25 minutes**
Cooking temperature **low**
Cooking time **6 to 8 hours**

2 **onions**, divided
2 **garlic cloves**, halved
1½-inch piece of **fresh ginger root**,
    peeled and sliced
1 **red chile**, quartered and seeded
low-calorie cooking oil spray
1½ tablespoons **medium curry powder**
1 teaspoon **fennel seeds**,
    coarsely crushed
1 cup **coconut milk**
1¼ cups **vegetable stock**
2 teaspoons **granulated sweetener**
1¼ lb **pumpkin**, peeled, seeded, and
    cut into 1½-inch chunks
14 oz can **chickpeas**, drained
1 teaspoon **black mustard seeds**
1 cup **cilantro**, coarsely torn
juice of 1 **lime**
salt and **pepper**

Preheat the slow cooker if necessary. Quarter 1 of the onions and place with the garlic, ginger, and chile in a food processor and blend until very finely chopped. Alternatively, chop the ingredients finely with a knife. Spray a large skillet with a little low-calorie cooking oil spray and place over high heat until hot. Add the onion paste and cook for 2 minutes, then stir in the curry powder and fennel seeds.

Add the coconut milk, stock, and sweetener, then season to taste. Bring to a boil, stirring. Place the pumpkin and chickpeas in the slow-cooker pot and pour the coconut mixture on top. Cover and cook on low for 6 to 8 hours until the pumpkin is tender.

When almost ready to serve, make a crispy onion topping. Slice the remaining onion. Heat a little low-calorie cooking oil spray in a clean skillet and cook the onion over medium heat for 5 minutes until softened. Stir in the mustard seeds and cook for a few minutes more until the onion is golden and crispy.

Stir the cilantro and lime juice into the curry, spoon into bowls, and serve topped with the crispy onions.

FOR CREAMY COCONUT, EGGPLANT & CHICKPEA CURRY, follow the recipe above, using 1¼ lb eggplant, trimmed and diced, instead of the pumpkin.

RED COOKED CHINESE DUCK

Serves **4**
Preparation time **20 minutes**
Cooking temperature **high**
Cooking time **5 to 6 hours**

4 **duck legs**, about 7 oz each
1 **onion**, sliced
2 tablespoons **all-purpose flour**
2 cups **chicken stock**
2 tablespoons **soy sauce**
1 tablespoon **red wine vinegar**
1 tablespoon **liquid honey**
2 teaspoons **tomato paste**
2 teaspoons **fish sauce**
½ teaspoon **crushed dried red chiles**
½ teaspoon **ground allspice**
4 **star anise**
¾ lb **red plums**, pitted and quartered

Preheat the slow cooker if necessary. Dry-fry the duck legs in a skillet over low heat at first until the fat begins to run, then increase the heat and brown on both sides. Lift out of the pan with a slotted spoon and transfer to the slow-cooker pot.

Pour off all but 1 tablespoon of the duck fat from the pan, then add the onion and fry, stirring, for 5 minutes or until just turning golden. Stir in the flour, then gradually mix in the stock. Add the remaining ingredients, except for the plums, and bring to a boil, stirring.

Pour the sauce over the duck, add the plums, and press the duck beneath the surface of the liquid. Cover with the lid and cook on high for 5 to 6 hours or until the duck is almost falling off the bones. Serve with rice or with Ginger Noodles (*see* below), if liked.

FOR GINGER NOODLES TO ACCOMPANY THE DUCK, heat 1 tablespoon sesame oil in a wok, add a 1-inch piece of peeled and finely chopped fresh ginger root, 3 cups finely shredded bok choy, ½ cup halved snow peas, and 3 5-oz packages of thick-cut, straight-to-wok noodles. Stir-fry for 3 to 4 minutes or until the bok choy has just wilted and the noodles are hot.

KEEMA MUTTER

Serves **4**
Preparation time 10 minutes
Cooking temperature **high** and **low**
Cooking time **8 to 10 hours**

1 lb **lean ground beef**
1 **onion**, finely chopped
14 oz can **diced tomatoes**
3 tablespoons **mild curry paste**
2 teaspoons **cumin seeds**
2 to 3 **green bird's-eye chiles**,
    seeded and sliced, plus extra
    to garnish
1-inch piece of **fresh ginger root**,
    peeled and finely chopped
2 **garlic cloves**, minced
2 oz **creamed coconut**, crumbled
½ cup boiling **beef stock**
1 cup **frozen peas**
chopped **cilantro**, to garnish

Preheat the slow cooker if necessary. Put the beef, onion, and tomatoes into the slow-cooker pot, then stir in the curry paste, cumin seeds, chiles, ginger, and garlic. Scatter with the coconut, then stir in the boiling stock.

Cover with the lid and cook on high for 30 minutes. Reduce the heat and cook on low for 7 to 9 hours, or set to auto for 7½ to 9½ hours. Stir the ground beef well to break up into small pieces, then mix in the peas and cook on high for 30 minutes or until cooked through.

When almost ready to serve, scatter with the chopped cilantro and extra sliced chiles. Serve with warmed chapatis and a tomato and red onion salad, if liked.

FOR KEEMA ALOO, make the recipe as above, replacing the ground beef with 1 lb ground lamb. Stir in 1½ cups finely diced potatoes, after adding the garlic. At the end of cooking, replace the peas with ¼ lb rinsed and drained torn spinach. Serve scattered with 4 finely sliced scallions and a little chopped cilantro.

SPICY TURKEY TORTILLAS ♥

Serves **4**
Preparation time **30 minutes**
Cooking temperature **low**
Cooking time **8 to 10 hours**

low-calorie cooking oil spray
13 oz **ground turkey breast**
1 **onion**, chopped
2 **garlic cloves**, minced
1 teaspoon **crushed dried red chiles**
1 teaspoon **cumin seeds**, crushed
1 teaspoon **mild paprika**
14 oz can **diced tomatoes**
7 oz can **red kidney beans**, drained
¾ cup **chicken stock**
1 tablespoon **tomato paste**
1 **red bell pepper**, cored, seeded,
   and diced

TO SERVE
4 x 8-inch **soft tortilla wraps**,
   1½ oz each
1 cup **lettuce leaves**
¼ cup **0% fat Greek yogurt**
½ cup shredded **reduced-fat**
   Cheddar cheese
torn **cilantro leaves**

Preheat the slow cooker if necessary. Spray a large skillet with a little low-calorie cooking oil spray and place over high heat until hot. Add the ground turkey and onion and fry for 4 to 5 minutes, stirring and breaking up the ground turkey with a wooden spoon, until it is just beginning to brown.

Stir in the garlic, chiles, cumin, and paprika, then add the tomatoes, kidney beans, stock, and tomato paste. Add the red bell pepper, season to taste, and bring to a boil. Transfer to the slow-cooker pot, cover, and cook on low for 8 to 10 hours until the turkey is cooked through.

Warm the tortillas in a hot dry skillet for 1 to 2 minutes each side, then place on 4 serving plates. Spoon the spicy turkey on top, then divide the salad leaves between each and add a spoonful of yogurt, a little Cheddar, and some torn cilantro leaves. Serve immediately.

FOR SPICY TURKEY THATCH, follow the recipe above to make and cook the spicy turkey mixture. Cut 1½ lb potatoes into chunks and cook in a saucepan of boiling water for 15 minutes or until soft. Drain and mash with ¼ cup vegetable stock, then season to taste. Place the turkey mixture in a shallow baking dish and spoon the mashed potatoes on top. Rough up the top with a fork, then brush with ½ beaten egg. Brown under a preheated hot broiler before serving.

THAI FISH CURRY

Serves **4**
Preparation time **15 minutes**
Cooking temperature **low**
Cooking time **2 to 3 hours**

1 **onion**, quartered
1 cup **cilantro leaves** and **stems**, plus
   extra to garnish
1-inch piece of **fresh ginger root**,
   peeled and sliced
1 **lemongrass stalk**, thickly sliced,
   or 1 teaspoon **lemongrass paste**
1 cup **light coconut milk**
1 cup **fish stock**
1 teaspoon **Thai fish sauce**
1 tablespoon **Thai red curry paste**
4 **salmon steaks**, 1 lb in total
low-calorie cooking oil spray
13 oz **ready-prepared mixed
   stir-fry vegetables**
grated zest and juice of 1 **lime**

Preheat the slow cooker if necessary. Place the onion, cilantro, ginger, and lemongrass in a food processor and blend until finely chopped. Transfer to a medium saucepan and stir in the coconut milk, stock, fish sauce, and curry paste. This mixture can be chilled until ready to use.

Arrange the salmon steaks in the bottom of the slow-cooker pot. Bring the coconut mixture to a boil, stirring, then pour over the salmon. Cover and cook on low for 2 to 3 hours until the salmon flakes easily when pressed in the center with a small knife.

When almost ready to serve, spray a large skillet with a little low-calorie cooking oil spray and place over high heat until hot. Add the vegetables and cook for 2 to 3 minutes until piping hot.

Break the salmon into large flakes and stir the lime zest and juice into the curry. Spoon into bowls and top with the vegetables and a little extra cilantro.

FOR THAI VEGETABLE CURRY, follow the recipe above to make the sauce, using 1 cup vegetable stock instead of the fish stock, and omitting the fish sauce if serving the curry to vegetarians. Place a 7 oz can bamboo shoots in the slow-cooker pot with 6 oz baby corn, 1 cup whole cherry tomatoes, and 1 diced zucchini. Pour over the sauce, cook, and serve with stir-fried vegetables as above.

TANDOORI CHICKEN

Serves **4**

Preparation time **20 minutes, plus
overnight marinating**

Cooking temperature **high**

Cooking time **3 to 4 hours**

¾ cup **0% fat Greek yogurt**

1½-inch piece of **fresh ginger root**,
peeled and grated

3 tablespoons chopped
cilantro leaves

3 teaspoons **medium-hot
curry powder**

½ teaspoon **ground turmeric**

1 teaspoon **paprika**

1¼ lb **boneless, skinless chicken
thighs**, cut into chunks

juice of ½ **lemon**

low-calorie cooking oil spray

salt and **pepper**

TO SERVE

1 cup **mixed salad greens**

¼ **cucumber**, diced

small handful of **cilantro leaves**

juice of ½ **lemon**

Place the yogurt in a bowl and stir in the ginger, cilantro, curry powder, turmeric, and paprika. Toss the chicken with the lemon juice, season lightly, and stir into the yogurt mixture until evenly coated. Cover with plastic wrap and marinate in the refrigerator overnight.

Preheat the slow cooker if necessary. Stir the chicken mixture, then transfer to the slow-cooker pot in an even layer. Cover and cook on high for 3 to 4 hours or until the chicken is tender and cooked through. (The yogurt will separate during cooking, but this will not affect the taste.)

Spray a large skillet with a little low-calorie cooking oil spray and place over high heat until hot. Transfer the chicken to the skillet a few pieces at a time until all the chicken is in the pan and cook for 2 to 3 minutes, turning once, until golden on both sides. This step can be omitted if you are short of time.

Toss the salad greens, cucumber, and cilantro leaves with the lemon juice, arrange on serving plates, and top with the chicken.

FOR GARLICKY TANDOORI CHICKEN, add 3 minced garlic cloves to the yogurt and spice mixture and continue as above.

TOMATO & SQUASH CURRY

Serves **4**
Preparation time **20 minutes**
Cooking temperature **low**
Cooking time **5 to 6 hours**

2 tablespoons **butter**

1 **onion**, chopped

2½ cups diced **butternut squash**, peeled and seeded

2 **garlic cloves**, minced

1½-inch piece of **fresh ginger root**, peeled and finely chopped

½ to 1 **mild red chile**, to taste, seeded and finely chopped

¼ cup **korma curry paste**

¾ cup **vegetable stock**

8 **plum tomatoes**, about 1¼ lb in total, halved

2 oz **creamed coconut**, crumbled

salt and **pepper**

coarsely chopped **cilantro**, to garnish

Preheat the slow cooker if necessary. Heat the butter in a large skillet, add the onion, and fry until softened.

Stir in the butternut squash, garlic, ginger, and chile and cook for 2 to 3 minutes. Mix in the curry paste and cook for 1 minute to release the curry flavor. Stir in the stock and bring to a boil.

Transfer the mixture to the slow-cooker pot. Arrange the tomatoes, cut-side up, in a single layer on top of the squash, then scatter with the coconut and season with a little salt and pepper. Cover with the lid and cook on low for 5 to 6 hours or until the squash is tender and the tomatoes are soft but still holding their shape.

Spoon into bowls, scatter with coarsely chopped cilantro, and serve with plain or Quick Pilau Rice (*see* below) and warmed naan bread, if liked.

FOR QUICK PILAU RICE TO ACCOMPANY THE CURRY, rinse 1¼ cups basmati rice with cold water several times, then drain. Heat 1 tablespoon butter and 1 tablespoon sunflower oil in a very large skillet. Add 1 chopped onion and fry until softened. Stir in 1 dried red chile, 1 cinnamon stick, halved, 1 teaspoon cumin seeds, 1 bay leaf, 6 crushed cardamom pods, ½ teaspoon ground turmeric, and some salt. Pour in 2 cups boiling water, cover with a lid, and simmer gently for 10 minutes. Take off the heat and let stand for 5 to 8 minutes (don't be tempted to lift the lid). When ready to serve, fluff up the rice with a fork and spoon onto plates.

FRAGRANT SPICED CHICKEN WITH CHILE

Serves **4 to 5**
Preparation time **15 minutes**
Cooking temperature **high**
Cooking time **5¼ to 6¼ hours**

3 lb **roasting chicken**
1 **onion**, chopped
1¾ cups sliced **carrots**
3-inch piece of **fresh ginger root**,
    peeled and sliced
2 **garlic cloves**, sliced
1 large **mild red chile**, halved
3 large **star anise**
¼ cup **soy sauce**
¼ cup **rice vinegar**
1 tablespoon **light brown sugar**
2 pints boiling **water**
small bunch of **cilantro**
7 oz **dried egg noodles**
¾ cup **snow peas**, thickly sliced
2 **bok choy**, about 5 oz, thickly sliced
salt and **pepper**

Preheat the slow cooker if necessary. Put the chicken, breast-side down, into the slow-cooker pot. Add the onion, carrots, ginger, garlic, chile, and star anise and spoon over the soy sauce, vinegar, and sugar.

Pour over the measurement boiling water. Cut the cilantro leaves from the stems, then add the stems to the pot, reserving the leaves. Season, cover, and cook on high for 5 to 6 hours or until the juices run clear when the thickest parts of the leg and breast are pierced with a sharp knife.

When almost ready to serve, cook the noodles following the package instructions. Lift the chicken out of the slow-cooker pot, transfer to a plate, cover with foil, and keep hot. Add the snow peas and bok choy to the slow-cooker pot, replace the lid and cook, still on high, for about 10 minutes or until just wilted.

Carve the chicken into bite-sized pieces. Drain the noodles and divide between 4 bowls. Top with the chicken and the reserved cilantro leaves, chopped, then ladle over the hot broth.

FOR ITALIAN-SPICED CHICKEN WITH PESTO, put the chicken into the pot with the onion, carrots, and garlic only and add 1 sliced fennel bulb and 1 sliced lemon. Continue as above, replacing the cilantro with basil. When the chicken is removed, add the snow peas, 3 diced tomatoes, 5 oz chopped broccolini, and 2 tablespoons pesto. Cover and cook for 5 to 10 minutes. Omit the bok choy. Cook an 8 oz package of fresh tagliatelle in a large saucepan of lightly salted boiling water following the package instructions until just tender. Drain and continue as above.

LAMB ROGAN JOSH ♥

Serves **4**
Preparation time **15 minutes**
Cooking temperature **low**
Cooking time **8 to 10 hours**

2 tablespoons **butter**
1½ lb **lamb fillet**, sliced
2 **onions**, chopped
3 **garlic cloves**, minced
1-inch piece of **fresh ginger root**,
    peeled and finely chopped
1 teaspoon **ground turmeric**
2 teaspoons **ground coriander**
2 teaspoons **cumin seeds**,
    coarsely crushed
2 teaspoons **garam masala**
½ teaspoon **crushed dried red chiles**
2 tablespoons **all-purpose flour**
14 oz can **diced tomatoes**
1¼ cups **lamb stock**
¼ cup **heavy cream**

TO GARNISH
small bunch of **cilantro**, leaves torn
shredded **red onion**

Preheat the slow cooker if necessary. Heat the butter in a skillet, add the lamb a few pieces at a time until all the meat is in the pan, then fry, stirring, over high heat until browned. Lift out of the pan with a slotted spoon and add to the slow-cooker pot.

Add the onions to the skillet and fry, stirring, for 5 minutes or until softened and just beginning to turn golden. Stir in the garlic, ginger, spices, and chiles and cook for 1 minute. Mix in the flour, then add the tomatoes and stock. Bring to a boil, stirring.

Pour the tomato mixture over the lamb, cover with the lid, and cook on low for 8 to 10 hours or until the lamb is tender. Stir in the cream, garnish with cilantro leaves, and serve with Pilau Rice (*see* below) and naan bread, if liked.

FOR PILAU RICE TO ACCOMPANY THE CURRY, rinse 1¼ cups basmati rice in a sieve several times, drain, then soak in cold water for 15 minutes. Heat 1 tablespoon butter in a saucepan, add 1 finely chopped onion, and fry for 3 minutes. Add 5 lightly crushed cardamom pods, 5 cloves, ½ cinnamon stick, ½ teaspoon ground turmeric, and ½ teaspoon salt. Cook for 1 minute. Drain the rice, add to the pan, and cook for 1 minute. Pour in 2 cups boiling water, bring back to a boil, cover tightly, and simmer gently for 10 minutes. Turn off the heat but do not remove the lid. Let stand for 8 to 10 minutes. Fluff up with a fork and serve.

NEW ORLEANS CHICKEN GUMBO

Serves **4**
Preparation time **20 minutes**
Cooking temperature **low** and **high**
Cooking time **8¼ to 10¼ hours**

2 tablespoons **olive oil**
1 lb **boneless, skinless chicken thighs**, cubed
3 oz **ready-diced chorizo**
3 oz **smoked bacon**, diced
1 **onion**, sliced
2 **garlic cloves**, chopped
2 tablespoons **all-purpose flour**
2 ½ cups **chicken stock**
2 **bay leaves**
2 **thyme sprigs**
¼ to ½ teaspoon **cayenne pepper**, to taste
3 **celery stalks**, sliced
½ each of 3 different **colored bell peppers**, cored, seeded, and sliced
¼ lb **okra**, thickly sliced (optional)
salt
chopped **parsley**, to garnish
boiled **rice**, to serve

Preheat the slow cooker if necessary. Heat the oil in a large skillet, add the chicken a few pieces at time until all the pieces are in the pan, then add the chorizo and bacon and fry, stirring, until the chicken is golden. Lift out of the pan with a slotted spoon and transfer to the slow cooker.

Add the onion to the skillet and fry until softened. Mix in the garlic, then stir in the flour. Gradually mix in the stock and add the herbs and a little salt and cayenne to taste. Bring to a boil, stirring.

Mix the celery and different colored bell peppers into the chicken, then pour over the hot onion mixture. Cover with the lid and cook on low for 8 to 10 hours or until the chicken is cooked through.

Stir the okra into the chicken gumbo, if using. Replace the lid and cook on high for 15 minutes or until the okra has just softened. Stir once more, then scatter with chopped parsley. Ladle into shallow rice-lined bowls and serve with a soup spoon and fork.

FOR CRAB GUMBO SOUP, omit the chicken and make the gumbo as above, replacing the chicken stock with 2½ cups fish stock and adding 2 sliced carrots, 2 diced sweet potatoes, and 1 diced zucchini to the slow-cooker pot with the celery and bell peppers. Add 7 oz cooked peeled jumbo shrimp, defrosted if frozen, rinsed with cold water and drained, and 7 oz drained canned white crab meat to the pot with the okra, if using, and cook on high for 20 to 30 minutes or until the fish is piping hot. Serve with rice.

CAULIFLOWER & SPINACH BALTI

Serves **4**
Preparation time **10 minutes**
Cooking temperature **low**
Cooking time **5¼ to 6¼ hours**

1 tablespoon **sunflower oil**
1 **onion**, chopped
1 lb 3 oz can or jar **ready-made balti sauce**
1 large **cauliflower**, trimmed and cut into large pieces,
    about 1½ lb prepared weight
14 oz can **green lentils**, drained
5 oz **spinach**, rinsed, drained, and torn into pieces

Preheat the slow cooker if necessary. Heat the oil
in a large skillet, add the onion, and fry, stirring, for
5 minutes or until softened. Add the balti sauce and
bring to a boil.

Put the cauliflower and lentils into the slow-cooker pot,
then pour in the hot sauce. Cover and cook on low for
5 to 6 hours or until the cauliflower is tender.

Stir the cauliflower and lentil mixture and scatter with
the spinach. Replace the lid and cook, still on low, for
10 to 15 minutes or until the spinach has just wilted.
Spoon into bowls and serve with warmed naan bread,
if liked.

FOR MUSHROOM & SWEET POTATO BALTI, make
the sauce as above. Replace the cauliflower with ¾ lb
quartered white mushrooms and 3 cups diced peeled
sweet potatoes and add to the slow-cooker pot with the
lentils. Pour in the sauce, cover with the lid, and cook
on low for 6 to 7 hours or until the sweet potatoes are
tender. Add the spinach and cook and serve as above.

CHICKEN & SWEET POTATO BALTI

Serves **4**
Preparation time **15 minutes**
Cooking temperature **high** and **low**
Cooking time **6 to 7 hours**

6 **boneless, skinless chicken thighs**, about 1 lb
    in total, cubed
1 **onion**, sliced
3 cups cubed **sweet potatoes**, cut into ¾-inch pieces
2 **garlic cloves**, minced
14 oz can or jar **balti sauce**
coarsely chopped **cilantro**, to garnish (optional)

Preheat the slow cooker if necessary. Arrange the
chicken, onion, and sweet potatoes in the bottom of
the slow-cooker pot in an even layer. Scatter with the
minced garlic.

Bring the balti sauce just to a boil in a small saucepan
or the microwave. Pour into the slow-cooker pot in an
even layer. Cover with the lid and cook on high
for 30 minutes. Reduce the heat and cook on low for
5½ to 6½ hours, or set to auto for 6 to 7 hours, until
the chicken is cooked through and the sauce piping hot.

Stir well, then scatter with coarsely chopped cilantro,
if liked. Spoon into bowls and serve with warmed naan
bread, if liked.

FOR HARISSA-BAKED CHICKEN WITH SWEET POTATO,
prepare the chicken and vegetables as above. Replace
the balti curry sauce with a 14 oz can diced tomatoes
and 2 teaspoons harissa. Continue as above.

SPICED DATE & CHICKPEA PILAF

Serves **4**
Preparation time **15 minutes**
Cooking temperature **low**
Cooking time **3 to 4 hours**

1 tablespoon **olive oil**
1 **onion**, chopped
1 to 2 **garlic cloves**, minced
1½-inch piece of **fresh ginger root**,
   peeled and finely chopped
1 teaspoon **ground turmeric**
1 teaspoon **ground cumin**, plus extra
   to garnish
1 teaspoon **ground coriander**
1 cup **converted long-grain
   brown rice**
14 oz can **chickpeas**, drained
½ cup **ready-chopped pitted dates**
2 pints **vegetable stock**
salt and **pepper**

ONION GARNISH
1 tablespoon **olive oil**
1 **onion**, thinly sliced
¾ cup **Greek yogurt**
chopped **cilantro**

Preheat the slow cooker if necessary. Heat the oil in a large skillet, add the onion, and fry, stirring, for 5 minutes or until softened and just beginning to turn golden.

Stir in the garlic, ginger, and ground spices and cook for 1 minute. Add the rice, chickpeas, dates, stock, and a little salt and pepper and bring to a boil, stirring. Pour into the slow-cooker pot, cover with the lid, and cook on low for 3 to 4 hours or until the rice is tender and almost all the stock has been absorbed.

When almost ready to serve, make the onion garnish. Heat the oil in a skillet, add the sliced onion, and fry over medium heat, stirring, until crisp and golden. Stir the pilaf, spoon into bowls, and top with a spoonful of the yogurt, a little extra cumin, the onions, and a little chopped cilantro.

FOR CHICKEN & ALMOND PILAF, add 1 lb diced boneless, skinless chicken thighs to the skillet with the onion. Continue as above, omitting the dates. To serve, replace the onion garnish with ½ cup sliced almonds, fried in the oil until golden, and a little chopped mint, if liked.

MEDITERRANEAN

VEGETABLE MOUSSAKA

Serves **4**
Preparation time **25 minutes**
Cooking temperature **low**
Cooking time **6¾ to 9¼ hours**

low-calorie cooking oil spray
1 **onion**, coarsely chopped
1 large **eggplant**, sliced
2 **garlic cloves**, minced
1 **red bell pepper**, cored, seeded,
    and cut into chunks
1 **yellow bell pepper**, cored, seeded,
    and cut into chunks
2 large **zucchini**, thickly sliced
2 cups **tomato purée**
¾ cup **vegetable stock**
½ cup **dried Puy lentils**, rinsed
    and drained
leaves from 3 **rosemary**
    sprigs, chopped
1 teaspoon **granulated sweetener**
salt and **pepper**

TOPPING
1 cup **0% fat Greek yogurt**
3 **eggs**
¼ cup freshly shredded
    Parmesan cheese

Preheat the slow cooker if necessary. Spray a large skillet with a little low-calorie cooking oil spray and place over high heat until hot. Add the onion and eggplant and fry for 4 to 5 minutes, stirring, until just beginning to brown. Add the garlic, bell peppers, and zucchini and cook for 2 minutes more, then add the tomato purée, stock, and lentils.

Add the rosemary and sweetener and season to taste. Bring to a boil, stirring, then transfer to the slow-cooker pot. Cover and cook on low for 6 to 8 hours until the lentils are tender.

Mix the yogurt, eggs, and a little pepper together in a bowl until smooth. Stir the vegetable mixture, then smooth the surface with the back of a spoon. Pour the yogurt mixture over the top in an even layer and sprinkle with the Parmesan. Cover and continue cooking for 45 minutes to 1¼ hours until the yogurt mixture has set.

Lift the pot out of the housing using oven mitts, then place under a preheated hot broiler for 4 to 5 minutes until the top is golden. Serve with a green salad, if liked.

FOR PENNE WITH MEDITERRANEAN VEGETABLES, make and cook the vegetable and lentil mixture as above. Cook 3¼ oz dried wholewheat penne in a saucepan of lightly salted boiling water following the package instructions until just tender. Drain and stir into the cooked vegetables, spoon into shallow dishes, and sprinkle with ¼ cup freshly grated Parmesan cheese.

TOMATO-BRAISED SQUID WITH CHORIZO

Serves **4**
Preparation time **20 minutes**
Cooking temperature **low**
Cooking time **3½ to 5½ hours**

1¼ lb **prepared squid tubes**, chilled
1 **onion**, thinly sliced
4 oz **ready-diced chorizo**
1¾ cups **white mushrooms**, sliced
1 **red bell pepper**, cored, seeded,
    and sliced
2 **garlic cloves**, minced
leaves from 2 to 3 **rosemary sprigs**
1 tablespoon **tomato paste**
1 teaspoon **superfine sugar**
14 oz can **diced tomatoes**
½ cup **red wine**
1 tablespoon **cornstarch**
salt and **pepper**
chopped **parsley**, to garnish

Preheat the slow cooker if necessary. Rinse the squid inside and out, pulling out the tentacles and reserving. Drain and slice the tubes. Put the tentacles in a bowl, cover with plastic wrap, and let chill in the refrigerator until required.

Put the onion, chorizo, mushrooms, and red bell pepper into the slow-cooker pot. Add the garlic, rosemary, tomato paste, and sugar, then stir in the sliced squid.

Pour the tomatoes and wine into a saucepan and bring to a boil or heat in the microwave. Add a little salt and pepper, then pour into the slow-cooker pot and stir well. Cover with the lid and cook on low for 3 to 5 hours or until the squid is tender.

Put the cornstarch in a small bowl with a little cold water and mix to a smooth paste. Stir into the slow-cooker pot, add the squid tentacles, then replace the lid and cook, still on low, for 30 minutes. Spoon into bowls and scatter with chopped parsley. Serve with thickly sliced bread or rice, if liked.

FOR TOMATO-BRAISED SQUID WITH RED ONION, replace the onion, mushrooms, and chorizo with 2 large thinly sliced red onions and add to the slow-cooker pot along with the red bell pepper, garlic, tomato paste, and sugar, adding 2 bay leaves instead of the rosemary. Add the squid and continue as above.

MOUSSAKA

Serves **4**
Preparation time **30 minutes**
Cooking temperature **low**
Cooking time **8¾ to 11¼ hours**

¼ cup **olive oil**, divided
1 large **eggplant**, thinly sliced
1 lb **ground lamb**
1 **onion**, chopped
2 **garlic cloves**, minced
1 tablespoon **all-purpose flour**
14 oz can **diced tomatoes**
1 cup **lamb stock**
1 teaspoon **ground cinnamon**
¼ teaspoon grated **nutmeg**
1 tablespoon **tomato paste**
salt and **pepper**

TOPPING
3 **eggs**
1 cup **plain yogurt**
½ cup crumbled **feta cheese**
pinch of grated **nutmeg**

Preheat the slow cooker if necessary. Heat half the oil in a skillet and fry the eggplant slices in batches, adding more oil as needed until they have all been fried and are softened and lightly browned on both sides. Drain and transfer to a plate.

Add the ground lamb and onion to the skillet and dry-fry, stirring and breaking up the lamb with a wooden spoon, until evenly browned. Stir in the garlic and flour, then mix in the tomatoes, stock, spices, tomato paste, and a little salt and pepper. Bring to a boil, stirring.

Spoon the lamb mixture into the slow-cooker pot and arrange the eggplant slices on top, overlapping. Cover and cook on low for 8 to 10 hours.

Make the topping. Mix together the eggs, yogurt, feta, and nutmeg and spoon evenly over the top of the eggplant. Replace the lid and cook, still on low, for ¾ to 1¼ hours or until set. Lift the pot out of the housing using oven mitts and brown under a preheated hot broiler. Serve with a salad, if liked.

FOR GREEK SHEPHERD'S PIE, prepare the meat mixture, top with the fried eggplant slices, and cook as above. Omit the topping and instead cut 1½ lb potatoes into chunks and cook in a saucepan of boiling water for 15 minutes or until soft. Drain and mash with 3 tablespoons Greek yogurt and some salt and pepper. Lift the pot out of the housing using oven mitts, spoon the mashed potatoes onto the eggplant, dot with 2 tablespoons butter, and brown under a preheated hot broiler.

SLOW-BRAISED PORK WITH RATATOUILLE

Serves **4**
Preparation time **20 minutes**
Cooking temperature **high**
Cooking time **7 to 9 hours**

1 tablespoon **olive oil**
1 **onion**, chopped
1 **red bell pepper**, cored, seeded, and cut into chunks
1 **yellow bell pepper**, cored, seeded, and cut into chunks
¾ lb **zucchini**, cut into chunks
2 **garlic cloves**, minced
14 oz can **diced tomatoes**
¾ cup **red wine** or **chicken stock**
1 tablespoon **cornstarch**
leaves from 2 to 3 **rosemary sprigs**
1¾ lb piece of **thick-end pork belly**, rind and any string removed
salt and **pepper**
mashed potatoes, to serve

Preheat the slow cooker if necessary. Heat the oil in a skillet, add the onion and fry, stirring, for 5 minutes or until just beginning to turn golden.

Add the bell peppers, zucchini, and garlic and fry for 2 minutes, then mix in the tomatoes and the wine or stock. Mix the cornstarch to a smooth paste with a little cold water, then stir into the pan with the rosemary leaves and some seasoning. Bring to a boil, stirring.

Tip half the mixture into the slow-cooker pot, add the unrolled pork belly, and cover with the rest of the vegetable mixture. Cover with the lid and cook on high for 7 to 9 hours or until the pork is almost falling apart. If you prefer a thicker sauce, ladle it out of the pot into a saucepan and boil for 5 minutes to reduce down. Cut the pork into 4 pieces, then spoon into shallow dishes and serve with mashed potatoes and the tomato sauce.

FOR BRAISED CHICKEN WITH RATATOUILLE, fry 4 chicken leg pieces in 1 tablespoon olive oil until browned on both sides. Drain and transfer to the slow-cooker pot. Make the ratatouille as above, spoon it over the chicken, and cook on high for 5 to 6 hours or until the chicken is tender and cooked through.

SAUSAGE TAGLIATELLE

Serves **4**
Preparation time **25 minutes**
Cooking temperature **low**
Cooking time **8 to 10 hours**

1 tablespoon **sunflower oil**
8 **chile-** or **spicy-flavored sausages**
1 **onion**, chopped
2 cups sliced **mushrooms**
2 **garlic cloves**, minced
14 oz can **diced tomatoes**
¾ cup **beef stock**
8 oz **dried tagliatelle**
salt and **pepper**

TO SERVE
torn **basil leaves**
freshly grated **Parmesan**
cheese (optional)

Preheat the slow cooker if necessary. Heat the oil in a large skillet, add the sausages, and fry until browned all over but not cooked through. Transfer to the slow-cooker pot with long-handled tongs.

Pour the excess fat out of the skillet but leave 2 teaspoons behind, then add the onion and fry until softened. Mix in the mushrooms and garlic and fry for 1 to 2 minutes.

Stir in the diced tomatoes, stock, and a little salt and pepper and bring to a boil, stirring. Pour the mixture over the sausages, cover with the lid, and cook on low for 8 to 10 hours or until cooked through.

When almost ready to serve, cook the tagliatelle in a large saucepan of lightly salted boiling water following the package instructions until just tender, then drain. Lift the sausages out of the slow-cooker pot and slice thickly, then return to the pot with the pasta and mix together. Scatter with torn basil leaves and serve with freshly shredded Parmesan and a green salad, if liked.

FOR CHICKEN & CHORIZO TAGLIATELLE, omit the sausages and fry 1 lb diced boneless chicken thighs in 1 tablespoon olive oil until golden. Drain and transfer to the slow-cooker pot. Continue as above, adding 3½ oz diced chorizo sausage to the skillet with the onions and replacing the beef stock with ¾ cup chicken stock.

HOT SPANISH BEANS

Serves **4**
Preparation time **10 minutes**
Cooking temperature **high**
Cooking time **4 to 5 hours**

4 oz **chorizo sausage**, sliced
1 **red onion**, chopped
2 x 14 oz cans **navy beans**, drained
2½ cups **cherry tomatoes**
2 **garlic cloves**, minced
leaves from 2 to 3 **rosemary sprigs**
¾ lb package **frankfurters**, chilled,
  drained, and thickly sliced
½ cup **marinated mixed
  olives** (optional)
1 cup boiling **vegetable stock**
1 tablespoon **tomato paste**
salt and **pepper**

Preheat the slow cooker if necessary. Put the chorizo, onion, and navy beans into the slow-cooker pot, add the tomatoes, garlic, and rosemary and mix together. Arrange the frankfurters and olives, if using, on the top.

Mix the boiling stock with the tomato paste and a little salt and pepper, then pour into the slow-cooker pot. Cover with the lid and cook on high for 4 to 5 hours. Stir the beans, then spoon into bowls. Serve with hot peppered foccacia or garlic bread and a green leafy salad, if liked.

FOR MUSTARD BEANS, put the onion, beans, tomatoes, and garlic in the slow-cooker pot, omitting the chorizo, rosemary, and olives. Add 1 cored, seeded, and diced red bell pepper. Mix the stock with 2 tablespoons each tomato paste and Worcestershire sauce, 1 tablespoon Dijon mustard, ½ teaspoon smoked paprika, and salt and pepper. Pour over the beans and add the frankfurters. Continue as above.

CHICKEN AVGOLEMONO

Serves **4**
Preparation time **30 minutes**
Cooking temperature **high** and **low**
Cooking time **6 to 8 hours**

8 **boneless, skinless chicken thighs**,
    about 1 lb 6 oz in total, each cut into
    3 or 4 pieces
1 **onion**, thinly sliced
2 to 3 **oregano** or **basil sprigs**
2 cups boiling **chicken stock**
grated zest and juice of 1 **lemon**
10 oz **dried macaroni** or **orzo**
2 **eggs**
2 **egg yolks**
¼ cup chopped **parsley**, plus extra
    to garnish (optional)
salt and **pepper**
lemon zest curls, to garnish (optional)

Preheat the slow cooker if necessary. Put the chicken, onion, and herbs into the slow-cooker pot. Mix the boiling stock, lemon zest and juice, and salt and pepper together, then pour over the chicken.

Cover with the lid and cook on high for 30 minutes. Reduce the heat and cook on low for 5½ to 7½ hours, or set to auto for 6 to 8 hours, until the chicken is cooked through and tender. When almost ready to serve, cook the pasta in a large saucepan of lightly salted boiling water following the package instructions until just tender, then drain.

Meanwhile, drain the stock from the slow-cooker pot into a second large saucepan and boil for 5 minutes until reduced by one-third or to approximately 1 cup. Beat the whole eggs and egg yolks in a bowl, then gradually beat in 2 ladlefuls of the stock until smooth. Pour into the reduced stock, then beat over very low heat until thickened slightly. Stir in the parsley.

Pour the sauce over the chicken. Spoon the pasta into bowls and top with the chicken. Sprinkle with lemon zest curls and extra chopped parsley, if liked.

FOR SALMON AVGOLEMONO, lower a thick piece of salmon, about 1 lb in weight, into the slow-cooker pot over a double-thickness strip of foil, add 6 thinly sliced scallions, and the oregano or basil. Pour in 1½ cups boiling fish stock mixed with the lemon zest and juice, as above, and salt and pepper. Cover and cook on low for 2½ to 3 hours or until the fish flakes easily when pressed in the center with a knife. Cook the pasta and make the sauce as above. Lift the salmon out with the foil, remove and discard the skin, flake the flesh into large chunks, then toss with the sauce and pasta.

FEIJOADA HAM ♥

Serves 4
Preparation time **20 minutes**
Cooking temperature **high**
Cooking time **5 to 6 hours**

1 **onion**, chopped
2 **celery stalks**, thickly sliced
1 cup diced **carrots**
12 oz can **black beans**, drained
1 **red chile**, halved and seeded
2 **thyme sprigs**
pared zest of 1 **orange**
1 lb **unsmoked ham**, trimmed of fat
1 teaspoon **mild paprika**
½ teaspoon **ground allspice**
2 cups hot **vegetable stock**
salt and **pepper**
¼ cup chopped **parsley**, to garnish
boiled **rice**, to serve (optional)

Preheat the slow cooker if necessary. Place the onion, celery, and carrot in the slow-cooker pot, then add the beans, chile, thyme, and orange zest. Nestle the ham in the center.

Stir the paprika and allspice into the hot stock, then season to taste and pour over the ham. Spoon some of the orange zest and thyme on top of the ham, cover with the lid, and cook on high for 5 to 6 hours until the ham is very tender.

When almost ready to serve, cook the rice in a saucepan of lightly salted boiling water following the package instructions until tender.

Cut the ham into pieces, then spoon into shallow bowls with the beans, vegetables, and sauce. Scatter with the parsley and serve with rice, if liked.

FOR FEIJOADA CHICKEN, substitute a 2 lb 10 oz roasting chicken for the ham and follow the recipe above. Cook on high for 5 to 6 hours or until the chicken is thoroughly cooked and the meat juices run clear when the thickest parts of the leg and breast are pierced with a sharp knife.

RIOJA-BRAISED LAMB WITH OLIVES

Serves **4**
Preparation time **20 minutes**
Cooking temperature **high**
Cooking time **5 to 6 hours**

2 tablespoons **olive oil**
4 **lamb shanks**, 3 lb in total
2 **red onions**, cut into wedges
4 large **garlic cloves**, halved
1¼ cups **Rioja** or **lamb stock**
14 oz can **diced tomatoes**
1 tablespoon **redcurrant jelly**
3 **rosemary sprigs**
1 cup **mixed pitted olives**
salt and **pepper**

Preheat the slow cooker if necessary. Heat 1 tablespoon of the oil in a large skillet, season the lamb shanks, then add them to the pan and brown on all sides. Lift them out of the skillet and put them in the slow-cooker pot with the meatiest parts downward.

Add the remaining oil and onion wedges to the skillet and fry for 3 to 4 minutes until just beginning to color. Add the garlic, wine or stock, tomatoes, redcurrant jelly, and rosemary. Season with salt and pepper and bring to a boil, stirring.

Scatter the olives over the lamb, then pour over the hot onion mixture. Cover with the lid and cook on high for 5 to 6 hours until the lamb is very tender.

When ready to serve, pour the liquid out of the slow cooker into a saucepan and boil for 10 minutes until reduced by half. Put the lamb into shallow bowls lined with some runny polenta flavored with butter and Parmesan cheese or mashed potatoes, if liked, spoon over the onions and olives, and serve with the Rioja sauce.

FOR RIOJA-BRAISED CHICKEN WITH OLIVES, substitute a 3 lb roasting chicken for the lamb shanks and cook as above, with the chicken cooked breast-side down in the liquid, until the chicken is cooked through and the juices run clear when the thickest parts of the leg and breast are pierced with a sharp knife.

BALSAMIC TOMATOES WITH SPAGHETTI

Serves **4**
Preparation time **10 minutes**
Cooking temperature **high**
Cooking time **3 to 4 hours**

1 tablespoon **olive oil**, for oiling
1½ lb **plum tomatoes**, halved
¼ cup **white wine**
4 teaspoons **good-quality**
    balsamic vinegar
12 oz **dried spaghetti**
salt and **pepper**
basil leaves, to garnish
Parmesan cheese shavings, to serve

Preheat the slow cooker if necessary. Brush the oil over the bottom of the slow-cooker pot, add the tomatoes, cut-side down, drizzle over the wine and vinegar, and add a little salt and pepper. Cover with the lid and cook on high for 3 to 4 hours or until the tomatoes are tender.

When almost ready to serve, cook the spaghetti in a large saucepan of lightly salted boiling water following the package instructions until just tender. Drain and mix into the sauce. Spoon the pasta into bowls and scatter with basil leaves and Parmesan shavings.

FOR PESTO-BAKED TOMATOES, oil the bottom of the slow-cooker pot as above, sprinkling with 2 minced garlic cloves before adding the tomatoes. Drizzle with the wine and 1 tablespoon pesto, omitting the vinegar. Cook and serve as above.

PHEASANT WITH PANCETTA

Serves **4**
Preparation time **35 minutes**
Cooking temperature **low**
Cooking time **2½ to 3 hours**

4 **pheasant breasts**, about 1¼ lb in total
small bunch of **sage**
3½ oz **smoked pancetta**, sliced
2 tablespoons **butter**
7 oz **shallots**, halved if large
2 tablespoons **all-purpose flour**
¾ cup **hard dry cider**
¾ cup **chicken stock**
1 teaspoon **Dijon mustard**
1 **apple**, cored and sliced
7¾ oz can **whole peeled
  chestnuts**, drained
salt and **pepper**
steamed **baby carrots**, to serve

Preheat the slow cooker if necessary. Rinse the pheasant breasts with cold water, pat dry with paper towels, and season well with salt and pepper. Top each pheasant breast with a few sage leaves, then wrap in pancetta slices until completely covered. Tie at intervals with kitchen string to keep the pancetta in place.

Heat the butter in a skillet, add the shallots, and fry for 4 to 5 minutes or until browned. Stir in the flour, then add the hard cider, stock, and mustard. Add the apple and chestnuts and a little extra salt and pepper. Bring to a boil, stirring.

Arrange the pheasant breasts in the slow-cooker pot. Pour the hot onion mixture over the top, cover with the lid, and cook on low for 2½ to 3 hours or until the pheasant is tender and cooked through to the center. Spoon onto plates, remove the string from the pheasant and serve with baby carrots.

FOR PHEASANT WITH BACON & RED WINE, lay 4 slices smoked bacon on a cutting board and stretch with the flat of a cook's knife until half as long again. Add a sage leaf to each pheasant breast, then wrap each one with a stretched bacon slice. Fry as above with the shallots until the bacon is browned. Stir in the flour, then add ¾ cup red wine in place of the hard cider, stock, and mustard. Omit the apple and instead add 8 halved ready-to-eat pitted prunes and the chestnuts. Cook as above.

PEASANT PAELLA ♥

Serves **4**
Preparation time **20 minutes**
Cooking temperature **high**
Cooking time **4¾ to 6 hours**

low-calorie cooking oil spray
1 lb **boneless, skinless chicken thighs,** cubed
1 **onion**, chopped
2¼ oz **chorizo sausage**, sliced
2 **garlic cloves**, minced
1 **red bell pepper**, cored, seeded, and diced
1 **orange bell pepper**, cored, seeded, and diced
2 **celery stalks**, diced
2 pinches of **saffron threads**
½ teaspoon **dried Mediterranean herbs**
3¼ cups hot **chicken stock**
1 cup **converted long-grain brown rice**
¾ cup **frozen peas**
salt and **pepper**
2 tablespoons chopped **parsley**, to garnish

Preheat the slow cooker if necessary. Spray a large skillet with a little low-calorie cooking oil spray and place over high heat until hot. Add the chicken a few pieces at a time until all the chicken is in the pan and cook for 5 minutes, stirring, until browned. Use a slotted spoon to transfer the chicken to the slow-cooker pot.

Add the onion, chorizo, and garlic to the skillet and cook for 3 to 4 minutes, stirring, until the onion is beginning to color. Add the bell peppers and celery, stir well, then transfer to the slow-cooker pot. Mix the saffron and dried herbs with the hot stock, season to taste, then pour into the slow-cooker pot and stir well. Cover and cook on high for 3 to 4 hours.

Place the rice in a sieve and rinse under cold running water, then drain and stir into the chicken mixture. Cover again and cook, still on high, for 1½ to 1¾ hours until the rice is tender. Stir in the peas and continue cooking for 15 minutes. Serve garnished with the chopped parsley.

FOR SEAFOOD PAELLA, follow the recipe above to cook the paella, omitting the chicken. Defrost 14 oz frozen mixed seafood from a package and pat dry on paper towels. Spray a large skillet with a little low-calorie cooking oil spray and place over high heat until hot. Add the seafood and fry for 4 to 5 minutes until piping hot. Stir into the finished paella and garnish with the parsley.

PORK PUTTANESCA

Serves **4**
Preparation time **20 minutes**
Cooking temperature **high**
Cooking time **7 to 8 hours**

low-calorie cooking oil spray
1¼ lb **lean pork**, diced
1 **onion**, chopped
2 **garlic cloves**, minced
14 oz can **diced tomatoes**
4 teaspoons **sherry vinegar**
½ oz **basil**, coarsely torn, plus extra
   to garnish
1 tablespoon drained **capers in**
   brine, chopped
¼ cup **pitted olives**, chopped
salt and **pepper**
chopped **parsley**, to garnish
6 oz **dried spaghetti**, boiled, to serve

Preheat the slow cooker if necessary. Spray a large skillet with a little low-calorie cooking oil spray and place over high heat until hot. Add the pork a few pieces at a time until all the meat is in the pan and cook for 5 minutes, stirring, until browned. Use a slotted spoon to transfer the pork to a plate.

Add a little more low-calorie cooking oil spray to the skillet if necessary, then add the onion and cook for 4 to 5 minutes, stirring, until just beginning to brown. Add the garlic, tomatoes, vinegar, and basil. Bring to a boil, stirring.

Mix the capers and olives together and add half to the sauce, reserving the rest for garnish.

Transfer the pork to the slow-cooker pot, then pour over the sauce. Cover and cook on high for 7 to 8 hours until the pork is tender. Stir, then scatter with the reserved capers and olives, some extra basil, and a little chopped parsley. Serve with the cooked spaghetti.

FOR PORK OSSO BUCCO, follow the recipe above, using 2 tablespoons chopped parsley mixed with the grated zest of 1 lemon and 2 minced garlic cloves instead of the capers and olives. Serve with 1 cup rice, boiled with a few saffron threads.

SKINNY SPAGHETTI BOLOGNESE ♥

Serves **4**
Preparation time **20 minutes**
Cooking temperature **low**
Cooking time **8 to 10 hours**

low-calorie cooking oil spray
1 lb **extra-lean ground beef**
1 **onion**, finely chopped
2 **garlic cloves**, minced
1 **carrot**, coarsely grated
2 **zucchini**, coarsely grated
2 cups sliced **baby mushrooms**
2 cups **tomato purée**
¾ cup **beef stock**
1 teaspoon **dried oregano**
salt and **pepper**

TO SERVE
10 oz **dried spaghetti**
handful of **oregano** or **basil leaves**

Spray a large skillet with low-calorie cooking oil spray and place over high heat until hot. Add the ground beef and onion and cook for 5 minutes, stirring and breaking up the beef with a wooden spoon, until evenly browned. Stir in the garlic, carrot, zucchini, and mushrooms. Add the tomato purée, stock, and oregano, then season to taste. Bring to a boil, stirring. Transfer to the slow-cooker pot, cover, and cook on low for 8 to 10 hours.

Cook the spaghetti in a large saucepan of lightly salted boiling water following the package instructions until just tender. Drain well, toss with the Bolognese sauce, and serve scattered with the oregano or basil leaves.

FOR ITALIAN SHEPHERD'S PIE, make the Bolognese sauce as above. Cook 1 lb potatoes and 1 lb turnips, cut into chunks, in a saucepan of lightly salted boiling water for 15 to 20 minutes until tender. Drain and mash with ¼ cup vegetable stock (or ¼ cup cooking water). Beat 1 egg and stir half into the mashed vegetables, then season to taste. Lift the pot out of the housing using oven mitts. Spoon the mashed vegetable mixture over the Bolognese sauce and rough up the top with a fork. Brush with the remaining beaten egg and brown under a preheated hot broiler before serving.

EGGPLANT PARMIGIANA ♥

Serves **4**
Preparation time **20 minutes**
Cooking temperature **high**
Cooking time **4 to 5 hours**

1 tablespoon **olive oil**
1 **onion**, chopped
2 **garlic cloves**, minced
¾ lb **tomatoes**, diced
14 oz can **diced tomatoes**
small handful of **basil**, torn, plus extra to garnish
2 teaspoons **granulated sweetener**
2 teaspoons **cornstarch**
2 large **eggplants**, sliced
¾ cup shredded **sharp Cheddar cheese**
salt and **pepper**
2 tablespoons freshly shredded **Parmesan cheese**, to garnish

Preheat the slow cooker if necessary. Heat the oil in a large skillet over medium heat, add the onion, and cook for 4 to 5 minutes until just beginning to soften. Add the garlic, fresh tomatoes, canned tomatoes, basil, and sweetener. Mix the cornstarch to a smooth paste with a little cold water and stir into the sauce. Season to taste and bring to a boil, stirring.

Spoon a little of the tomato sauce over the bottom of the slow-cooker pot and arrange one-third of the eggplant slices, overlapping, on top. Spoon over a thin layer of the sauce and scatter with a little shredded Cheddar. Repeat to make 3 eggplant layers, finishing with a generous layer of sauce and shredded Cheddar.

Cover and cook on high for 4 to 5 hours until the eggplant is soft. Sprinkle with the Parmesan, scatter with the extra basil, and serve.

FOR MUSHROOM PARMIGIANA, follow the recipe above to make the tomato sauce, then layer in the slow-cooker pot with 8 large flat field mushrooms, in 2 layers, and the Cheddar. Cook and serve as above.

CHICKEN CACCIATORE ♥

Serves **4**
Preparation time **20 minutes**
Cooking temperature **low**
Cooking time **8 to 9 hours**

low-calorie cooking oil spray
1 lb **boneless, skinless chicken thighs**, cubed
1 **onion**, chopped
2 **garlic cloves**, minced
1 **red bell pepper**, cored, seeded, and diced
1 **orange bell pepper**, cored, seeded, and diced
2 **celery stalks**, diced
¾ cup **chicken stock**
14 oz can **diced tomatoes**
1 tablespoon **tomato paste**
1 tablespoon **balsamic vinegar**
leaves from 2 **rosemary sprigs**, chopped
7 oz **dried tagliatelle**
salt and **pepper**
2 tablespoons chopped **parsley**, to garnish

Preheat the slow cooker if necessary. Spray a large skillet with a little low-calorie cooking oil spray and place over high heat until hot. Add the chicken a few pieces at a time until all the chicken is in the pan and cook for 3 to 4 minutes, stirring, until just beginning to brown. Add the onion and continue to cook until the chicken is golden and the onion has softened.

Stir in the garlic, bell peppers, and celery, then add the stock, tomatoes, tomato paste, balsamic vinegar, and rosemary. Season generously and bring to a boil, stirring. Transfer to the slow-cooker pot, cover, and cook on low for 8 to 9 hours until the chicken is tender and cooked through.

When almost ready to serve, cook the tagliatelle in a large saucepan of lightly salted boiling water following the package instructions until just tender. Drain, then toss with the chicken mixture and serve garnished with the parsley.

FOR POTATO-TOPPED CACCIATORE, follow the recipe above and place all the ingredients in the slow-cooker pot. Thinly slice 1¼ lb potatoes and arrange them on top of the chicken mixture, overlapping. Press the potatoes down into the liquid, then cover and cook on high for 5 to 6 hours until the potatoes and chicken are cooked through. If liked, lift the pot out of the housing using oven mitts, spray the potatoes with a little extra low-calorie cooking oil spray, and place under a preheated hot broiler until the potatoes are golden.

DESSERTS

CHERRY & COCONUT SPONGE PUDDING

Serves **4 to 6**
Preparation time **15 minutes**
Cooking temperature **high**
Cooking time **3 to 3½ hours**

butter, for greasing
¾ cup **desiccated coconut**, divided
14 oz can **cherry pie filling**
16 oz package **vanilla cake mix**
¼ cup **sunflower oil** or 1 **egg**,
   according to the cake
   mix instructions

Preheat the slow cooker if necessary. Lightly butter a 3-pint pudding bowl and line the bottom with a disk of nonstick parchment paper, checking first that it will fit in the slow-cooker pot. Sprinkle in a little of the coconut, then tilt and turn the bowl until the buttery sides are lightly coated. Spoon half the cherry pie filling into the bottom of the bowl.

Add the cake mix to another bowl and beat in the oil or egg and water following the package instructions. Stir in the remaining coconut to combine, then spoon the batter into the bowl with the cherry pie filling, spreading the batter evenly. Cover the top with buttered, domed foil and lower the bowl into the slow-cooker pot.

Pour boiling water into the pot to come halfway up the sides of the bowl. Cover with the lid and cook on high for 3 to 3½ hours or until the cake is well risen, feels dry, and springs back when pressed with a fingertip.

Lift the bowl out of the slow-cooker pot using a dish towel and remove the foil. Loosen the edge of the cake with a knife, turn out onto a plate, and peel off the lining paper. Heat the remaining pie filling in a small saucepan or the microwave until hot. Serve in bowls drizzled with the warm cherries and vanilla ice cream on the side, if liked.

FOR SPICED CHOCOLATE CHERRY SPONGE PUDDING, line the pudding bowl with cherry pie filling as above, omitting the coconut. Make a 16-oz package of chocolate-flavored cake mix adding 1 teaspoon ground cinnamon and the sunflower oil or egg, and continue as above.

HOT CHOCOLATE MOUSSES

Serves **4**
Preparation time **25 minutes**
Cooking temperature **high**
Cooking time **1 to 1¼ hours**

7 oz **semisweet chocolate**,
   broken into pieces
½ stick **butter**, plus extra for greasing
4 **eggs**, separated
¼ cup **superfine sugar**
1 tablespoon warm **water**
sifted **powdered sugar**, to decorate

MINT CREAM
¼ cup **heavy cream**
4 teaspoons chopped **mint**

Preheat the slow cooker if necessary. Put the chocolate and butter in a bowl set over a saucepan of very gently simmering water, ensuring that the water does not touch the bottom of the bowl, and let stand until just melted.

Meanwhile, butter 4 mugs, each with a 1-cup capacity, checking first that they will fit in the slow-cooker pot.

Beat the egg whites in a bowl until soft peaks form, then gradually beat in the sugar a teaspoonful at a time until it has all been added and the meringue is thick and glossy. Carefully lift the bowl of melted chocolate and butter off of the saucepan, stir in the egg yolks and measurement water to combine, then gently fold in a spoonful of the egg whites to loosen the mixture. Fold in the remaining egg whites, then divide between the mugs.

Cover the tops with domed foil and place in the slow-cooker pot. Pour boiling water into the pot to come halfway up the sides of the mugs. Cover with the lid and cook on high for 1 to 1¼ hours or until the puddings are softly set in the center.

Lift the mugs out of the slow-cooker pot using a dish towel and remove the foil. Mix the cream and mint together and pour into a pitcher. Dust the mousses with powdered sugar and serve immediately with the mint cream.

FOR GINGER AND CHOCOLATE MOUSSES WITH ORANGE CREAM, add 4 teaspoons drained, finely chopped stem ginger to the mousse mixture and cook as above. To serve with the hot mousses, stir an extra 2 teaspoons drained, finely chopped stem ginger and the finely grated zest of 1 orange into ¼ cup crème fraîche in a bowl.

APRICOT & ORANGE FOOL

Serves **6**
Preparation time **20 minutes**,
   plus cooling
Cooking temperature **low**
Cooking time **3 to 4 hours**

8 oz **ready-to-eat dried apricots**
grated zest and juice of 1 **orange**
2 tablespoons **superfine sugar**
1¼ cups cold **water**
2 x 4½ oz cartons **ready-made custard**
   or **vanilla pudding**
2 cups **plain yogurt**

Preheat the slow cooker if necessary. Put the apricots, orange zest and juice, and sugar into the slow-cooker pot and pour over the measurement water. Cover and cook on low for 3 to 4 hours or until the apricots are plump.

Lift the pot out of the housing using oven mitts and let the apricots cool, then purée with a hand-held stick blender or transfer to a blender and blend until smooth.

Fold the custard (or pudding) and yogurt together until just mixed, then add the apricot purée and very lightly mix for a marbled effect. Spoon into glass dessert dishes and serve with dainty cookies, if liked.

FOR PRUNE & VANILLA FOOL, put 8 oz ready-to-eat pitted prunes, 1 teaspoon vanilla extract, 2 tablespoons liquid honey, and 1¼ cups cold water in the slow-cooker pot and then cook, cool, and make the fool as above.

ICED JAMAICAN GINGER CAKE

Serves **6**

Preparation time **25 minutes**, **plus cooling** and **setting**

Cooking temperature **high**

Cooking time **4½ to 5 hours**

1 stick **butter**, plus extra for greasing

½ cup **dark brown sugar**

½ cup **light corn syrup**

½ cup chopped **pitted dates**

¾ cup **wholewheat flour**

¾ cup **all-purpose flour**, sifted with
    ¾ teaspoon **baking powder**

½ teaspoon **baking soda**

2 teaspoons **ground ginger**

3 pieces of **stem ginger**, drained
    of syrup, 2 chopped and 1 cut
    into strips

2 **eggs**, beaten

½ cup **milk**

1 cup **powdered sugar**

3 to 3½ teaspoons **water**

Preheat the slow cooker if necessary. Butter a soufflé dish 5½ inches in diameter and 3½ inches deep and line the bottom with a disk of nonstick parchment paper, checking first that it will fit in the slow-cooker pot.

Put the butter, sugar, syrup, and dates into a saucepan and heat gently, stirring, until the butter and sugar have melted. Remove the pan from the heat, add the flours, baking soda, ground and chopped ginger, eggs, and milk and beat until smooth. Pour into the lined dish and cover the top loosely with buttered foil.

Lower the dish carefully into the slow-cooker pot. Pour boiling water into the pot to come halfway up the sides of the dish, cover with the lid, and cook on high for 4½ to 5 hours or until a skewer comes out cleanly when inserted into the center of the ginger cake.

Lift the dish out of the slow-cooker pot using a dish towel and let stand for 10 minutes, then remove the foil and loosen the edge of the cake with a knife. Invert onto a wire rack, peel off the lining paper, and let cool.

Sift the powdered sugar into a bowl and mix in just enough of the measurement water to make a smooth, thick icing. Spoon over the top of the cake, letting it drizzle down the sides, then decorate with the strips of ginger. Let set. Serve in wedges.

FOR BANANA GINGER CAKE, omit the dates from the ginger cake and add 1 small mashed banana mixed with 1 tablespoon lemon juice when adding the chopped stem ginger. Cook and frost as above.

SAFFRON PEARS WITH CHOCOLATE

Serves **4**
Preparation time **20 minutes**
Cooking temperature **low**
Cooking time **3 to 4 hours**

1¼ cups **cloudy apple juice**
3 tablespoons **superfine sugar**
large pinch of **saffron threads**
4 **cardamom pods**, coarsely crushed
4 **firm**, **ripe pears**

CHOCOLATE SAUCE
¼ cup **chocolate and hazelnut spread**
2 tablespoons **heavy cream**
2 tablespoons **milk**

Preheat the slow cooker if necessary. Pour the apple juice into a small saucepan and add the sugar, saffron, and cardamom pods and their black seeds. Bring to a boil, then tip into the slow-cooker pot.

Cut each pear in half lengthwise, leaving the stalk on. Remove the pear cores with a melon baller, if you have one, or a teaspoon. Add the pears to the slow-cooker pot, pressing them beneath the surface of the liquid as much as you can. Cover with the lid and cook on low for 3 to 4 hours or until the pears are tender and pale yellow.

When ready to serve, put all the ingredients for the sauce into a small saucepan and warm together, stirring until smooth. Spoon the pears and some of the saffron sauce into shallow dishes, pour the chocolate sauce into a small pitcher, and allow dinner guests to drizzle the sauce over the pears just before eating. Serve with vanilla ice cream or crème fraîche, if liked.

FOR SPICED PEARS WITH RED WINE, warm ¾ cup red wine with ¾ cup water, ¼ cup superfine sugar, the pared zest of ½ small orange, 1 small cinnamon stick, halved, and 4 cloves in a saucepan. Pour into the slow-cooker pot, add 4 halved, peeled, and cored pears, then cover and cook as above. Serve with spoonfuls of crème fraîche.

LEMON CUSTARD CREAMS

Serves **6**
Preparation time **15 minutes, plus
    cooling** and **chilling**
Cooking temperature **low**
Cooking time **2 to 2½ hours**

2 **eggs**
3 **egg yolks**
½ cup **superfine sugar**
grated zest of 2 **lemons** and the juice
    of 1 **lemon**
1¼ cups **heavy cream**
1 cup **blueberries**, to serve

Preheat the slow cooker if necessary. Put the whole eggs and egg yolks, sugar, and lemon zest into a bowl and beat together until just mixed.

Pour the cream into a small saucepan and bring just to a boil, then gradually beat into the egg mixture. Strain the lemon juice and gradually beat into the cream mixture.

Pour the mixture into 6 small coffee cups, checking first that they will fit in the slow-cooker pot. Put them in the pot, then pour hot water into the pot so that it comes halfway up the sides of the cups. Loosely cover the tops of the cups with a piece of foil, cover with the lid, and cook on low for 2 to 2½ hours or until the custards are just set.

Lift the cups carefully out of the slow cooker with a dish towel and let cool. Transfer to the refrigerator to chill for 3 to 4 hours or overnight.

Set the cups on their saucers and decorate the tops of the custard creams with the blueberries.

FOR LIME & ELDERFLOWER CUSTARD CREAMS, make the dessert as above but with the grated zest and juice of 2 limes and 2 tablespoons undiluted elderflower cordial instead of the lemon zest and juice. Cook in coffee cups as above, then serve chilled with fresh strawberries drizzled with a little extra elderflower cordial.

BAKED APPLES WITH DATES

BAKED PEACHES WITH GINGER ♥

Serves **4**
Preparation time **20 minutes**
Cooking temperature **low**
Cooking time **3 to 4 hours**

½ stick **butter**, at room temperature
¼ cup **light brown sugar**
½ teaspoon **ground cinnamon**
grated zest of ½ small **orange**
1 tablespoon finely chopped **candied** or drained
    stem **ginger**
¼ cup chopped **pitted dates**
4 large **sweet, crisp apples**
¾ cup **cloudy apple juice**
hot **custard** or **cream** to serve

Preheat the slow cooker if necessary. Mix together the butter, sugar, cinnamon, and orange zest until smooth, then stir in the chopped ginger and dates.

Trim a thin slice off the bottom of the apples, if needed, so that they will stand up without rolling over, then cut a thick slice off the top of each and reserve for later. Using a small knife, remove the apple core to leave a cavity for the stuffing.

Divide the date mixture into 4 and press a portion into each apple cavity, spreading it over the top cut edge of the apple if it won't all fit in. Replace the apple lids and then put the apples into the slow-cooker pot. Pour the apple juice into the bottom of the pot, cover, and cook on low for 3 to 4 hours or until the apples are tender.

Lift the apples carefully out of the slow cooker and serve in shallow dishes with the sauce spooned over and a drizzle of hot custard or cream.

FOR BAKED APPLES WITH CHERRIES AND GINGER, follow the recipe as above, but omit the cinnamon, replace the orange zest with lemon zest, and replace the dates with ¼ cup chopped candied cherries.

Serves **4**
Preparation time **10 minutes**
Cooking temperature **low**
Cooking time **1½ to 2½ hours**

1-inch piece of **fresh ginger root**, peeled
    and finely chopped
6 **ripe peaches**, halved and stoned
¼ cup **cloudy apple juice**
1 tablespoon **superfine sugar**
½ cup **blueberries**
¾ cup **0% fat Greek yogurt**

Preheat the slow cooker if necessary. Arrange the chopped ginger on the bottom of the slow-cooker pot, then place the peaches, cut-sides down, on top in a single layer. Pour over the apple juice, then sprinkle with the sugar and scatter with the blueberries.

Cover and cook on low for 1½ to 2½ hours until the peaches are piping hot and the juices are beginning to run from the blueberries. Spoon into serving bowls and serve warm or cold with the Greek yogurt.

FOR BAKED PEACHES WITH ROSÉ WINE, arrange 8 peach halves, cut-sides down, in the bottom of the slow-cooker pot and pour over ¼ cup rosé wine, sprinkle with 1 tablespoon superfine sugar, and scatter with 1 cup raspberries instead of the blueberries. Cover, cook, and serve as above.

MINI BANANA & DATE PUDDINGS

PLUM & BLUEBERRY SWIRL

Serves **4**
Preparation time **20 minutes**
Cooking temperature **high**
Cooking time **2 to 3 hours**

1 stick **butter**, at room temperature, plus extra
   for greasing
½ cup **light brown sugar**
2 **eggs**, beaten
1 cup **all-purpose flour**, sifted with
   1 teaspoon **baking powder**
1 small **ripe banana**
½ cup chopped **pitted dates**
1 cup **ready-made toffee sauce**
2 oz **semisweet chocolate**, broken into pieces

Preheat the slow cooker if necessary. Butter 4 metal
pudding molds, each with a 1-cup capacity, and line the
bottom of each with a disk of nonstick parchment paper,
checking first that they will fit in the slow-cooker pot.
Beat the butter and sugar in a bowl until soft and creamy.
Gradually add alternate spoonfuls of egg and flour until
both have all been added and the mixture is smooth.
Mash the banana on a plate, then beat into the pudding
mixture. Stir in the dates, then divide between the molds.

Cover each one with a square of foil and set them in the
slow-cooker pot. Pour boiling water into the pot to come
halfway up the sides of the molds. Cover with the lid
and cook on high for 2 to 3 hours or until the tops of the
puddings spring back when pressed with a fingertip. Lift
the molds from the slow-cooker pot using a dish towel
and remove the foil. Loosen the edges with a knife,
invert onto plates, and peel off the lining paper. Pour the
toffee sauce into a small saucepan, add the chocolate,
and warm through, stirring, until the chocolate has just
melted. Drizzle over the puddings to serve.

FOR MINI CHOCOLATE & BANANA PUDDINGS, make
the puddings with the butter, sugar, and eggs as above.
Substitute 2 tablespoons unsweetened cocoa powder for
the same quantity of flour, then add with the remaining
flour, mashed banana, and dates. Cook as above. Warm
¼ cup chocolate and hazelnut spread with 2 tablespoons
each heavy cream and milk in a saucepan, stirring until
smooth, and serve with the puddings.

Serves **4**
Preparation time **15 minutes**, **plus cooling** and **chilling**
Cooking temperature **high**
Cooking time **2¼ to 2¾ hours**

10 oz **ripe red plums**, halved, stoned, and
   cut into chunks
1 cup **blueberries**
1 tablespoon **granulated sweetener**
juice of ½ **orange**
3 tablespoons **water**
1 tablespoon **cornstarch**

YOGURT
1 cup **0% fat Greek yogurt**
finely grated zest of ½ **orange**
1 tablespoon **granulated sweetener**

Preheat the slow cooker if necessary. Place the plums
and blueberries in the slow-cooker pot, sprinkle
with the sweetener, then add the orange juice and
measurement water. Cover and cook on high for 2 to
2½ hours until the fruit is soft.

Mix the cornstarch to a smooth paste with a little cold
water and stir into the pot. Cover again and cook, still
on high, for another 15 minutes until thickened. Stir the
fruit and let cool.

Mix the yogurt with the orange zest and sweetener.
Divide the fruit between 4 serving glasses, top with the
yogurt, then swirl together with a teaspoon. Chill until
ready to serve.

FOR STRAWBERRY & BLUEBERRY SWIRL WITH MINT,
place 2 cups ripe strawberries, hulled, in the slow-
cooker pot with 1 cup blueberries, 1 tablespoon
granulated sweetener, and the juice of ½ orange.
Cook as above, then thicken with the cornstarch,
cook for 15 minutes, and let cool. Mix 1 cup 0% fat
Greek yogurt with 1 tablespoon chopped fresh mint
and 1 tablespoon granulated sweetener, then swirl with
the fruit as above.

STRAWBERRY CHEESECAKE

Serves **4 to 5**
Preparation time **30 minutes**,
   plus cooling and **chilling**
Cooking temperature **high**
Cooking time **2 to 2½ hours**

4 **ready-made plain sponge cakes**
1¼ cups **regular cream cheese**
¼ cup **superfine sugar**
¾ cup **heavy cream**
3 **eggs**
grated zest and juice of ½ **lemon**
butter, for greasing

TOPPING
2 tablespoons **strawberry jam**
1 tablespoon **lemon juice**
1¼ cups **strawberries**, hulled
   and sliced

Preheat the slow cooker if necessary. Line the bottom and sides of a soufflé dish 5½ inches in diameter and 3½ inches deep with nonstick parchment paper, checking first that it will fit in the slow-cooker pot. Line the bottom with the sponge cakes, trimming them to fit in a single layer.

Put the cream cheese and sugar in a bowl, then gradually beat in the cream until smooth and thick. Gradually beat in the eggs 1 at a time, then mix in the lemon zest and juice. Pour the mixture into the dish, spreading it evenly.

Cover the top with buttered foil and lower it into the slow-cooker pot. Pour boiling water into the pot to come halfway up the sides of the dish. Cover with the lid and cook on high for 2 to 2½ hours or until the cheesecake is well risen and softly set in the center.

Lift the dish out of the slow-cooker pot using a dish towel and let cool and get firm. The cheesecake will sink quickly as it cools to about the size that it was before cooking. Transfer to the refrigerator to chill for at least 4 hours.

When ready to serve, loosen the edge of the cheesecake with a knife, invert onto a serving plate, peel off the lining paper, and turn it the right way up. Mix the jam and lemon juice in a bowl until smooth, add the sliced strawberries, and toss together. Spoon on top of the cheesecake and serve.

CHOCOLATE BROWNIE PUDDINGS

Serves 4
Preparation time **20 minutes**
Cooking temperature **high**
Cooking time **1¼ to 1½ hours**

4 oz **semisweet chocolate**, plus 8
  extra small squares
¾ stick **butter**
2 **eggs**
2 **egg yolks**
¼ cup **superfine sugar**
½ teaspoon **vanilla extract**
¼ cup **all-purpose flour**

TO DECORATE
sifted **powdered sugar**
mini **pastel-colored marshmallows**
vanilla ice cream or **crème fraîche**

Preheat the slow cooker if necessary. Break the 4 oz chocolate into pieces, put into a saucepan with the butter, and heat gently, stirring occasionally, until melted. Take off the heat and set aside. Meanwhile, butter 4 individual metal pudding molds, each with a 1-cup capacity, and line the bottom with disks of nonstick parchment paper, first checking that they will fit in the slow-cooker pot.

Beat together the whole eggs, egg yolks, sugar, and vanilla extract in a large mixing bowl with a hand-held electric beater for 3 to 4 minutes or until light and frothy. Gradually beat in the melted chocolate mixture.

Sift the flour into the chocolate mixture and fold together. Divide between the pudding molds. Press 2 squares of chocolate into the center of each, then loosely cover the tops with squares of buttered foil. Transfer the pudding molds to the slow-cooker pot and pour boiling water into the pot to come halfway up the sides of the molds. Cover and cook on high for 1¼ to 1½ hours until well risen and the tops spring back when lightly pressed with a fingertip.

Lift the molds out of the pot using a dish towel. Loosen the puddings with a knife, invert into shallow serving dishes, and remove the lining paper. Dust with sifted powdered sugar. Serve with marshmallows and vanilla ice cream or crème fraîche.

FOR CHERRY BROWNIE PUDDINGS WITH BRANDY, soak 8 drained, canned pitted black cherries in 1 tablespoon brandy for at least 2 hours (longer if possible). Make the brownie mixture as above and drop 2 cherries into the center of each instead of the squares of chocolate.

BLUEBERRY & PASSION FRUIT CHEESECAKE

Serves **4**
Preparation time **25 minutes, plus cooling** and **chilling**
Cooking temperature **high**
Cooking time **2 to 2½ hours**

1 tablespoon **sunflower margarine**, plus extra for greasing
¾ cup **graham cracker crumbs**
10 oz **extra-light soft cheese**
¾ cup **0% fat Greek yogurt**
1 tablespoon **cornstarch**
finely grated zest and juice of ½ **lime**
1 teaspoon **vanilla extract**
3 tablespoons **granulated sweetener**
3 tablespoons **superfine sugar**
2 **eggs**
1 cup **blueberries**
2 **passion fruit**, halved

Preheat the slow cooker if necessary. Grease the bottom and sides of a 6-inch, round baking dish, about 2½ inches deep, with a little margarine and line the bottom with a disk of nonstick parchment paper.

Melt the margarine in a small saucepan and stir in the graham cracker crumbs. Spoon into the dish and press down firmly to make a thin, even layer. Place the cheese, yogurt, and cornstarch in a mixing bowl and beat until smooth. Add the lime zest and juice, vanilla, sweetener, sugar, and eggs and beat again until smooth.

Pour the mixture into the dish, spreading it evenly. Cover with greased foil and put in the slow-cooker pot. Pour boiling water into the slow-cooker pot to come halfway up the sides of the dish, cover, and cook on high for 2 to 2½ hours or until the cheesecake is set but with a slight wobble in the center. Lift the dish out of the slow-cooker pot using a dish towel and let cool, then chill in the refrigerator for 3 to 4 hours or overnight.

Loosen the edge of the cheesecake with a knife, turn out of the dish, and peel away the lining paper. Place on a serving plate, pile the blueberries on top, then scoop the passion fruit seeds out of the halved fruits with a teaspoon and scatter them onto the cheesecake. Serve cut into wedges.

FOR SUMMER BERRY CHEESECAKE, follow the recipe above to make the cheesecake but using the grated zest and juice of ½ lemon instead of the lime. Gently toss ¾ cup hulled, sliced strawberries and 1 cup raspberries with 2 tablespoons reduced-sugar strawberry jam and 1 tablespoon lemon juice instead of the blueberries and passion fruit. Turn out the cheesecake and top with the berry mixture just before serving.

DATE, GINGER & SYRUP PUDDINGS

Serves **4**
Preparation time **20 minutes**
Cooking temperature **high**
Cooking time **3½ to 4 hours**

¾ cup chopped **pitted dates**
½ cup boiling **water**
¼ teaspoon **baking soda**
¼ cup **light corn syrup**
¼ cup **sunflower margarine**, plus
   extra for greasing
¼ cup **light brown sugar**
¾ cup **all-purpose flour**, sifted with
   ¾ teaspoon **baking powder**
1 **egg**
1 teaspoon **vanilla extract**
1 teaspoon **ground ginger**
2 small scoops of **low-fat vanilla
   ice cream**

Preheat the slow cooker if necessary. Place the chopped dates, measurement boiling water, and baking soda in a bowl, stir, and let soak for 10 minutes.

Meanwhile, lightly grease 4 metal pudding bowls, each with a 1-cup capacity, and line the bottoms with disks of nonstick parchment paper. Divide the light corn syrup between the bowls.

Place the margarine, sugar, flour, egg, vanilla, and ginger in a food processor and blend until smooth. Drain the dates, add to the processor, and blend briefly to mix. Divide the batter between the pudding bowls, cover the tops with greased foil, and set them into the slow-cooker pot.

Pour boiling water into the slow-cooker pot to come halfway up the sides of the bowls, cover, and cook on high for 3½ to 4 hours until the sponge is well risen and springs back when pressed with a fingertip.

Lift the bowls out of the pot using a dish towel. Remove the foil, loosen the edges of the puddings with a knife, and turn out into shallow bowls. Peel away the lining paper and serve immediately with the ice cream.

FOR GINGER & BANANA PUDDINGS, omit the dates, boiling water, and baking soda. Follow the recipe above, adding 1 ripe banana to the food processor with the remaining ingredients. Blend and continue as above.

PLUM & POLENTA CAKE

Serves **6**
Preparation time **30 minutes**
Cooking temperature **high**
Cooking time **3 to 3½ hours**

½ lb **sweet red plums**, stoned
  and halved
1½ sticks **butter**, at room
  temperature, plus extra
  for greasing
¾ cup **superfine sugar**
2 **eggs**, beaten
1 cup **ground almonds**
¼ cup **fine polenta (cornmeal)**
½ teaspoon **baking powder**
grated zest and juice of ½ **orange**

TO DECORATE
2 tablespoons toasted
  sliced almonds
sifted **powdered sugar**

Preheat the slow cooker if necessary. Butter a 2½-pint oval or round baking dish that will fit comfortably in your slow-cooker pot and line the bottom with a disk of nonstick parchment paper. Arrange the plum halves, cut-side down, in rings in the bottom of the dish.

Cream together the butter and superfine sugar in a mixing bowl until light and fluffy. Gradually beat the eggs and ground almonds alternately into the mixture. Stir in the polenta, baking powder, and orange zest and juice and beat until smooth.

Spoon the batter over the plums and smooth with a knife. Cover the dish with buttered foil, then stand it on an upturned saucer in the slow-cooker pot. Pour boiling water into the pot to come halfway up the sides of the dish. Cover with the lid and cook on high for 3 to 3½ hours or until the top of the cake is dry and springs back when pressed with a fingertip.

Remove the dish carefully from the slow cooker using a dish towel. Take off the foil and let cool slightly. Run a knife around the inside edge of the dish to loosen the cake and invert it onto a serving plate. Remove the lining paper, sprinkle the top with toasted flaked almonds, and dust with a little sifted powdered sugar to decorate. Cut into wedges and serve warm or cold with spoonfuls of whipped cream, if liked.

FOR APPLE & POLENTA CAKE, follow the recipe as above, but replace the plums with 2 apples, peeled, cored, and thickly sliced, then tossed with the grated zest and juice of ½ lemon.

SPICED PEARS ♥

Serves **4**
Preparation time **15 minutes**
Cooking temperature **low**
Cooking time **3 to 4 hours**

1¼ cups hot **water**
4 **cardamom pods**, crushed
3-inch **cinnamon stick**, halved
1-inch piece of **fresh ginger root**, peeled and thinly sliced
2 teaspoons **granulated sweetener**
4 **pears with stalks**, peeled, halved lengthwise, and cored
pared zest and juice of 1 **lemon**
pared zest and juice of 1 **orange**

Preheat the slow cooker if necessary. Pour the measurement hot water into the slow-cooker pot, then stir in the cardamom pods and their black seeds, the cinnamon, ginger, and sweetener.

Add the pears and the lemon and orange juice, then gently turn the pears in the liquid to coat and arrange them, cut-sides down, in a single layer. Cut the pared lemon and orange zest into very thin strips and scatter on top.

Cover and cook on low for 3 to 4 hours until the pears are tender. The cooking time will depend on their ripeness. Serve warm.

FOR MULLED WINE PEARS, follow the recipe above, using ¾ cup red wine and ¾ cup hot water instead of 1¼ cups hot water, and using 4 cloves instead of the cardamom pods. Increase the granulated sweetener to 3 teaspoons, or to taste, and cook as above.

HOT TODDY ORANGES

Serves **4**
Preparation time **15 minutes**
Cooking temperature **low**
Cooking time **2 to 3 hours**

8 **clementines**
2½ tablespoons liquid **honey**
½ cup **light brown sugar**
grated zest and juice of ½ **lemon**
¼ cup **whisky**
1¼ cups boiling **water**
1 tablespoon **butter**

Preheat the slow cooker if necessary. Peel the clementines, leaving them whole. Put the remaining ingredients in the slow-cooker pot and mix together.

Add the clementines. Cover with the lid and cook on low for 2 to 3 hours or until piping hot. Spoon into shallow bowls and serve with just-melting scoops of vanilla ice cream, if liked.

FOR HOT TODDY APRICOTS, put all the ingredients, omitting the clementines and sugar, into the slow-cooker pot as above. Add 10 oz ready-to-eat dried apricots and continue as above. Serve warm with crème fraîche or vanilla ice cream.

CHOCOLATE CROISSANT PUDDING

Serves **4**
Preparation time **15 minutes**,
  plus soaking
Cooking temperature **low**
Cooking time **4 to 4½ hours**

½ stick **butter**, plus extra for greasing
4 **chocolate croissants**
¼ cup **superfine sugar**
¼ teaspoon **ground cinnamon**
½ cup **pecans**, coarsely crushed
1¼ cups **milk**
2 **eggs**
2 **egg yolks**
1 teaspoon **vanilla extract**
sifted **powdered sugar**, to decorate

Grease the inside of a 2½-pint straight-sided baking dish with the extra butter, checking first that the dish will fit into the slow-cooker pot.

Slice the chocolate croissants thickly and spread 1 side of each slice with the remaining butter. Mix together the superfine sugar and cinnamon. Arrange the croissants in layers in the dish, sprinkling each layer with the spiced sugar and the pecans.

Beat the milk, whole eggs, egg yolks, and vanilla extract together in a mixing bowl. Pour into the dish with the croissants and let soak for 15 minutes. Meanwhile, preheat the slow cooker if necessary.

Cover the top of the dish loosely with buttered foil and lower it into the slow-cooker pot. Pour boiling water into the pot to come halfway up the sides of the dish, cover with the lid, and cook on low for 4 to 4½ hours or until the custard is set and the pudding well risen. Lift the dish out of the slow-cooker pot using a dish towel. Dust with sifted powdered sugar. Scoop into bowls and serve with vanilla ice cream, if liked.

FOR BREAD & BUTTER PUDDING, spread 3 tablespoons butter onto 4 thick slices of bread, cut into triangles, and layer in the buttered dish with 3 tablespoons high-quality mixed dried fruit and the superfine sugar. Pour the custard evenly over the bread and continue as above.

STICKY TOFFEE APPLE PUDDING

Serves **4 to 5**
Preparation time **30 minutes**
Cooking temperature **high**
Cooking time **3 to 3½ hours**

1¼ cups **all-purpose flour**, sifted with
   1¼ teaspoons **baking powder**
½ stick **butter**, diced, plus extra
   for greasing
¾ cup **dark brown sugar**
2 **eggs**
2 tablespoons **milk**
1 **apple**, cored and finely chopped
crème fraîche, vanilla ice cream,
   or **light cream**, to serve

SAUCE
1 cup **dark brown sugar**
2 tablespoons **butter**, diced
1¼ cups boiling **water**

Preheat the slow cooker if necessary. Butter the inside of a soufflé dish 5½ inches in diameter and 3½ inches deep, checking first that it will fit into the slow-cooker pot. Put the flour in a bowl, add the diced butter, and rub in with the fingertips until the mixture resembles fine bread crumbs. Stir in the sugar, then mix in the eggs and milk until smooth. Stir in the chopped apple.

Spoon the batter into the soufflé dish and spread it level. Sprinkle the sugar for the sauce over the top and dot with the 2 tablespoons diced butter. Pour the measurement boiling water over the top, then cover loosely with foil.

Lower the dish carefully into the slow-cooker pot. Pour boiling water into the pot so that it comes halfway up the sides of the soufflé dish. Cover with the lid and cook on high for 3 to 3½ hours or until the pudding is well risen and the sauce is bubbling around the edges.

Lift the dish out of the slow cooker using a dish towel. Remove the foil and loosen the sides of the pudding. Cover with a dish that is large enough to catch the sauce, then invert and remove the soufflé dish. Serve with vanilla ice cream, crème fraîche, or light cream.

FOR STICKY BANANA PUDDING, prepare the pudding as above, but replace the chopped apple with 1 small ripe and coarsely mashed banana and ½ teaspoon ground cinnamon. Make the sauce and cook as above.

DARK CHOCOLATE & COFFEE POTS

Serves **4**
Preparation time **25 minutes,**
   plus cooling and **chilling**
Cooking temperature **low**
Cooking time **3 to 3½ hours**

2 cups **milk**
¾ cup **heavy cream**
7 oz **semisweet chocolate**,
   broken into pieces
2 **eggs**
3 **egg yolks**
¼ cup **superfine sugar**
¼ teaspoon **ground cinnamon**
chocolate curls, to decorate

TOPPING
¾ cup **heavy cream**
3 fl oz **coffee cream liqueur**

Preheat the slow cooker if necessary. Pour the milk and cream into a saucepan and bring just to a boil. Remove from the heat, add the chocolate pieces, and set aside for 5 minutes, stirring occasionally, until the chocolate has melted.

Put the whole eggs, egg yolks, sugar, and cinnamon in a mixing bowl and beat until smooth. Gradually beat in the warm chocolate milk, then strain the mixture into 4 heatproof ramekins or mugs, each with a 1-cup capacity.

Cover the tops with foil and set the dishes in the slow-cooker pot. Pour hot water into the slow-cooker pot to come halfway up the sides of the ramekins or mugs. Cover with the lid and cook on low for 3 to 3½ hours or until set.

Lift the dishes carefully out of the slow-cooker pot using a dish towel. Let cool at room temperature, then transfer to the refrigerator for at least 4 hours until well chilled.

Just before serving, whip the cream for the topping until soft swirls form. Gradually beat in the liqueur, then spoon the flavored cream over the tops of the desserts. Scatter with chocolate curls and serve.

FOR CAPPUCCINO POTS WITH COFFEE CREAM LIQUEUR, add 2 teaspoons instant coffee to the just-boiled cream and milk when adding the chocolate. Continue as above, but omit the cinnamon.

EVE'S PUDDING

Serves **4**
Preparation time **25 minutes**
Cooking temperature **high**
Cooking time **3 to 3½ hours**

¼ cup **sunflower margarine**, plus extra
   for greasing
¼ cup **superfine sugar**
½ cup **all-purpose flour**
¼ cup **ground almonds**
¾ teaspoon **baking powder**
1 **egg**
grated zest and juice of 1 **lemon**
1 **apple**, quartered, cored, and sliced
1 tablespoon **apricot jam**
¾ cup **instant powdered custard**
   or vanilla pudding mix with
   sweetener, to serve

Preheat the slow cooker if necessary. Grease the bottom and inside of a 6-inch, round baking dish, about 2½ inches deep, with a little margarine, checking first that it will fit in the slow-cooker pot. Place the margarine, sugar, flour, almonds, and baking powder in a food processor, add the egg and lemon zest, and blend until smooth. Spoon into the dish, spreading the batter evenly.

Toss the apple slices with the lemon juice, then overlap in a ring on top of the batter. Cover the dish with greased foil and put in the slow-cooker pot. Pour boiling water into the slow-cooker pot to come halfway up the sides of the dish, cover, and cook on high for 3 to 3½ hours until a knife comes out cleanly when inserted into the center.

Dot the top of the pudding with the apricot jam, then gently spread into an even layer. Place under a preheated hot broiler for 3 to 4 minutes until the top is lightly caramelized. Make the custard with boiling water following the package instructions and serve with the pudding.

FOR CHOCOLATE & PEAR PUDDING, follow the recipe above to make the pudding batter, using 1 tablespoon unsweetened cocoa powder instead of the lemon zest. Quarter, core, and slice 1 small pear, toss with the lemon juice, then arrange on top of the pudding batter. Cover and bake as above, then dust the top with a little sifted powdered sugar before serving.

JAM ROLY-POLY PUDDING

Serves **4**
Preparation time **25 minutes**
Cooking temperature **high**
Cooking time **3½ to 4 hours**

2½ cups **all-purpose flour**, sifted with
   2½ teaspoons **baking powder**,
   plus extra flour for dusting
¾ cup **shredded suet**
¼ cup **superfine sugar**
grated zest of 2 **lemons**
pinch of **salt**
1 cup **milk** or **milk and water mixed**
¼ cup **strawberry jam**
hot **custard**, to serve

Preheat the slow cooker if necessary. Put the flour, suet, sugar, lemon zest, and a pinch of salt in a bowl and mix well. Gradually stir in the milk or milk and water to make a soft but not sticky dough. Knead lightly, then roll out on a piece of floured nonstick parchment paper to a rectangle about 9 x 12 inches. Turn the paper so that the shorter edges are facing you.

Spread the jam evenly over the pastry, leaving ¾ inch around the edges. Roll up, starting at a shorter edge, using the paper to help. Wrap in the paper, then in a sheet of foil. Twist the ends together tightly, leaving space for the pudding to rise.

Transfer the pudding to the slow-cooker pot and raise off the bottom by standing it on 2 ramekin dishes. Pour boiling water into the pot to come a little up the sides of the pudding, being careful that the water cannot seep through any joins. Cover with the lid and cook on high for 3½ to 4 hours or until the pudding is light and fluffy. Lift out of the pot, unwrap, and cut into thick slices. Serve with hot custard.

FOR SPOTTED DICK, grate the zest of 1 large orange and reserve. Squeeze the juice into a saucepan, bring to a boil, add 1 cup raisins, and let soak for 30 minutes. Make the pastry as above, adding the orange zest, the grated zest of 1 lemon, and the soaked raisins before mixing with enough milk to make a soft dough. Shape into a 9-inch long log. Wrap in nonstick parchment paper and foil, then cook as above.

TOPSY TURVY PLUM PUDDING

Serves **6**
Preparation time **25 minutes**
Cooking temperature **high**
Cooking time **4 to 5 hours**

¾ cup **blackberries**, thawed if frozen
7 oz **ripe red plums**, halved, stoned,
    and sliced
2 tablespoons **red berry jam**
1 stick **butter**, at room temperature,
    plus extra for greasing
½ cup **superfine sugar**
¾ cup **all-purpose flour**, sifted with
    ¾ teaspoon **baking powder**
2 **eggs**, beaten
½ cup **ground almonds**
few drops of **almond extract**
toasted **flaked almonds**, to decorate

Preheat the slow cooker if necessary. Lightly butter a 2½-pint soufflé dish and line the bottom with a disk of nonstick parchment paper, checking first that the dish will fit in the slow-cooker pot. Arrange the blackberries and plums in the bottom, then dot with the jam.

Beat together the butter and sugar in a mixing bowl until soft and creamy. Gradually mix in alternate spoonfuls of the flour and beaten egg, and continue adding and beating until the mixture is smooth. Stir in the almonds and almond extract. Spoon the batter over the fruit, spread it evenly, and cover the top with foil.

Lower the dish into the slow-cooker pot and pour boiling water into the pot to come halfway up the sides of the dish. Cover with the lid and cook on high for 4 to 5 hours or until the pudding is well risen and springs back when pressed with a fingertip.

Lift the dish out of the slow-cooker pot using a dish towel and remove the foil. Loosen the edges of the pudding with a knife, invert onto a plate with a rim, and remove the lining paper. Decorate with toasted sliced almonds and serve hot with custard, if liked.

FOR PEACH & CHOCOLATE PUDDING, arrange 2 (or 1, if very large) halved, stoned, and sliced ripe peaches in the bottom of the dish and dot with 2 tablespoons apricot jam. Make the batter as above, adding 1 tablespoon unsweetened cocoa powder and an extra 2 tablespoons all-purpose flour instead of the ground almonds and almond extract. Continue as above.

LEMON & POPPY SEED DRIZZLE CAKE

Serves **6 to 8**
Preparation time **25 minutes, plus**
    cooling and **soaking**
Cooking temperature **high**
Cooking time **4½ to 5 hours**

1¼ sticks **butter**, at room
    temperature, plus extra
    for greasing
½ cup **superfine sugar**
1 cup **all-purpose flour**, sifted with
    1 teaspoon **baking powder**
2 **eggs**, beaten
2 tablespoons **poppy seeds**
grated zest of 1 **lemon**
lemon zest curls, to decorate
crème fraîche, to serve

LEMON SYRUP
juice of 1½ **lemons**
½ cup **superfine sugar**

Preheat the slow cooker if necessary. Lightly butter a soufflé dish 5½ inches in diameter and 3½ inches deep, and line the bottom with a disk of nonstick parchment paper, checking first that it will fit in the slow-cooker pot.

Beat together the butter and sugar in a mixing bowl until soft and creamy. Gradually mix in alternate spoonfuls of the flour and beaten egg, and continue adding and beating until the batter is smooth. Stir in the poppy seeds and lemon zest, then spoon the batter into the soufflé dish, spreading it evenly. Cover the top of the dish loosely with buttered foil and then lower into the slow-cooker pot.

Pour boiling water into the slow-cooker pot so that it comes halfway up the sides of the dish. Cover with the lid and cook on high for 4½ to 5 hours or until the cake is dry and springs back when pressed with a fingertip.

Lift the dish carefully out of the slow cooker using a dish towel, remove the foil, and loosen the edge of the cake with a knife. Invert onto a plate or shallow dish with a rim and remove the lining paper. Quickly warm the lemon juice and sugar together for the syrup and, as soon as the sugar has dissolved, pour the syrup over the cake. Let stand to cool and to allow the syrup to soak in. Cut into slices and serve with spoonfuls of crème fraîche, decorated with lemon zest curls.

FOR CITRUS DRIZZLE CAKE, omit the lemon zest and poppy seeds from the cake batter and stir in the grated zest of ½ lemon, ½ lime, and ½ small orange. Bake as above. Make the syrup using the juice of the grated fruits and sugar as above.

CHERRY & CHOCOLATE PUDDINGS

Serves **4**
Preparation time **25 minutes**
Cooking temperature **high**
Cooking time **1½ to 2 hours**

½ stick **butter**, plus extra for greasing
¼ cup **superfine sugar**
½ cup **all-purpose flour**
1 **egg**
1 tablespoon **unsweetened
   cocoa powder**
¾ teaspoon **baking powder**
¼ teaspoon **ground cinnamon**
14 oz can **pitted dark sweet
   cherries**, drained

CHOCOLATE SAUCE
3½ oz **white chocolate**, broken
   into pieces
¾ cup **heavy cream**

Preheat the slow cooker if necessary. Butter the insides of 4 metal, 1-cup capacity pudding molds, and line the bottoms with a disk of nonstick parchment paper, checking first that they will fit in the slow-cooker pot.

Put the butter, sugar, flour, egg, cocoa, baking powder, and cinnamon in a mixing bowl and beat them together with a wooden spoon until smooth.

Arrange 7 cherries in the bottom of each pudding mold. Roughly chop the remainder and stir them into the pudding batter. Spoon the batter into the pudding molds and spreading the batter evenly. Loosely cover the tops of the molds with foil and put them in the slow-cooker pot. Pour boiling water into the pot so that it comes halfway up the sides of the molds, cover with the lid, and cook on high for 1½ to 2 hours or until the puddings are well risen and the tops spring back when pressed with a fingertip. Lift the puddings out of the slow-cooker pot using a dish towel.

Put the chocolate and cream in a small saucepan and heat gently, stirring occasionally, until melted. Loosen the edges of the puddings, turn them out into shallow bowls, peel away the lining paper, and pour the sauce around them to serve.

FOR CHERRY & ALMOND PUDDINGS, prepare the pudding batter as above, omitting the unsweetened cocoa powder and ground cinnamon and instead adding 2 tablespoons ground almonds and a few drops of almond extract. Cook as above, turn out onto serving dishes, and serve with vanilla ice cream.

RASPBERRY & RHUBARB OATY CRISP

Serves **4 to 5**
Preparation time **15 minutes**
Cooking temperature **low**
Cooking time **2 to 3 hours**

13 oz trimmed **rhubarb**
1 cup **frozen raspberries**
¼ cup **superfine sugar**
3 tablespoons **water**

TOPPING
1 tablespoon **butter**
3 tablespoons **flaked almonds**
7 oz **ready-made granola bars**
  (about 4)

Preheat the slow cooker if necessary. Cut the rhubarb into slices 1 inch thick and add to the slow-cooker pot with the raspberries (do not defrost), the sugar, and measurement water. Cover with the lid and cook on low for 2 to 3 hours or until the rhubarb is just tender.

When almost ready to serve, heat the butter in a skillet, add the almonds, and crumble in the granola bars. Fry, stirring, for 3 to 4 minutes or until hot and lightly browned. Spoon the fruit into bowls, scatter the crisp over the top, and serve with heavy cream, if liked.

FOR PEACH & MIXED BERRY CRISP, dice 3 fresh peaches, discarding the stones, and add to the slow-cooker pot with 5 oz mixed frozen summer fruits, the sugar, and water as above. Cook and scatter with the granola crisp, as above.

COMPOTE WITH MASCARPONE

Serves **4**
Preparation time **20 minutes**
Cooking temperature **high**
Cooking time **1 to 1¼ hours**

4 **nectarines**, halved, stoned, and diced
2 cups **strawberries**, hulled, halved (or quartered, depending on size)
¼ cup **superfine sugar**, plus 2 tablespoons, divided
finely grated zest and juice of 2 **oranges**
½ cup cold **water**
¾ cup **mascarpone cheese**
1½ oz **amaretti cookies**, plus a few for decoration

Preheat the slow cooker if necessary. Put the fruit in the slow-cooker pot with the ¼ cup sugar, the zest of 1 orange, the juice of 1½ oranges, and the measurement water. Cover and cook on high for 1 to 1¼ hours or until the fruit is tender. Serve warm or cold.

When almost ready to serve, mix the mascarpone with the remaining 2 tablespoons sugar and orange zest and juice. Reserve some of the amaretti cookies for decoration. Crumble the rest into the bowl with the mascarpone and stir to combine. Spoon the fruit into glass dessert dishes, top with spoonfuls of the orange mascarpone mixture, and scatter with amaretti cookie crumbs to decorate.

FOR PLUM & CRANBERRY COMPOTE WITH ORANGE MASCARPONE, replace the nectarines and strawberries with 1¼ lb plums, quartered and stoned, and 1¼ cups cranberries (no need to defrost if frozen). Increase the sugar to ⅓ cup, then follow the recipe above, using cranberry and raspberry juice instead of water, if liked.

STICKY MARMALADE SYRUP PUDDING

Serves **4 to 5**
Preparation time **20 minutes**
Cooking temperature **high**
Cooking time **3 to 3½ hours**

butter, for greasing
¼ cup **light corn syrup**
3 tablespoons **orange marmalade**, divided
1¾ cups **all-purpose flour**, sifted with
    1½ teaspoons **baking powder**
½ cup **shredded vegetable shortening**
¼ cup packed **light brown sugar**
1 teaspoon **ground ginger**
grated zest and juice of 1 **orange**
2 **eggs**
2 tablespoons **milk**

Preheat the slow cooker if necessary. Lightly butter a 2½-pint pudding bowl and line the bottom with a disk of nonstick parchment paper, checking first that it will fit in the slow-cooker pot. Spoon the light corn syrup and 2 tablespoons of the marmalade into the bowl.

Put the flour, shortening, sugar, and ginger in a bowl and mix together. Add the remaining marmalade, orange zest and juice, the eggs, and milk and beat until smooth. Spoon the batter into the bowl, spread it evenly, and cover the top with buttered foil.

Lower the bowl into the slow-cooker pot and pour boiling water into the pot to come halfway up the sides of the bowl. Cover with the lid and cook on high for 3 to 3½ hours or until the pudding is well risen and feels firm and dry when the top is pressed with a fingertip. Lift the bowl out of the slow-cooker pot using a dish towel and remove the foil. Loosen the edge of the pudding with a knife, turn out onto a plate, and peel off the lining paper. Serve scoops of the pudding in bowls with custard or vanilla ice cream, if liked.

FOR STICKY BANANA PUDDING, spoon ¼ cup light corn syrup and 3 tablespoons light brown sugar into the bottom of the lined bowl. Cut 2 bananas in half lengthwise, then in half again across. Toss in the juice of ½ lemon and arrange, cut-side down, in the bowl. Make the pudding batter, spoon it over the bananas, spreading it evenly, and continue as above.

COCONUT & ROSE RICE PUDDING

PEPPERMINT & RASPBERRY BRÛLÉE

Serves **4**
Preparation time **10 minutes**
Cooking temperature **high**
Cooking time **2½ to 3 hours**

¼ cup **short-grain sweet white rice**, rinsed and drained
¼ cup **superfine sugar**
¼ cup **desiccated coconut**, plus 2 teaspoons
2½ cups **skim milk**
½ to 1 teaspoon **rosewater**, to taste
1 cup **raspberries**, to serve

Preheat the slow cooker if necessary. Place the rice, sugar, and the ¼ cup coconut in the slow-cooker pot, add the milk, and stir well. Cover and cook on high for 2½ to 3 hours until the rice is tender.

Stir well, then add the rosewater. Spoon into bowls, top with the raspberries and the remaining 2 teaspoons coconut, and serve immediately.

FOR VANILLA & ORANGE RICE PUDDING, split 1 vanilla bean lengthwise and scrape out the seeds with a small knife. Follow the recipe above, adding the vanilla seeds to the rice and milk in the slow-cooker pot with the vanilla bean and the finely grated zest of ½ orange. Stir well, cover, and cook as above. Stir again and remove the vanilla bean before serving with raspberries and a sprinkling of coconut.

Serves **4**
Preparation time **30 minutes**, **plus cooling** and **chilling**
Cooking temperature **low**
Cooking time **2½ to 3½ hours**

4 **egg yolks**
¼ cup **superfine sugar**
1¾ cups **heavy cream**
¼ teaspoon **peppermint extract**
1¼ cups **raspberries**
2 tablespoons **powdered sugar**

Preheat the slow cooker if necessary. Beat the egg yolks and sugar in a bowl for 3 to 4 minutes until frothy, then gradually beat in the cream. Stir in the peppermint extract. Strain the mixture into a pitcher.

Pour into 4 ramekin dishes, each ¾ cup in capacity, checking first that they will fit in the slow-cooker pot. Put the dishes into the slow-cooker pot, pour boiling water into the pot to come halfway up the sides of the dishes, then loosely cover the top of each dish with foil.

Cover with the lid and cook on low for 2½ to 3½ hours or until the custard is set with a slight quiver to the middle. Lift the dishes carefully out of the slow cooker and let cool. Let chill in the refrigerator for 4 hours.

When ready to serve, pile a few raspberries in the center of each serving and sift over the powdered sugar. Caramelize the sugar with a chef's torch.

FOR PEPPERMINT & WHITE CHOCOLATE BRÛLÉE, bring 1½ cups heavy cream just to a boil in a saucepan, then remove from the heat, add 4 oz good-quality white chocolate, broken into pieces, and let stand until melted. Beat the egg yolks with 2 tablespoons superfine sugar, then gradually mix in the chocolate cream and the peppermint extract. Continue as above. Replace the raspberries with blueberries and serve as above.

DRINKS

SKIER'S HOT CHOCOLATE

Serves **4**
Preparation time **10 minutes**
Cooking temperature **low**
Cooking time **2 to 3 hours**

3½ oz **good-quality chocolate**
2 tablespoons **superfine sugar**
3¼ cups **milk**
few drops of **vanilla extract**
small pinch **ground cinnamon**
3 tablespoons **Kahlúa coffee
    liqueur** (optional)
mini marshmallows, to serve

Preheat the slow cooker if necessary. Put the chocolate and sugar in the slow-cooker pot, then add the milk, vanilla extract, and cinnamon.

Cover with the lid and cook on low for 2 to 3 hours, beating once or twice, until the chocolate has melted and the drink is hot. Stir in the Kahlúa, if using. Ladle into mugs and top with a few mini marshmallows.

FOR HOT CHOCOLATE WITH BRANDY CREAM, make the hot chocolate as above, replacing the Kahlúa with 3 tablespoons brandy. Whip ½ cup heavy cream with 2 tablespoons sifted powdered sugar until soft peaks form, then gradually beat in 3 tablespoons brandy. Pour the hot chocolate into mugs, then top with spoonfuls of the whipped cream and dust lightly with chocolate powder drink mix or grated chocolate.

FOR MEXICAN HOT CHOCOLATE, put ½ cup unsweetened cocoa powder and 4 teaspoons instant coffee into the slow-cooker pot. Measure 2 pints boiling water. Make a smooth paste by mixing a little of the boiling water with the cocoa and coffee. Add the rest of the water, 6 fl oz rum, ½ cup superfine sugar, ½ teaspoon ground cinnamon, and 1 dried red chile, cut in half. Cover and cook on low for 3 to 4 hours. Discard the chile halves and ladle into 4 cups. Top with ¾ cup heavy cream.

LEMON CORDIAL

HOT JAMAICAN PUNCH

Serves about **20**
Preparation time **10 minutes**, plus cooling
Cooking temperature **high** and **low**
Cooking time **3 to 4 hours**

3 **lemons**, washed and thinly sliced, seeds discarded
3 cups **granulated sugar**
2 pints boiling **water**
2½ tablespoons **cream of tartar**
ice cubes, to serve

Preheat the slow cooker if necessary. Add the lemon slices to the slow-cooker pot with the sugar and measurement boiling water and stir well until the sugar has almost all dissolved. Cover with the lid and cook on high for 1 hour.

Reduce the heat and cook on low for 2 to 3 hours or until the lemons are almost translucent. Switch off the slow cooker and stir in the cream of tartar. Let cool.

Remove and discard some of the sliced lemons using a slotted spoon. Transfer the cordial and remaining lemon slices to 2 sterilized screw-top, wide-neck bottles or food storage jars. Seal well, label, and store in the refrigerator for up to 1 month.

Dilute the cordial with water in a ratio of 1:3, adding a few of the sliced lemons for decoration, ice cubes, and mint or lemon balm sprigs, if liked.

FOR LEMON & LIME CORDIAL, prepare the cordial using 2 lemons and 2 limes, washed and thinly sliced, instead of 3 lemons. Serve diluted with sparkling mineral water and mint sprigs.

Serves **6**
Preparation time **10 minutes**
Cooking temperature **high** and **low**
Cooking time **3 to 4 hours**

juice of 3 **limes**
10½ fl oz **dark rum**
1¼ cups **ginger wine**
2½ cups cold **water**
¼ cup **superfine sugar**

TO DECORATE
1 **lime**, thinly sliced
2 slices of **pineapple**, cored, skin left on, cut into pieces

Preheat the slow cooker if necessary. Strain the lime juice into the slow-cooker pot and discard the seeds. Add the rum, ginger wine, measurement water, and sugar. Cover and cook on high for 1 hour.

Reduce the heat and cook on low for 2 to 3 hours until the punch is piping hot or until you are ready to serve. Stir well, then ladle into heatproof glasses and add a slice of lime and 2 pieces of pineapple to each glass.

FOR RUM TODDY, put the grated zest of 1 lemon and 1 orange and the juice of 3 lemons and 3 oranges into the slow cooker. Add ½ cup honey and ½ cup superfine sugar. Increase the water to 3¼ cups and reduce the rum to 6 fl oz. Cook and serve as above.

MULLED CRANBERRY & RED WINE

Makes **8 to 10 glasses**
Preparation time **10 minutes**
Cooking temperature **high** and **low**
Cooking time **4 to 5 hours**

750 ml bottle **inexpensive red wine**
2½ cups **cranberry juice**
3½ fl oz **brandy**, **rum**, **vodka**, or **orange liqueur**
½ cup **superfine sugar**
1 **orange**, cut into segments
8 **cloves**
1 to 2 **cinnamon sticks** (depending on size)

TO SERVE
1 **orange**, cut into segments
2 to 3 **bay leaves**
few **cranberries**

Preheat the slow cooker if necessary. Pour the red wine, cranberry juice, and brandy or other alcohol into the slow-cooker pot. Stir in the sugar.

Stud each orange segment with a clove. Break the cinnamon sticks into large pieces and add to the pot with the orange pieces. Cover with the lid and cook on high for 1 hour. Reduce the heat and cook on low for 3 to 4 hours.

Replace the orange segments with new ones and add the bay leaves and cranberries. Ladle into heatproof glasses, keeping back the fruits and herbs, if liked.

FOR MULLED ORANGE & RED WINE, prepare the wine as above, but omit the cranberry juice and add 1¼ cups orange juice from a carton and 1¼ cups water. Serve the mulled wine decorated with extra herbs and fruit.

HOT SPICED BERRY PUNCH

Serves **6**
Preparation time **10 minutes**
Cooking temperature **high** and **low**
Cooking time **3 to 4 hours**

2 pints **cranberry and raspberry drink**
2 cups **frozen berry fruits**
¼ cup **superfine sugar**
2 fl oz **crème de cassis** (optional)
4 small **star anise**
1 **cinnamon stick**, halved
raspberries, to decorate (optional)

Preheat the slow cooker if necessary. Pour the cranberry and raspberry drink into the slow-cooker pot. Add the frozen fruits, sugar, and crème de cassis, if using. Stir together, then add the star anise and cinnamon.

Cover with the lid and cook on high for 1 hour. Reduce the heat and cook on low for 2 to 3 hours, or set to auto for 3 to 4 hours, until piping hot.

Strain, if liked, then put the star anise and cinnamon into small heatproof glasses. Ladle the hot punch into the glasses and add a few raspberries, if liked.

FOR BOOZY BERRY PUNCH, replace the crème de cassis with 6 fl oz vodka and then make the recipe as above.

FOR SPICED BERRY AND PEAR COMPOTE, make the punch as above. Peel, core, and slice 4 ripe pears and arrange in a heatproof serving dish. Pour over 1¼ cups of the hot punch and let cool. Serve as a dessert or breakfast accompaniment topped with spoonfuls of Greek yogurt flavored with a little honey. Serve the remaining punch in glasses as above.

HOT MEXICAN COFFEE

Serves **4**
Preparation time **10 minutes**
Cooking temperature **low**
Cooking time **3 to 4 hours**

½ cup **unsweetened cocoa powder**
4 teaspoons **instant coffee granules**
2 pints boiling **water**
6 fl oz **dark rum**
½ cup **superfine sugar**
½ teaspoon **ground cinnamon**
1 large **dried** or **fresh red**
  chile, halved
¾ cup **heavy cream**

TO DECORATE
2 tablespoons grated
  semisweet chocolate
4 **dried red chiles** (optional)

Preheat the slow cooker if necessary. Put the cocoa and instant coffee in a bowl and mix to a smooth paste with a little of the measurement boiling water.

Pour the cocoa paste into the slow-cooker pot. Add the remaining measurement boiling water, the rum, sugar, cinnamon, and red chile. Stir to combine, cover with the lid, and cook on low for 3 to 4 hours until piping hot or until the coffee is required.

Stir well, then ladle into heatproof glasses. Whip the cream until it is just beginning to hold its shape and spoon a little into each glass. Decorate each drink with a little of the grated chocolate and a dried chile, if liked.

FOR HOT MOCHA COFFEE, use 1 teaspoon vanilla extract instead of the rum and chile. Cook as above, then whisk in 1¼ cups milk. Pour the drink into heatproof glasses, top with cream as above, and decorate each glass with a few mini marshmallows.

CIDER TODDY

Serves **6**
Preparation time **10 minutes**
Cooking temperature **high** and **low**
Cooking time **3 to 4 hours**

2 pints (35 fl oz) **hard dry cider**
4 fl oz **whisky**
½ cup **orange juice**
¼ cup **spun honey**
2 **cinnamon sticks**
orange wedges and curls,
   to decorate (optional)

Preheat the slow cooker if necessary. Add all the ingredients to the slow-cooker pot, cover with the lid, and cook on high for 1 hour.

Reduce the heat and cook on low for 2 to 3 hours, or set to auto for 3 to 4 hours, until piping hot. Stir, then ladle into heatproof old-fashioned glasses. Add orange wedges and curls to decorate, if liked.

FOR CIDER & GINGER TODDY, replace the whisky with 4 fl oz ginger wine and 2 tablespoons drained, finely chopped stem ginger and make the recipe as above.

FOR CITRUS TODDY, pour 5 fl oz whisky into the slow-cooker pot, add ½ cup honey, ½ cup superfine sugar, and 3¼ cups cold water, then add the grated zest of 1 orange, the juice of 3 oranges, the grated zest of 1 lemon, and the juice of 3 lemons. Coarsely crush 8 cardamom pods and add the pods and their black seeds to the slow-cooker pot. Cover with the lid and cook as above.

HOT BUTTERED RUM

Serves **6**
Preparation time **5 minutes**
Cooking temperature **high** and **low**
Cooking time **3 to 4 hours**

2 pints **apple juice**
5 fl oz **dark rum**
2 tablespoons **spun honey**
2 tablespoons **dark brown sugar**
2 tablespoons **butter**
6 **cloves**
1 **apple**, cored and thickly sliced, to decorate

Preheat the slow cooker if necessary. Put all the ingredients into the slow-cooker pot, cover with the lid, and cook on high for 1 hour. Reduce the heat and cook on low for 2 to 3 hours, or set to auto for 3 to 4 hours, until piping hot.

Stir, fish out the cloves, then ladle the punch into heatproof old-fashioned glasses. Decorate with the apple slices.

FOR HOT BUTTERED CALVADOS, replace the rum with 6 fl oz calvados (French apple brandy) and make the recipe as above.

FOR POACHED APPLES WITH BUTTERED RUM, once the punch is made, pour into a serving pitcher, keeping 1¼ cups in the slow-cooker pot. Add 4 apples that have been quartered, cored, and peeled, cover with the lid, and cook on high for 1 to 1½ hours until the apples are tender. Serve as a dessert with some vanilla ice cream.

BLACKBERRY MULLED WINE

Serves **6**
Preparation time **5 minutes**
Cooking temperature **high** and **low**
Cooking time **3 to 4 hours**

750 ml bottle **red wine**
6 fl oz **dark rum**
1 cup **orange juice**
1¾ cups cold **water**
¾ cup **superfine sugar**
1¼ cups **blackberries**
1 **cinnamon stick**, halved
1 **orange**, halved and sliced, to serve

Preheat the slow cooker if necessary. Pour the wine, rum, orange juice, and measurement water into the slow-cooker pot. Add the sugar, blackberries, and cinnamon and stir together.

Cover with the lid and cook on high for 1 hour, then reduce the heat and continue to cook on low for 2 to 3 hours. Ladle into heatproof old-fashioned glasses and serve each with a half slice of orange.

FOR TRADITIONAL MULLED WINE, omit the blackberries and rum. Heat the red wine, orange juice, and water with the sugar and 2 cinnamon sticks, adding 1 orange, cut into chunks and spiked with 4 cloves, plus a little grated nutmeg and a 1-inch piece of fresh ginger root, peeled and thinly sliced. Cook as above.

MULLED WINE

Serves **6**
Preparation time **5 minutes**
Cooking temperature **high** and **low**
Cooking time **3 to 4 hours**

750 ml bottle **inexpensive red wine**
1¼ cups **clear apple juice**
1¼ cups cold **water**
juice of 1 **orange**
1 **orange**, sliced
½ **lemon**, sliced
1 **cinnamon stick**, halved
6 **cloves**
2 **bay leaves**
½ cup **superfine sugar**
5 fl oz **brandy**

Preheat the slow cooker if necessary. Pour the wine, apple juice, measurement water, and orange juice into the slow-cooker pot.

Add the orange and lemon slices, the cinnamon stick, cloves, and bay leaves, then mix in the sugar and brandy.

Cover with the lid and cook on high for 1 hour. Reduce the heat and cook on low for 2 to 3 hours, or set to auto for 3 to 4 hours, until piping hot. Ladle into heatproof old-fashioned glasses.

FOR CRANBERRY MULLED WINE, replace the apple juice with 1¼ cups cranberry juice and 1¼ cups cranberries and make the recipe as above.

FOR MULLED WINE JELLY, cook the mulled wine as above. Spoon 6 tablespoons cold water into a bowl, sprinkle with a 1-oz package unflavored powdered gelatin, and let soak for 5 minutes. Strain the mulled wine, stir in the gelatin mixture until dissolved, and let cool. Pour into 8 wine glasses and chill in the refrigerator until set. Top each of the mulled wine jellies with whipped cream.

PRESERVES

APPLE, THYME & ROSEMARY JELLY

Makes **3 jars of assorted sizes**
Preparation time **40 minutes**
Cooking temperature **high**
Cooking time **2 to 3 hours**

2¼ lb **cooking apples** (not peeled
    or cored), washed and diced
½ cup **red wine** or **apple cider vinegar**
2½ cups boiling **water**
about 3¼ cups **granulated sugar**
1 tablespoon **thyme leaves**, stripped
    from the stems
2 tablespoons finely chopped
    rosemary leaves

Preheat the slow cooker if necessary. Put the apples and wine or vinegar into the slow-cooker pot and pour over the measurement boiling water. Cover with the lid and cook on high for 2 to 3 hours or until the apples are tender. Don't worry if the apples discolor.

Ladle the apples and their juices into a jelly straining bag. Allow the juice to strain through the jelly bag overnight into a bowl set beneath it.

Measure the juice and pour it into a large saucepan; for every 2½ cups liquid add 2½ cups sugar. Heat gently, stirring occasionally, until the sugar has dissolved, then boil rapidly for about 15 minutes until setting point is reached. Check with a jam thermometer or spoon a little of the jelly onto a saucer that has been chilled in the refrigerator. Let stand for 1 to 2 minutes, then run a finger through the jelly. If a finger space is left and the jelly has wrinkled, it is ready; if not, boil for 5 to 10 minutes more and then retest. Skim off any scum with a slotted spoon, then stir in the herbs. Let the jelly stand for 5 minutes.

Warm 3 sterilized jars in a slow oven (300 to 325°F) for 5 minutes. Ladle the jelly into the warm jars, cover the surface with waxed disks, add cellophane jam jar covers, and secure with elastic bands or screw the jar lids in place. Label and let cool. Store in a cool place until required. Once opened, store in the refrigerator. Serve with lamb.

FOR APPLE & BLACKBERRY JELLY, put 1½ lb cooking apples, washed and diced, into the slow-cooker pot with 1¾ cups blackberries, ½ cup lemon juice, and the boiling water. Continue as above, omitting the herbs. Serve with scones or freshly baked soda biscuits and butter.

TANGY CITRUS CURD

APRICOT & PEACH CONSERVE

Makes **2 × 13-oz jars**
Preparation time **25 minutes**
Cooking temperature **low**
Cooking time **3 to 4 hours**

1¼ sticks **unsalted butter**
2 cups **superfine sugar**
grated zest and juice of 2 **lemons**
grated zest and juice of 1 **orange**
grated zest and juice of 1 **lime**
4 **eggs**, beaten

Preheat the slow cooker if necessary. Put the butter and sugar in a saucepan, add the fruit zests, then strain in the juice. Heat gently for 2 to 3 minutes, stirring occasionally, until the butter has melted and the sugar has dissolved.

Pour the mixture into a heatproof bowl that will fit comfortably in your slow-cooker pot. Let cool for 10 minutes, then gradually strain in the eggs and mix well. Cover the bowl with foil and lower into the slow-cooker pot. Pour hot water into the cooker pot to come halfway up the sides of the bowl. Cover with the lid and cook on low for 3 to 4 hours or until the mixture is very thick. Stir once or twice during cooking if possible.

Warm the 2 sterilized jars in a slow oven (300 to 325°F) for 5 minutes. Spoon in the citrus curd, place a waxed disk on top, and let cool.

Seal each jar with a screw-top lid or a cellophane jam jar cover and an elastic band, label, and store in the refrigerator. Use within 3 to 4 weeks.

FOR LEMON CURD, prepare as above, but omit the orange and lime and use 3 lemons instead of 2. Cook and store as above.

Makes **3 jars of assorted sizes**
Preparation time **15 minutes**
Cooking temperature **high**
Cooking time **3 to 5 hours**

1¾ cups diced **ready-to-eat dried apricots**
4 **peaches**, halved, stoned, and diced
1¼ cups **superfine sugar**
1¼ cups boiling **water**

Preheat the slow cooker if necessary. Put all the ingredients into the slow-cooker pot and stir together.

Cover with the lid and cook on high for 3 to 5 hours, stirring once during cooking and then again at the end, until the fruit is soft and the liquid thick and syrupy, with a texture like chutney.

Warm 3 sterilized jars in a slow oven (300 to 325°F) for 5 minutes. Ladle the conserve into the warm jars. Cover the surface with waxed disks, add cellophane jam jar covers, and secure with elastic bands or screw the jar lids in place. Label and let cool. The conserve can be stored for up to 2 months in the refrigerator.

FOR APRICOT & ORANGE CONSERVE, put 2¼ cups diced ready-to-eat dried apricots, the grated zest and juice of 1 large orange, the sugar, and the boiling water in the slow cooker, omitting the peaches. Continue as above.

CHILE, TOMATO & GARLIC CHUTNEY

Makes **5 × 13-oz jars**
Preparation time **30 minutes**
Cooking temperature **high**
Cooking time **6 to 8 hours**

2¼ lb **tomatoes**, skinned and
    coarsely chopped
1 large **onion**, chopped
2 **cooking apples**, about 1 lb, peeled,
    cored, and chopped
2 **red bell peppers**, cored, seeded,
    and diced
½ cup **golden raisins**
½ cup **distilled malt vinegar**
1¼ cups **granulated sugar**
2 to 3 large **mild red chiles**, halved,
    seeded, and finely chopped
6 to 8 **garlic cloves**, minced
1 **cinnamon stick**, halved
½ teaspoon **ground allspice**
1 teaspoon **salt**
pepper

Preheat the slow cooker if necessary. Put all the ingredients in the slow-cooker pot and mix together. Cover with the lid and cook on high for 6 to 8 hours or until thick and pulpy, stirring once or twice.

Warm the 5 sterilized jars in a slow oven (300 to 325°F) for 5 minutes. Spoon in the chutney, place a waxed disk on top, and let cool. Seal each jar with a screw-top lid, then label. Store in a cool place for up to 2 months. Once opened, store in the refrigerator.

FOR SPICED GREEN TOMATO CHUTNEY, replace the tomatoes with 2¼ lb green tomatoes (chopped but not skinned) and replace the onion and bell peppers with 3 onions weighing 1 lb in total. Mix the tomatoes and onions with the cooking apples, vinegar, sugar, chiles, and salt. Decrease the garlic cloves to 2 and replace the cinnamon and allspice with 1 teaspoon each ground ginger and ground turmeric and 1 teaspoon coarsely crushed cloves. Cook and store as above.

ORANGE MARMALADE

Makes **6 jars of assorted sizes**
Preparation time **45 minutes, plus
 overnight cooling**
Cooking temperature **low**
Cooking time **8 to 10 hours**

2¼ lb **Seville oranges**
2½ pints boiling **water**
4½ lb **granulated sugar**

Preheat the slow cooker if necessary. Put the whole oranges into the slow-cooker pot, cover with the measurement boiling water, and put an upturned saucer on top of the oranges to keep them submerged in the liquid.

Cover with the lid and cook on low for 8 to 10 hours or until the oranges are tender. Lift the pot out of the housing using oven mitts and let cool overnight. The next day, lift the oranges out of the slow-cooker pot, draining well. Cut into quarters, scoop out and discard the seeds, then thinly slice the oranges.

Put the sliced oranges and the liquid from the slow-cooker pot into a stockpot or large saucepan, add the sugar, and heat gently, stirring occasionally, until the sugar has completely dissolved. Increase the heat, and boil for 20 to 30 minutes or until setting point is reached (*see* page 277).

Warm 6 sterilized jars in a slow oven (300 to 325°F) for 5 minutes. Ladle the hot marmalade into the warm jars, cover the surface with waxed disks, add cellophane jam jar covers, and secure with elastic bands or screw the jar lids in place. Label and let cool. Store in a cool place until required.

FOR DARK GINGER ORANGE MARMALADE, cook the Seville oranges with ¾ cup finely chopped peeled fresh ginger root in the slow cooker as above. Make the marmalade with the sliced oranges and ginger as above, using 3¼ lb granulated sugar and 1 lb light brown sugar.

PICKLED PLUMS

Makes **2 × 3¼-cup**
    and **1 × 2-cup preserving jars**
Preparation time **20 minutes**
Cooking temperature **high**
Cooking time **2 to 2½ hours**

3¼ cups **white wine vinegar**
2½ cups **superfine sugar**
7 **rosemary sprigs**, divided
7 **thyme sprigs**, divided
7 small **bay leaves**, divided
4 **lavender sprigs** (optional)
4 **garlic cloves**, unpeeled
1 teaspoon **salt**
½ teaspoon **black peppercorns**
3 lb **firm red plums**, washed
    and pricked

Preheat the slow cooker if necessary. Pour the vinegar and sugar into the slow-cooker pot, then add 4 sprigs each of the rosemary and thyme and the bay leaves, all the lavender, if using, the garlic cloves, salt, and peppercorns. Cover and cook on high for 2 to 2½ hours, stirring once or twice.

Warm the 3 sterilized jars in a slow oven (300 to 325°F) for 5 minutes. Pack the plums tightly into the jars. Tuck the remaining fresh herbs into the jars. Strain in the hot vinegar, making sure that the plums are completely covered, then seal tightly with the rubber seals and jar lids.

Label the jars and let cool. Transfer to a cool, dark cupboard and store for 3 to 4 weeks before using. Once opened, store in the refrigerator.

FOR PICKLED SHALLOTS, trim a little off of the tops and roots of 2½ lb small shallots. Put them in a bowl and cover with boiling water, let soak for 3 minutes, then pour off the water and recover with fresh cold water. Lift the shallots out 1 at a time and peel off the brown skins. Drain and layer in a second bowl with 2½ tablespoons salt. Let stand overnight. Make the vinegar mixture in the slow cooker as above, but use 1¼ cups superfine sugar and 1¾ cups light brown sugar (not packed) and omit the lavender. Transfer the shallots to a colander and drain off as much liquid as possible. Rinse with cold water, drain, and pat dry with paper towels. Pack tightly into the warmed jars, adding a few extra herbs. Pour in the hot, strained vinegar, add some crumpled wax paper to keep the shallots beneath the surface of the liquid, and finish as above.

PASSION FRUIT & LIME CURD

Makes **3 small jars**
Preparation time **15 minutes**
Cooking temperature **low**
Cooking time **3 to 4 hours**

1¼ sticks **unsalted butter**, diced
2 cups **superfine sugar**
4 **eggs**, beaten
grated zest and juice of 2 **limes**
grated zest of 2 **lemons**
juice of 1 **lemon**
3 **passion fruit**, halved

Preheat the slow cooker if necessary. Put the butter and sugar in a large bowl, checking first that it will fit into the slow-cooker pot, then heat in the microwave until the butter has just melted. Alternatively, heat the butter and sugar in a saucepan and pour into the bowl.

Stir the sugar mixture, then gradually beat in the eggs, and then the fruit zest and juice. Cover the bowl with foil and lower into the slow-cooker pot. Pour boiling water into the pot to come halfway up the sides of the bowl. Cover with the lid and cook on low for 3 to 4 hours, stirring once during cooking, until thick.

Stir once more, then scoop the passion fruit seeds out of the halved fruit with a teaspoon and stir them into the curd mixture.

Warm the 3 sterilized jars in a slow oven (300 to 325°F) for 5 minutes. Ladle the preserve into the warm jars, cover the surface with waxed disks, add cellophane jam jar covers, and secure with elastic bands or screw the jar lids in place. Label and let cool. The preserve can be stored for up to 2 weeks in the refrigerator.

FOR LEMON CURD, make as above, using the zest and juice of 3 lemons and omitting the lime zest and juice and passion fruit.

FIERY TROPICAL CHUTNEY

Makes **4 x 12-oz jars**
Preparation time **25 minutes**
Cooking temperature **high**
Cooking time **4 to 5 hours**

1 cup **distilled malt vinegar**
1¼ cups **granulated sugar**
2 large **red chiles**, halved, seeded, and finely chopped
1½-inch piece of **fresh ginger root**, peeled and finely chopped
2 teaspoons **black mustard seeds**
1 teaspoon **cumin seeds**, coarsely crushed
1 teaspoon **coriander seeds**, coarsely crushed
½ teaspoon **ground turmeric**
½ teaspoon **salt**
2 large **mangoes**, peeled, seeded, and diced
1 large **pineapple**, peeled, cored, and diced
2 **onions**, finely chopped
pepper

Preheat the slow cooker if necessary. Put the vinegar and sugar in a nonreactive saucepan and heat gently, stirring, until the sugar has dissolved. Mix in the red chiles, ginger root, mustard seeds, crushed spices, turmeric, salt, and pepper to taste.

Put the mangoes, pineapple, and onions into the slow-cooker pot, add the hot vinegar mixture, then cover with the lid and cook on high for 4 to 5 hours until the fruit is almost translucent.

Warm the 4 sterilized jars in a slow oven (300 to 325°F) for 5 minutes. Mash the fruit slightly, if liked, then ladle the chutney into the warm jars to the very top and press down well, ensuring there are no air pockets. Seal each jar with a screw-top lid, label, and let cool. Store in a cool, dry place for up to 3 months. Once opened, store in the refrigerator and consume within 2 weeks.

FOR SWEET TROPICAL MANGO & PINEAPPLE CHUTNEY, omit the chiles and continue as above.

SPICY TOMATO "SANDWICH" CHUTNEY

Makes **5 x 12-oz jars**
Preparation time **20 minutes**
Cooking temperature **high**
Cooking time **6 to 7 hours**

1 lb **cooking apples**, peeled, cored, and diced
1 lb **butternut squash**, peeled, seeded, and diced
1 lb **onions**, finely chopped
1 lb **tomatoes**, coarsely chopped (no need to skin, unless preferred)
1 cup **golden raisins**
1 teaspoon **crushed dried red chiles**
1 teaspoon **ground ginger**
1 teaspoon **ground turmeric**
1 teaspoon **cumin seeds**, coarsely crushed
1 teaspoon **salt**
1¾ cups **light brown sugar** (not packed)
1 cup **red wine vinegar**

Preheat the slow cooker if necessary. Add the apples, vegetables, and golden raisins to the slow-cooker pot. Sprinkle with the spices, salt, and sugar and stir together.

Add the vinegar, cover with the lid, and cook on high for 6 to 7 hours, stirring the chutney once and again at the end, until the vegetables are soft. If you prefer a finer texture, mash the cooked chutney.

Warm the 5 sterilized jars in a slow oven (300 to 325°F) for 5 minutes. Spoon the hot chutney into the warm jars to the very top and press down well, ensuring there are no air pockets. Seal each jar with a screw-top lid, label, and let cool. Store in a cool, dry place for up to 3 months. Let the chutney stand for at least 2 to 3 days before serving so that the flavors have had time to mellow. Once opened, store in the refrigerator and consume within 2 weeks. Serve with cheese and a salad, in a ham sandwich, or try it in hot toasted sandwiches, if liked.

FOR SPICY TOMATO & ZUCCHINI CHUTNEY, omit the butternut squash and replace with ¾ lb zucchini, trimmed and diced, and 1 red bell pepper, cored, seeded, and diced. Continue as above.

BEST BARBECUE SAUCE EVER

Makes **about 2 lb**
Preparation time **15 minutes**
Cooking temperature **high**
Cooking time **5 to 6 hours**

2 **onions**, finely chopped
2 small **cooking apples**, 14½ oz in total, peeled, cored, and finely chopped
2 cups **tomato purée**
¼ cup **dark brown sugar**
2 tablespoons **sherry vinegar**
1 tablespoon **Worcestershire sauce**
1 teaspoon **mustard powder**
salt and **pepper**

Preheat the slow cooker if necessary. Add all the ingredients to the slow-cooker pot. Stir to combine, cover with the lid, and cook on high for 5 to 6 hours, stirring once during cooking and again at the end.

Warm sterilized jars in a slow oven (300 to 325°F) for 5 minutes. Pour the sauce into the warm jars to the very top. Seal each jar with a screw-top lid, then label and let cool. Store in the refrigerator for up to 1 month. Alternatively, pack into plastic containers and freeze for up to 3 months. Thaw in the refrigerator overnight. Serve with burgers, sausages, or steak, if liked.

FOR CAJUN SAUCE, add 1 teaspoon each ground allspice and cinnamon, ½ teaspoon smoked hot paprika, and 1 teaspoon crushed dried red chiles to the other barbecue sauce ingredients. Cook as above.

INDEX

thighs 13
chickpeas
  & chorizo soup 71
  coconut & pumpkin curry 207
  with dum aloo 187
  Indian chicken curry 204
  & lemon couscous 158
  & lentil tagine 198
  & spiced date pilaf 219
  in turkey tagine 102–3
chile
  beef 47, 147, 154
  black bean stew 80
  corn/mushroom 55
  sweet potato & Quorn 206
Chinese-style dishes 81, 105, 173, 178, 179, 180, 208
chocolate
  & banana mini puddings 247
  brownie puddings 250
  & cherry puddings 239, 264
  & coffee pots 258
  croissant pudding 255
  hot 269
  mousses, hot 240–1
  & pear pudding 259
  & peppermint brûlée 267
  sauce 244, 264
chorizo
  with baked bell peppers 34
  caldo verde 61
  in chicken gumbo 217
  & chicken soup 71
  & chicken tagliatelle 226
  hot Spanish beans 227
  in peasant paella 234
  & red bell pepper tortilla 54
  in shakshuka 168
  in skinny cassoulet 91
  with Spanish chicken 89
  tapenade-topped cod 120
  & tomato braised squid 222
chowder 61, 65
chutney 279, 282, 283
cobbler, mushroom & walnut 199
coconut 239, 267
  cream 64, 209, 214
  milk 98, 99, 207, 211
cod
  in fish dumplings 74
  fish terrine 39
  herb-topped 120
  salmon-wrapped, with leeks 129
  tapenade-topped 120
  in three-fish gratin 130
cod, smoked
  with buttered leeks 129
  & corn chowder 61
  with mashed beans 126
  & spinach salad 119
coffee 258, 272
coleslaw 173
compote 25, 27, 266, 271
cordial, lemon/lime 270
corn 55, 61, 65, 89, 116
cottage pie, Indian-spiced 141
couscous 111, 158, 163, 188
crab 61, 65, 72, 217
cranberries
  with braised duck 108
  in compote with mascarpone 266

in drinks 271
sauce with lamb steaks 157
in turkey curry 100
& turkey meatloaf 40
in turkey & sausage stew 82
cream
  cooking 11
  lemon custard creams 245
  mustard cream 127
  peppermint & raspberry brûlée 267
  rosemary 152
  syllabub with berry compote 25
crepes 27
crisp, raspberry & rhubarb 265
cucumber, pickled 179
curd 278, 282
curry
  cauliflower & spinach balti 218
  chicken & sweet potato balti 218
  coconut, pumpkin & chickpea 207
  creamy chicken korma 104
  Indian chicken 204–5
  lamb rogan josh 216
  mushroom & sweet potato balti 218
  sweet potato & egg/paneer 191
  sweet potato & Quorn chili 206
  Thai fish 211
  Thai green/red chicken 99
  Thai vegetable 211
  tomato & squash 214
  turkey 100
  vegetable & chicken soup 70

dairy products 8, 9, 11
dates 219, 246, 247, 252
desserts 239–67
drinks 269–75
duck 33, 36–7, 108, 208
dum aloo 187
dumplings
  fish 74
  horseradish 136
  with lamb stew 86
  mustard 136
  parsley 82
  ricotta 189
  rosemary 170
  sage 170

eggplant
  & apricot pilaf 200
  baba ganoush 53
  with baked eggs 195
  coconut & chickpea curry 207
  in moussaka 221, 224
  & mushroom dahl 203
  parmigiana 236
  in ratatouille 189
  sauce, with broiled steaks 53
  timbale 30–1
eggs
  baked, with eggplant 195
  baked, with toast fingers 19
  benedict 19
  en cocotte, with salmon 16–17
  mixed vegetable shakshuka 48
  poached, & haddock 20–1
  red bell pepper & chorizo tortilla 54
  safety advice 4
  shakshuka 168
  & sweet potato curry 191

zucchini & fava bean frittata 48
Eve's pudding 259

fajitas, turkey, with guacamole 47
fennel 75, 106
figs 24, 158
fish 113–31
  cooking 8, 9, 10
  dumplings, with Thai broth 74
  kedgeree 122
  pie 113, 130
  & spinach gratin 113
  terrine 39
  Thai curry 211
  three-fish gratin 130
  see also types of fish
flatbreads, cilantro 107
fondue, cheese and beer 35
fool, apricot & orange 242
freezing food 13
frittata, zucchini 48

ginger 240, 243, 246, 252, 280
gnocchi, pumpkin & cheese 190
goulash 134, 201
granola 23
gravy, onion 172, 196
Greek dishes 142, 151, 221, 224, 228
guacamole, with turkey fajitas 47
guinea fowl, pot-roast, with prunes 109
gumbo 72, 217

haddock 39, 113
haddock, smoked
  & bacon chowder 65
  & chive terrine 39
  in kedgeree 122, 128
  with macaroni 116
  & poached eggs 20–1
  in three-fish gratin 130
ham
  bacon & leek suet pudding 176
  & cider hotpot 90
  in cola 90, 171
  feijoada 229
  honey-roast, with baked eggs 19
  honey-glazed 174–5
  with parsley sauce 171
  pea & ham soup 62
  with pease pudding 174
hard cider 90, 170, 177, 273
harissa 93, 102, 121, 218
health & safety 4, 8, 9, 10, 13
heart symbol 4
heat settings 9
herbs 4
herrings 121
hot toddy 254, 270, 273
Hungarian chorba 68

Indian-style dishes
  black pepper chicken 204–5
  creamy chicken korma 104
  dum aloo 187
  keema aloo 209
  keema mutter 109, 209
  lamb rogan josh 216
  spiced cottage pie 141
  sweet potato & egg curry 191
  tarka dahl 200
  turkey curry 100, 109

ACKNOWLEDGMENTS

Senior Commissioning Editor: Eleanor Maxfield
Editorial Assistant: Natalie Bradley
Design: Tracy Killick and Jaz Bahra
Production Controller: Allison Gonsalves

Photography: Fotolia Barbara Dudzińska 5, 238; Claudia
Paulussen 132; daffoldilred 14; Daria Minaeva 56, 92; dusk 268;
geargodz 28; Jiri Hera 164; juliasudnitskaya 220; katrinshine 42;
marylooo 182; strixcode 202; victoria p 150; weyo 276; zzayko 112.
iStock twohumans 76. **Octopus Publishing Group** Stephen
Conroy 2, 6 left, 10 left, 10 right, 11 left, 11 right, 17, 19, 22, 24, 25,
26, 31, 33, 37, 38, 39, 40, 41, 45, 46, 47, 51, 52, 54, 55, 57, 59, 62, 63,
64, 65, 67, 68, 69, 70, 71, 72, 73, 75, 77, 80, 82, 87, 89, 93, 97, 98, 99,
103, 104, 105, 107, 110, 111, 113, 115, 116, 117, 118, 123, 124, 125,
126, 127, 129, 136, 137, 138, 139, 140, 141, 143, 144, 145, 146, 147,
149, 153, 155, 159, 163, 165, 170, 171, 172, 173, 175, 176, 177, 178,
179, 185, 186, 187, 188, 189, 191, 193, 194, 195, 199, 208, 209, 214,
215, 216, 217, 219, 223, 224, 225, 226, 227, 228, 232, 233, 239, 241,
242, 243, 244, 245, 249, 250, 253, 255, 257, 258, 260, 261, 263, 264,
265, 269, 272, 273, 275, 277, 279, 280, 281; William Shaw 6 right, 7, 9
left, 9 right, 12, 15, 21, 23, 27, 29, 32, 34, 43, 49, 53, 79, 81, 83, 84, 85,
88, 91, 95, 96, 101, 106, 119, 130, 131, 133, 135, 151, 154, 156, 157,
160, 161, 167, 168, 169, 181, 183, 196, 197, 198, 203, 205, 206, 207,
210, 211, 213, 221, 229, 231, 234, 235, 237, 251, 252, 259.